Everyday Magic

How to Live a Mindful, Meaningful, Magical Life

Marie D. Jones & Denise A. Agnew

DETROIT

Everyday
Magic

How to Live a Mindful, Meaningful, Magical Life

Marie D. Jones & Denise A. Agnew

VISIBLE
INK
PRESS

DETROIT

ABOUT THE AUTHORS

Marie D. Jones is the author of over 20 non-fiction books, including Visible Ink Press' *Earth Magic, Natural Health* and *The Afterlife Book*. A former radio show host, she has been interviewed on more than 2,000 radio programs worldwide, including *Coast-to-Coast AM*, *The Shirley MacLaine Show*, and *Midnight in the Desert*. She has also been interviewed for and  contributed to dozens of print and online publications. She makes her home in San Diego County, California and is the mom to one very brilliant son, Max.

Denise A. Agnew is the award–winning author of over 70 multi–genre novels and has collaborated with Marie D. Jones on several projects, including screenplays. Fascinated  since childhood with all things esoteric, Denise is also a paranormal investigator, reiki master, psychic medium, and certified creativity coach. She lives in Arizona with her husband.

OTHER VISIBLE INK PRESS BOOKS
BY MARIE D. JONES

The Afterlife Book: Heaven, Hell, and Life After Death
with Alan Flaxman
ISBN: 978-1-57859-761-1

The Disaster Survival Guide: How to Prepare for and Survive Floods, Fires, Earthquakes and More
ISBN: 978-1-57859-673-7

Disinformation and You: Identify Propaganda and Manipulation
ISBN: 978-1-57859-740-6

Celebrity Ghosts and Notorious Hauntings
ISBN: 978-1-57859-689-8

Demons, the Devil, and Fallen Angels
with Larry Flaxman
ISBN: 978-1-57859-613-3

Earth Magic: Your Complete Guide to Natural Spells, Potions, Plants, Herbs, Witchcraft, and More
ISBN: 978-1-57859-697-3

Natural Health: Your Complete Guide to Natural Remedies and Mindful Well-Being
ISBN: 978-1-57859-555-6

The New Witch: Your Guide to Modern Witchcraft, Wicca, Spells, Potions, Magic, and More
ISBN: 978-1-57859-555-6

Toxin Nation: The Poisoning of Our Air, Water, Food, and Bodies
ISBN: 978-1-57859-709-3

ALSO FROM VISIBLE INK PRESS

American Ghost Stories: True Tales from All 50 States
by Michael A. Kozlowski
ISBN: 978-1-57859-799-4

Angels A to Z, 2nd edition
by Evelyn Dorothy Oliver and James R. Lewis
ISBN: 978-1-57859-212-8

The Astrology Book: The Encyclopedia of Heavenly Influences, 2nd edition
by James R. Lewis
ISBN: 978-1-57859-144-2

The Astrology Guide: Understanding Your Signs, Your Gifts, and Yourself
by Claudia Trivelas
ISBN: 978-1-57859-738-3

The Big Book of Facts
by Terri Schlichenmeyer
ISBN: 978-1-57859-720-8

The Book of Facts and Trivia: American History
by Terri Schlichenmeyer
ISBN: 978-1-57859-795-6

The Book of Facts and Trivia: Science (From Earthquakes to Moonscapes to Back Aches)
by Terri Schlichenmeyer
ISBN: 978-1-57859-797-0

The Dream Encyclopedia, 2nd edition
by James R. Lewis and Evelyn Dorothy Oliver
ISBN: 978-1-57859-216-6

The Dream Interpretation Dictionary: Symbols, Signs, and Meanings
by J. M. DeBord
ISBN: 978-1-57859-637-9

The Encyclopedia of Religious Phenomena
by J. Gordon Melton, Ph.D.
ISBN: 978-1-57859-209-8

The Fortune-telling Book: The Encyclopedia of Divination and Soothsaying
by Raymond Buckland
ISBN: 978-1-57859-147-3

The Handy Communication Answer Book
by Lauren Sergy
ISBN: 978-1-57859-587-7

Please Visit Us at visibleinkpress.com

Everyday Magic: How to Live a Mindful, Meaningful, Magical Life

Visible Ink Press®
43311 Joy Rd., #414
Canton, MI 48187-2075
Visible Ink Press is a registered trademark of Visible Ink Press, LLC.

Most Visible Ink Press books are available at special quantity discounts when purchased in bulk by corporations, organizations, or groups. Customized printings, special imprints, messages, and excerpts can be produced to meet your needs. For more information, contact Special Markets Director, Visible Ink Press, www.visibleinkpress.com, or 734-667-3211.

Managing Editor: Kevin S. Hile
Cover Design: John Gouin, Graphikitchen, LLC
Page Design: Mary Claire Krzewinski
Typesetting: Marco Divita
Proofreaders: Christa Brelin and Suzanne Goraj
Indexer: Larry Baker
Cover and chapter images: Shutterstock.

ISBNs
Paperback: 978-1-57859-721-5
Hardbound: 978-1-57859-858-8
eBook: 978-1-57859-859-5

Cataloging-in-Publication data is on file at the Library of Congress.

Printed in the United States of America.

10 9 8 7 6 5 4 3 2 1

CONTENTS

Photo Sources xiii

Acknowledgments xvii

Introduction xix

The Magic of Self–Love 1

The Magic of Relationships 27

The Magic of Connecting to Source .49

The Magic of Well–Being 79

The Magic of Nature 99

The Magic of Universal Laws 125

The Magic of Gratitude 149

The Magic of Giving and Service . . . .·. . . .167

The Magic of Passion and Purpose 183

The Magic of Creativity and Imagination 203

The Magic of Miracles 225

The Magic of Death 249

Conclusion: Everyday Magic Is Right Where You Are 261

Further Reading 267

Index 271

PHOTO SOURCES

Archives des Jésuites de France: p. 255.

BBeagTeam (Wikicommons): p. 34.

Jake Beech: pp. 208–209.

Sophie Delar: p. 54.

Factoryjoe (Wikicommons): p. 25.

Joan Halifax: p. 30.

Heritage–images.com: p. 237.

Einar Einarsson Kvaran: p. 129.

Library of Congress: p. 196.

Luxvandag (Wikicommons): p. 3.

Marie Forleo International: p. 190.

NASA/JPL: p. 73.

NBC Television: p. 192.

Philosovieth.de: p. 126.

Shutterstock: pp. 2, 5, 6, 7, 8, 10, 11, 13, 15, 17, 19, 21, 27, 29, 31, 33, 36, 37, 39, 41, 42, 44, 46, 51, 53 (top), 56, 58, 59, 61, 62, 65, 66, 67, 69, 75, 77, 80, 81, 83, 85, 88, 90, 91, 92, 94, 96, 97, 101, 103, 104, 105, 107, 109, 112, 114 (top and bottom), 115, 118, 120, 122, 133, 135, 136, 138, 145, 147, 150, 153, 155, 156, 157, 159, 165, 166, 168, 170, 172, 173, 175, 178, 180, 185, 188, 194, 197, 200, 204, 206, 207, 212, 214, 216, 217, 220, 226, 227, 231, 233, 235, 240, 242, 245, 246, 250, 252, 254, 259, 262, 263.

Derek Smith: p. 238.

Supearmesh (Wikicommons): p. 229.

U.S. Department of Defense: p. 193.

Franz Vesely: p. 140.

Matthew Yohe: p. 53 (bottom).

Ralph Zuranski: p. 186.

Public Domain: pp. 100, 128, 130.

DEDICATIONS

Marie

To Max. May your life be filled
with everyday magic in every way.

Denise

Special thanks and love go to my husband Terry, who
has always supported my creative journey every step
of the way. You're the best, my love.

Also, to my good buddies Stacy Chitwood and Selena
Robins, amazing people who have encouraged me
through all the ups and downs of a writer's life and
added to the magic of my experience. I cherish our
friendship.

ACKNOWLEDGMENTS

We would like to thank Roger Jänecke and his wonderful team at Visible Ink Press for championing this book and being such a supportive force behind so many great books in the world today. You guys are such a pleasure to write for and work with! We would also like to thank Lisa Hagan for agenting the deal and for all the years of wonderful support and friendship. You are absolutely amazing and always look out for your writers. We truly are blessed to have such a magical crew on this book.

I, Marie, would like to thank my family and my friends, my writer pals and colleagues, and the many readers and supporters I have had the pleasure to interact with over the years. You truly make writing these books worthwhile. I thank all of the people who have read my books and listened to me on radio or television. I do this for you guys. I would also like to thank all of the people I've met over the years who have brought their own special touches of magic into my life or allowed me to share mine with them. Many of you may no longer be in my daily life, but you exist within my heart forever.

Denise, as a writing partner and a friend, you just absolutely rock! It has been such an incredible pleasure working with you over the last few years, and I look forward to so many more! We really do make such a great team!

Most of all, I'd like to thank my son, Max, for inspiring everything I do. He may not know it but having him in my life is the best magic there is.

I, Denise, don't know where to begin. Over my life I've learned more and more each year about how to create magic in my life. In this book, we've talked so much about using the magic we're capable of to give us the utmost chance at living our best lives. When I write, I discover new things about living every single day, and this book has only enriched the experience for me, giving me brand new insights. I am truly blessed to have had this opportunity.

Copious thanks to Marie for bringing me on to this project. You've been amazing to work with on this book and the many other projects we've put together over the last several years. Thanks for believing in me as a writer and a person. Here's to many, many more writing adventures together!

INTRODUCTION: WHAT IS EVERYDAY MAGIC?

"And above all, watch with glittering eyes the whole world around you because the greatest secrets are always hidden in the most unlikely places. Those who don't believe in magic will never find it."

Roald Dahl

"That's the thing with magic. You've got to know it's still here, all around us, or it just stays invisible for you."

Charles de Lint

"We have buried so much of the delicate magic of life."

D. H. Lawrence

"Do you believe in magic?"

Usually when someone asks us this question, we think of the pull-a-rabbit-out-of-a-top-hat Las Vegas magic show or the esoteric magic of wizards and mages in movies or novels. We look at magic as something detached and external to us that exists within the realm of fantasy and imagination, a place like Disneyland, where all kinds of dreams do come true—at least, in an illusory sense.

We usually believe we have five senses and do not possess the ability to bend time, shape energy, or pull anything out of our hats, unless it is the price tag we forgot to remove.

There is magic in words; understanding the etymology of a word can tell us so much about its true meaning and intent. According to etymonline.com, the word "magic" can be defined this way:

magic (n.)

late 14c., *magike*, "art of influencing or predicting events and producing marvels using hidden natural forces," also "supernatural art," especially the art of controlling the actions of spiritual or super-human beings; from Old French *magique* "magic; magical," from Late Latin *magice* "sorcery, magic," from Greek *magike* (presumably with *tekhnē*) "art"), fem. of *magikos* "magical," from *magos* "one of the members of the learned and priestly class," from Old Persian *magush*, which is possibly from PIE root *magh– "to be able, have power."

Magic can mean using hidden natural forces or having supernatural powers the way a sorcerer might. Merriam–Webster.com defines "magic" as a noun meaning:

1a: the use of means (such as charms or spells) believed to have supernatural power over natural forces.

b: magic rites or incantations

2a: an extraordinary power or influence seemingly from a supernatural source Both pitchers, although they are older, haven't lost their magic.

b: something that seems to cast a spell: EN-CHANTMENT

The emphasis appears to be on a supernatural power or sleight–of–hand trickery, but real magic is something that we all possess and can tap into. We influence our surroundings and our environment, and we have the ability to feel charmed and enchanted as well as to charm and enchant others.

It doesn't require an external force or box full of tricks but rather an internal understanding of our connectivity with the source of life.

But there is another kind of magic that does exist, and each and every one of us has experienced it at some point in our lives, even if we have forgotten it or it happened so long ago that it feels like it was just a dream.

Everyday magic.

This is the kind of magic that comes upon us suddenly, taking us out of our little ego bubble and making us feel a part of everything. The magic that slices us open so that we spill out joy and love and a feeling of being one with everything around us. The magic that makes us feel huge and expansive, yet it also drops us to our knees as we realize the grandeur of the universe of which we are but a teeny, tiny part. This is the kind of magic that feels ecstatic, yet even when it dissipates, we remain in a state of absolute grace and connectedness and experience a joy from just being alive that is not attached to any one thing or person or experience. It's just THERE.

This is the magic we experience as little children looking at the world through fresh eyes. The kind evoked by seeing or experiencing something for the first time, whether it be watching a majestic lion at the zoo or running downstairs to see a pile of colorfully wrapped presents under the Christmas tree. Or perhaps our childhoods contained traumas that made that childlike ability to bounce back harder than it was for other kids in more stable situations. We might have fallen into adulthood far sooner than we should have.

If the latter were the case, we might have dreamed of how much better things would be when we grew up. We might have said to ourselves that we'd do things differently than the adults we knew. We would plan and keep those dreams alive. We would show everyone how amazing we could be and the things we could accomplish once we reached that magic age of 18 or 21.

As children, it's all magic because it's all so incredible. We see the wonder of a caterpillar creeping up a leaf and feel awe under a night sky filled with too many stars to count. We have not yet learned to explain it all away, ignore it, get distracted from it, or label it as a "childish thing" as we strive to become more mature adults. Magic is for kids, not grown-ups. We have jobs and families and bills to pay. We have hard times and bad times and deaths in the family and career losses and betrayals and illnesses and bankruptcies. Who can possibly think about magic when there are the hard truths of life staring us in the face, demanding our attention?

We might have occasional glimpses of that everyday magic when we fall in love with someone, or see a gorgeous sunset on an ocean cruise, or when we step out of our comfort zone and try zip-lining or skydiving on a vacation. But even these exciting experiences lose their magic after a while as we become comfortable with them, and they are added to our "been there, done that" list. We may still get a kick out of these experiences, but the magic tends to last only as long as the initial thrill does. Once it's over, we seek out another kick, like sugar addicts looking for the next doughnut or cookie hit.

Feelings of awe and wonder may be more intense during certain times, such as when we hold our newborn child for the first time, receive a great bonus at work, or buy that dream house up in the hills with the lazy river pool, but eventually the novelty wears off. Those peak magic moments of pure wonder, when we stop existing as separate from everything and feel ourselves soaring in the sky, seeing all and knowing all, or when we become like a child again in abject awe ... become fewer and farther between. We can look at the same things we did as a child and not feel that sense of amazement. And trying to force the sensation is a fruitless pursuit.

Magic can never be forced.

The challenge is to feel it for longer than just a fleeting few seconds and being able to recreate that feeling more often rather than waiting for something to trigger it.

The truth is, magic is our natural state of being, and it exists everywhere we are. It exists within us and all around us, and we can cultivate and sustain a magical connection and perspective when we understand what everyday magic is.

The world needs more magical people having magical moments. We live in a whirlwind of activity, doing things and then posting about what we are doing, of achieving and comparing notes about who is achieving more or less than we are. We wake up and jump out of bed to race to the bathroom and off to school, work, or a day of chores, grumbling and complaining as we sit in traffic or spill coffee on our pants. We work and work for our pay-checks, then we watch the money vanish as we pay off stacks of bills. Then we do it all again the next day.

If we are lucky, we have the finances to take a few weeks off here or there for a vacation to some exotic port of call, but even our vacays can be stressful. Amidst mo-ments of bliss we worry about crime, money, what's hap-pening at home with the kids or our jobs, and whether or not we'll get sick on the cruise ship or get stuck on a layover in some airport for three hours. We stress about everything from dawn to dusk to dawn again.

There is little, if any, time to just be–to immerse our-selves in nature, stand in the sun, walk barefoot on the grass, or enjoy a glass of wine without a care in the world. Everything we do is centered on doing and get-ting things done, and there is always something else to be done the next day.

Where the heck is the everyday magic in THAT? The truth is, magic doesn't abandon us as we get older. We abandon it. We decide that because we are adults, we can't believe in magic anymore. It's childish and immature.

Magic is still there, and the funny thing is that all it takes to experience it is a shift in perspective. Slowing down long enough to look back at it because it is always look-ing at us. Stopping long enough to let our senses experi-ence it for the sheer joy of doing so, not to accomplish another check mark on our to-do list. Experiencing magic requires the ability to stop resisting, denying, and ignoring the little whispers in your heart, soul, and in-tuition and pay them the attention they deserve, because they speak the language of everyday magic.

With some tools, insights, and exercises, you can turn every mundane act, every trivial moment, into something worthy of awe and wonder. You can find grace and gratitude in the smallest things and allow yourself to get lost in the majestic grandeur of the biggest things without any concern for "wasting time" or whether or not you are being "productive." Finding your magical life is probably the most miraculous thing you can do, because it opens a whole new universe of possibilities you may not have been able to see before.

There is magic afoot, calling you to come and play, but you must first be willing to get off the hamster wheel and out of the rat race for a while.

Just be. Observe. Listen.

Otherwise, you will never hear the call.

Because it's in the "being" where everyday magic is found waiting for us. And when we rediscover it and learn how to cultivate it, we then bring it into all aspects of our lives, from the being to the doing.

Will you heed its call?

The poet Mary Oliver said, "Tell me, what is it you plan to do with your one wild and precious life?"

But if everyday magic is really "a thing," how do we tap back into it when we've gone so long without it? How do we find our magical mojo again when we've come to believe it was lost for good? How do we, being so jaded and experienced and having "been there, done that," see the world around us in new ways and with fresh eyes?

Our hope is that this book will help you rediscover the magic all around you. It's there. We know it is. But we cannot see it for you or experience it for you. What we can do is provide some insights, wisdom, and exercises to help you move from being closed off to the possibility that magic exists to allowing yourself to believe it and open yourself to it a little at a time. Habits are not created overnight but born of practice and time, and it might take time for you to return to the magical state of believing that you had as a child.

As you go through these chapters, we ask that you open your mind and heart to the possibilities. You can be skeptical, but just allow one little corner to say, "Hey, what if?" Do the exercises and see if you don't start feeling a little lighter in step and brighter in tone. One day you might just step outside and be blown away in awe at the sun reflecting off the treetop leaves or the majesty of the night sky or feel a sense of joy watching the neighbor's dog chase a butterfly. One day you might wake up and feel (dare we say it?) excited about life again. One day you might realize that synchronicities are popping up everywhere, ideas are flowing like a river, and intuition is strong and guiding you to where you need to be and with whom you need to be. You might tell a friend, "This happened … and it felt just like magic." Or perhaps you will post on social media, "Isn't life so magical and wonderful?" Some will agree, and others will think you've gone off the deep end.

Go ahead. Dive off the deep end. That's where the magic is.

One day, you might open your eyes and realize with a huge smile that you have fallen back in love with your one wild and precious life again.

The Magic of Self-Love

*We are each gifted in a unique and important way.
It is our privilege and our adventure to discover our own special light.*

Mary Dunbar

*You yourself, as much as anybody in the entire universe,
deserve your love and affection.*

Buddha

You can't build joy on a feeling of self-loathing.

Ram Dass

Whitney Houston's smash hit "The Greatest Love of All," written for her 1986 self–titled album by the late Linda Creed, who wrote the song during her battle with breast cancer, compels us to look inside ourselves first to find the most power-ful love there is. The lyrics urge us to work for a better future for our children by learning to never walk in anyone's shadow, to look inside and come to the realization that learning to love our-selves is the greatest love of all. If we could teach this to children the world over, they would know the beauty they possessed. Creed's heartfelt lyrics, sung with such power, passion, and pur-pose by Ms. Houston, served as an anthem to millions to stop looking outside themselves for the truest form of love, and to first go within. Once we learn to love ourselves, then and only then can we love others.

Sadly, this is a lesson that many of us did not learn as children, and struggle with even as adults.

Everything begins within. Each of us was but a thought in the minds of our parents before we took on physical form. Every dream, every goal, every action and behavior, habit and pattern, feeling and emotion, begins within.

One might wonder what self–love has to do with magic, but the truth is, it has everything to do with magic. Before we can venture into the world and interact in a respectful, loving way with others, we must first know who we are, what we want, and why we are here. Without that pertinent information, we are simply shells of humans floating on the surface of a river, without direction or purpose, going where the current takes us. There is no magic in that. Then we must learn to accept who we are and love ourselves as we are, even as we strive for growth and improvement.

We do not discover who we are from the outside in but from the inside out, and we then perceive our world from that standpoint. If we loathe ourselves, our external world reflects that, with little to no room for magical maneuverings. If we are ashamed of ourselves, we are not open to the gifts that life offers because we have closed ourselves off to it, afraid to trust ourselves, let alone others or the universe at large. Our internal thermostat dictates the magical temperature of life on the "outside," and when we do not love who we are, we see little in the way of love from others. Our sensors are always on high alert, waiting for the other shoe to drop and reacting with the confirmation bias that says life sucks and people and situations are to be feared for a variety of reasons. Expect bad things to happen, and you'll find bad things. This isn't to

Magic begins with you and your ability to love and appreciate yourself. Without self-respect, we can't learn to appreciate the gifts all around us.

say that unfortunate situations never happen to people with a healthy self-worth and positive outlook. But expecting and looking for more good things to occur in your life and the world in general is guaranteed to generate creativity, resources, and opportunities for life to flow more smoothly and increase your chances for happiness and success.

Examining whether we love ourselves is one of the first steps required to gauge where we are on the self-love scale. Do you love yourself? Heck, do you even like yourself? When was the last time you looked into a mirror and approved of the image looking back at you? Oh, we are not talking about how good your body looked or how few wrinkles you had, but how much you cared for and appreciated that person staring back. How much you admired how far he or she had come, how much he or she had experienced and been through, and how he or she was still standing strong.

American author and motivational speaker Louise L. Hay (1926–2017) once said, "Love is the great miracle cure. Loving ourselves works miracles in our lives." Otherwise, we are just going through the motions or faking it until we make it, and it usually backfires because others know when we are being authentic, especially those we are in close relationships with.

The relationship we have with ourselves (and with a higher power, if you believe in one) is the only one that we are born with, live with every day, and die with. We are our own "loves of our lives," and until we come to fully embrace this, the love we have for anyone or anything else is not whole, or even healthy. Sometimes people who irk us the most are reflecting back to us things that irritate us about ourselves.

While society reinforces the idea that self-worth and self-esteem are both good things to possess, there are plenty of forces outside us that can damage our ability to recognize this. From the time we are children, these influences can cause

The late motivational speaker Louise Hay wrote a number of self-help books, including 1984's *You Can Heal Your Life*.

us to develop beliefs in certain untruths about ourselves. Trauma in childhood, including experiencing sustained bullying or physical or emotional abuse, can have a powerful impact on the young mind. Children who experience this type of trauma may develop CPTSD (Complex Post-Traumatic Stress Disorder). This is not to be confused with Post-Traumatic Stress Disorder. CPTSD is not a formal diagnosis in the DSM-5 manual, but many mental health-care professionals recognize it as a distinct diagnosis with specific symptoms. Many individuals with CPTSD will be on the extreme end of the scale in shame, self-loathing, guilt, and the use of various non-healthy coping mechanisms to deal with people and the outside world. While that could make another whole book, it is worth noting here as a significant impact on many people's ability to love themselves.

You can claim to love others even if you suffer with self-loathing, but there will always be some dysfunction attached to the love you are giving. It is based on past trauma, beliefs, and perceptions about who you are that have been carried into your present with every relationship you have, and it will be carried into the future unless you root it out.

WHAT SELF-LOVE IS NOT

Loving yourself completely is not about arrogance, narcissistic behavior, or spoiled and selfish tendencies. True self-love is not about what we can get from others, whether it be their love, attention, or approval. It is not about wanting to control others and force them to be what we think they should be and control all outcomes.

Self-love means treating ourselves as our best friend or perhaps our child. We afford ourselves kindness, understanding, compassion, patience, tolerance, and respect. Loving the self is not one-upping everyone else, but seeing yourself as you are, so you can then relate to others authentically by seeing them as they are.

Self-love is not delusional. It does not ask us to trick ourselves into thinking we are already perfect and cannot grow and become better people. It does not mean that we don't need to take responsibility for our actions and behaviors or for how we treat others because we think we are fabulous.

Self-love is not using addictions to fill the emptiness. It's not latching on to a spouse or lover for dear life because "they complete me." It's not living through our children or our jobs because if we stop for one moment, the truth of our emptiness will bring us to our knees. Many of us just don't believe we are worthy of loving ourselves, yet we plead for and pursue the love of others to assure ourselves of that worth. Then if we get any semblance of love or attention, we wonder why we still don't feel worthy.

Being in a codependent relationship with someone because you *need* them in your life is a strong indication that you are lacking in self-love. You shouldn't need someone else to "complete" you.

Most of us were not provided good models of self-love by our parents, teachers, and peers, so we grew up believing it was all the things it was not, and avoided cultivating the love of self we had when we were small and open and our hearts were full. Instead, we were probably scolded by authority figures to stop being "so full of ourselves" and tone it down. We were told it wasn't nice to brag or be too happy or ask for what we wanted. We had it hammered into our heads that love was about making other people happy and satisfying their needs, otherwise we were selfish and uncharitable, greedy and self-centered.

As adults we continued to believe these disparaging messages and to spend the rest of our lives pursuing wealth, possessions, and extreme external validation bestowed upon us by others. We were looking for love in all the wrong places.

We were not taught that real love must begin with loving ourselves, because our parents were not taught it, and their parents were not taught it. It's a brainwashing of multigenerational proportions. We often hear how domestic violence tends to be passed down from generation to generation, and how the pattern must be broken or it will continue. Creating magic within ourselves, if not taught to us by our parents or other individuals, is not recognized as a legitimate and healthier way to live. War, strife, poverty, racism, sexism, ageism, conflict, drug and alcohol addiction, depression, anxiety—they all have their roots in a lack of understanding of our own magic. Given this knowledge, we must generate that change from within by taking a vow to fix it for ourselves here and now.

Then and only then do we access the magic of authentic love and the beauty of discovering how it can change everything in your life for the better.

SELF–CARE

Do you take time out of each day to do something for yourself? "I'm too busy." "I have too much to do with getting the spouse and kids off to work and school." "Who has the time?" Why do we put ourselves last? We put our health last, our relaxation last, our exercise last, our alone time last. Then we wonder why we are depleted and our passion for life is dampened.

We don't have to plan a week at an expensive resort or spa to give ourselves a bit of me–time. It does not require a lot of money, or even time, yet those are the two biggest excuses made for not taking care of ourselves. It can be anything from stopping to do breathing exercises for five minutes to taking a morning walk before work to reading a chapter at night from a favorite novel.

There is a difference between being selfish and caring for oneself. You need to be healthy and mentally and emotionally balanced not only to function in the world but also to have the energy to help others. Go ahead and indulge a litte.

Self-care should start with taking better care of our health. That includes physical, emotional, and mental health. If we need more water, we drink more water. We might need a day off, so we take it without shame or guilt. Maybe what our souls beg for is a night on the town, so we find someone to trip the light fantastic with, or we go trip it ourselves.

Maybe it's a bubble bath after dinner, a book we've been longing to read, or an evening binging on a new show while the kids are asleep. It can be anything that nourishes us on any level. It is just for us, and not always what our loved ones want us to do. Again, we cannot pour of ourselves from an empty cup, so we need to take the time to fill the well.

SOMATICIZING

Not loving yourself has physical consequences beyond feelings of low self-worth, depression, and anxiety. When negative energy is stored in the body, it manifests in illness and disease. The more intense and ongoing that negativity is, the more likely you are going to suffer from physical symptoms such as stomach problems, headaches, tense muscles, lack of good sleep, overeating, and more.

Soma is the Latin word for body; when we somaticize, we are moving emotional and mental energy into the body. If we don't face our feelings and process our pain and suffering, our bodies pay the price. Lacking self-love and self-awareness is like living with a virus that eats away at us until we confront it. When we choose instead to deny, suppress, or ignore our fears and concerns, they store up in our bodies until we reach a breaking point, at which time we get sick or even end up in the hospital with a heart attack. We talk about nervous breakdowns, but we can also have bodily breakdowns when

Mental and emotional stress such as anxiety, worries, and fears can somaticize into physical symptoms, including insomnia, headaches, stomach aches, ulcers, high blood pressure, and other illnesses that could become serious.

emotions and anxieties create a perfect breeding ground inside us for cancer and other major diseases and disorders.

Even if we don't end up with cancer or a heart attack, when we somaticize it's like storing up clutter to the point where we can no longer move or breathe or feel free.

SETTING BOUNDARIES

Oh, there's that B–word. Boundaries. Unless we have them in place, people can take too much from us, disrespect our time, energy, and patience, and basically use us up because we are willingly giving too much of ourselves. In some cases, people do not even know they are asking too much of us. If we aren't setting the boundaries, they don't know what is acceptable to us and what is not. Setting firm boundaries about how we expect to be treated and what we are and are not willing to do is critical to self–love and self–care.

Boundaries are only as good as our determination to enforce them. We offer ourselves the space and energy we need when we are firm, yet compassionate, about where our boundaries are and what will happen if they are crossed or disrespected. Too many times we say we have boundaries, but then someone begs us for something or plays upon our generosity and we have difficulty saying "No."

Personal boundaries are important. It's okay to stand, maintain your values, and not allow yourself to be used or taken advantage of. You don't have to do this in a rude way, but be firm.

Having strong boundaries is a way for us to define our values and expectations to ourselves and to others. They help us cultivate better and stronger relationships that are built on mutual trust and respect and are not about who can get what from whom. Again, the key here is to inform others of our boundaries. They are not mind readers. We tell them with kindness and love, explaining what we will and will not tolerate, and those who respect our boundaries are keepers who are worthy of our time and efforts.

Think of it as advocating for yourself the way you might advocate for your child if told they needed major surgery. Be your own best friend and ally by putting boundaries in place that do not keep people out of your heart and your life but do screen out the time-suckers and energy vampires. Boundaries allow you to refuse to put up with anything that harms or diminishes you, such as abusive behavior, being used for money, and generally being treated as if you don't matter.

A boundary is like a door. It's not open to everyone and everything, but it is also not locked.

FORGIVE AND LET GO

It is impossible to love yourself if you are constantly regretting the past and beating yourself up for choices you made or didn't make. Regret, anger, resentment, and the inability to let go of the past anchor you to things that are no longer real and sap energy, freedom, and joy from your life.

Learning to release regrets by forgiving ourselves is key to finding that magic again. We pull up the anchor weighing us down and cut the line, letting the heaviness drop down to the bottom of the ocean where it belongs. We face our sadness, grief, and anger and process it, and then we forgive ourselves for all our mistakes and poor choices and let it go.

We have the power to reframe and reclaim the past, recognize what happened to us but work through the things that happened toward a greater enlightenment and better life.

We have the power to reframe and reclaim the past, recognize what happened to us but work through the things that happened toward a greater enlightenment and better life. We can release what no longer serves us and allow ourselves to be forgiven as we also forgive others involved.

How to Live a Mindful, Meaningful, Magical Life

You are not a barnacle attached to the past anymore.

Forgiveness might be the most important thing anyone can do to access the magic life has to offer, because without it, we are chained to people, events, and circumstances that weigh us down and don't allow us to step forward in freedom of body, mind, and spirit. Forgiveness is not about letting someone off the hook for something awful they may have done, but about letting ourselves off the hook of the attachment we still have that is keeping us from being happy again.

According to Nancy Colier, L.C.S.W., in "What Is Forgiveness and How Do You Do It," a March 15, 2018, *Psychology Today* blog post: "We imagine that not forgiving is a form of punishment, a way of being in control of a situation we didn't feel we had control over. At a primal level, we imagine that not forgiving is a way of taking care of our wound, proclaiming that suffering exists, and still and forever matters." But when we think of it in this way, all we succeed in doing is making sure the pain and hurt continue.

Forgiving others, even ourselves, does not mean we condone the behaviors or actions we are forgiving. We don't. We never will. Instead, it's about letting ourselves be free of the burden of the past and the suffering we believed the other person caused us. We do not forgive and forget; we forgive and move forward, because life can only be lived forward.

Forgiveness is different from condoning bad behavior, but we can recognize that people are not perfect, and we need to recognize this and keep moving forward.

This is especially important when it comes to things that we did that were stupid, painful, or harmful to ourselves. We can learn to forgive the worst offenses others perpetrated upon us, but often we can never forgive ourselves for the stupid stuff we did when we were more … well … stupid. We continue to beat ourselves up for bad decisions and rotten behaviors that, had we known better, we would never have engaged in. That is key, because at the time, we did not know better. We were probably doing the best we could with the mindset we had.

Colier also wrote: "Forgiveness, ultimately, is about freedom. When we need someone else to change in order for us to be OK, we are a prisoner." She describes us as being shackled to our anger and resentment when we do not forgive. We keep hoping that, if we hang on to the hurt, it will change things, but the past cannot be undone. "Forgiveness is ultimately about choosing to offer ourselves love—and with it—freedom."

ALL YOU NEED IS ... SELF-LOVE

Loving the self is not about trying to be perfect. There is no such thing as perfection, so stop chasing it. Instead, strive to be authentically you and honor, cherish, and celebrate who that is.

In "The Importance of Self-Love" for the January 17, 2019, *Psychology Today*, author Beverly D. Flaxington wrote: "It means recognizing that someone else who didn't learn unconditional love has a hard time giving it.… Understanding this can help you turn your attention from waiting and wanting someone to make you

One trait that really attracts people to one another is kindess. People who are genuine and care about others and not just themselves are respectful and nonjudgmental. A nice smile doesn't hurt, either!

whole, to realizing you have that ability inside you." When we understand that hurt people pass on that hurt to others, we can see that they did not have the self-love they so sorely needed, but that we can give that gift to ourselves."

Once we awaken to who we genuinely are and show our authenticity to the world, we make it easier to love ourselves and give love to others. People who meet a confident person recognize that confidence down deep, even if they do not know why.

Think of someone you met when you were a child or an adult that you felt completely comfortable with and wanted to spend more time being around. What was it about them? Did you notice their kindness, the genuine way they spoke, their smile? The way they accepted you and seemed to be totally capable, loving, non-judgmental and respectful to others? This isn't to say people cannot have these qualities and still be working through difficulties and trying to figure out their lives. Remember, we are not talking about perfect people. We are talking about people who are on the path of discovering self-love. Because that journey never ends.

Magic is like a head cold. It spreads quickly and easily, but only when people are susceptible to it. That requires a love of self and belief in ourselves that is strong enough to set free our own magic within so we can then experience it, express it, and share it with everyone we come in contact with. Alan Cohen said, "To love yourself right now, just as you are, is to give yourself heaven." Once you have the gift of heaven, you can then be an example to others who seek that same heaven for themselves.

That's how magic goes pandemic. You are patient zero. It begins with you and within you.

Do not feel lonely. The entire universe is inside you.
Rumi

AUTHOR INSIGHTS

Marie's Story

As a child, up until about the age of seven or eight, I loved who I was and expressed myself without worry or fear of being liked or disliked. I didn't care what others thought. I was a caring child, but my main concern was exploring the world around me and processing my feelings through writing. I was happy and joyful. I spent tons of time in nature, which was filled with magic to me. The starry night skies, the woods behind our house where I was sure Bigfoot lived, the birds in the trees that I identified with my binoculars and field guide, the animal tracks in the backyard that I drew and wrote about in my many journals, and the stories I made up to tell anyone who would listen.

Life was magic. I was magic. I was ME and I loved who that was.

Then I got a little older and suddenly I was filled with shame over my skinny legs and how my friend Finola had great calf muscles. I was made to feel awful for telling my auntie I wanted a cookie when it was too close to dinner time. I was made fun of for the crazy stories I told and wrote about and often told to stop talking so much. I was told I couldn't wear pants to school because girls wore dresses, and I hated dresses.

And as I got even older, things happened, traumatic things, that stripped me of all joy for a long, long time. Along the way, I forgot who I was and fell prey to addiction and depression.

To make a long story short, I am now at an age where I can look back and see how a lack of self-love derailed my life and my dreams and how I sought to fill that incredible black hole within with so many external people, things, achievements, and situations. Sadly, as with any drug or addiction, what works for a while stops working and you need more and more to fill that void until you hit bottom, or worse.

The push to conform and behave in certain ways has a way of stifling our creativity, our joy, and even our personality. Bullying, teasing, and judgment from adults can have lasting impacts on our lives as we become adults.

By the time I got where I am today, I had already done a lot of self-love and addiction work–for over a decade, in fact–and I was suddenly very much aware of how the answer to all my problems was always self–love. My health, my finances, my relationships, my goals and dreams, all were exactly as they were because I never loved myself enough to make things better. I didn't believe I was worth it or deserved it.

That realization was all I needed to stop putting time and energy into fixing others and focus on myself. It allowed me to re-group and redirect back onto my own path after being detoured by the paths of so many others. I am still a work in progress as I enter my sixties, but those feelings of magic have returned. They were always there, but I had buried them under years and years of distraction and deflection and refusing to look within, always so certain the problems as well as the answers were outside of me.

I can proudly say magic is afoot again and that it comes from first facing my own lack of self–love and learning to fall back in love with myself and my life again, the way I was when I was small and carefree and joyful in the world around me and my own presence in it.

I can proudly say magic is afoot again and that it comes from first facing my own lack of self-love and learning to fall back in love with myself and my life again....

Denise's Story

I was like most kids. Well, that's only partially true. As a child I definitely found the wonder, curiosity, and joy of playing with dolls, jacks, trucks and cars (yeah, a group of us little girls liked play-ing with toy trucks and cars). I read like crazy, loving books so much. I liked to do the twist (I'm aging myself here) and enjoyed the ad-miration and laughs of others watching me. Most of the time, though, I didn't like being noticed and went out of my way to avoid it. At the same time there was a yearning inside me for love and at-tention, to be thought of as special. All kids need that and want it.

On the outside looking in, I'm pretty sure everyone thought we had a model family of the time in many ways, with the homemaker mother and hardworking sheriff's deputy father. Sociology would say I was an only child and youngest child at the same time because of the large spread in age between my siblings and me. I took on the traits of only child and youngest at the same time. We didn't have a ton of money, but there was food on the table and a roof over our heads, and I lived in a beautiful pine forest. What more could I want? Hidden within all that was a dysfunctional family with a variety of issues, and eventually that spilled over into me developing CPTSD, which I wouldn't even know until I reached my fifties and the lightbulb went on and I could start working on it.

One of my earliest memories as a child, probably somewhere around three or four, was being acutely aware of what other people were feeling. As a child, I understood the energy in a room and other people's emotions. Especially if they were distressed and hiding it. Sometimes I'd tell people what their emotions were and surprise them with my accuracy. People would feel comfortable telling me everything, and I knew something had changed by the time we'd finished talking. They'd feel lighter, better, smiling. Yeah, this happened even when I was in grade school. When I became a teenager, and later as an adult, people would often tell me they felt like a weight had been lifted away from them after they'd chatted with me. People in general spilled their guts to me.

Was I just an empathic and sensitive child? Absolutely, yes. I didn't like loud noises (and noise has always been loud for me sometimes when it isn't for others) or bright light or crowds of people. One thing that impacted me significantly was the learning disability dyscalculia, which is the inability to process and understand numbers in certain ways and difficulty doing math. A host of other complications can result because of this disability.

Some people demonstrate a high propensity for empathy, which is a very nice trait to have when helping other people, but being very sensitive to others and one's surroundings can have its challenges, too.

My sensitivity as a child made people point it out as a fault. "She's so sensitive." "She's too sensitive."

"She cries too easily when she hears certain music. What is that all about?" "She hides behind her mother all the time." "Why can she do math and retain multiplication tables?" Some of the messages I received from adults and even other kids was, "What is wrong with her?" "She's too different." "She's weird." "She's just shy." "Oh, she's so mature for her age." "She's such a good little girl."

As a result, I was an easy target for bullies and suffered extensive bullying up through junior high. In high school that calmed down a lot, although there was the occasional bullying incident.

A sensitive child with elements in her life leading to CPTSD meant I created coping mechanisms to survive the world. I thought the way to survive was to accommodate everyone else's needs way more than my own. In my head other people were allowed to be angry and I wasn't. I became extremely fixated on the idea that for people never to be angry with me or disapprove of me and to like me, I must do, act, and be whatever was required in order to accomplish that goal. It wasn't until many decades later I realized my entire life had been centered around this one goal. So many things authentic and genuine to my own personality were subverted for this objective.

The fact that I did understand people very well helped me accomplish my goal of being a person who was praised extensively for being conscientious, hardworking and "nice." I developed the ability to calm angry people and those with mental health issues and communicate with almost anyone on a high level. People still spill their guts to me, but I've found I genuinely enjoy helping others find their best selves. It has drawn me to creativity coaching, intuitive readings, and mediumship. My imagination became huge, too, and my interest in writing at an early age blossomed into becoming a novelist and screenplay writer.

Have I rid myself of the dyscalculia? No, that's always going to be there. What about the sensitivity? While I'll always be "sensitive," I've learned several techniques to help myself and those who are empaths like me. In the chapter "The Magic of Connecting to Source," I talk more extensively about this.

While still a work in progress, I am more confident and capable and working toward becoming my most authentic self.

Only by being my full self, accepting my foibles and faults and loving my abilities, can I also assist others in finding their own path to self–worth and self–love.

MAGICAL TIPS

Twelve Ways to Love Yourself More

1. Practice self–care and take care of your own physical, emotional, spiritual, and mental needs.

2. Let go of the past, including past traumas and regrets, and clear the slate for your magical future.

3. Put your own well–being first and foremost. As with oxygen masks on a plane, you must put yours on first if you ever hope to help anyone else.

4. Surround yourself with loving, supportive, and positive people and eliminate negative relationships that drain and diminish you.

5. Set and keep boundaries. Adopt a "no matter what" attitude to protect your time and sanity.

Set yourself up for feeling more love about yourself by surrounding yourself with family and friends who support you and care about you. It's important to not allow yourself to be brought down by someone just because they are a relative or say they are a friend when they really aren't. Be choosy when it comes to the company you keep.

How to Live a Mindful, Meaningful, Magical Life

6. Practice gratitude and keep focused on the good in your life in order to see more of it.

7. Celebrate your small and big wins and be proud of what you achieve.

8. Do the things that bring you joy even if they don't seem "productive."

9. Surround your environment with beauty such as flowers, photos of loved ones, or art. Make where you live a place worth living and a reflection of who you are.

10. Meditate and practice mindfulness to stay in touch with your inner being and increase your intuition and self-awareness.

11. Exercise and eat nutritiously to take care of your physical being for a long and healthy life.

12. Get out in nature more often and let your spirit soar.

The Mirror Exercise

The experience of looking at yourself in the mirror can be incredibly uncomfortable. Most of us go through our days avoiding glimpses of ourselves, whether because we feel too old or fat or frumpy or just because we hate ourselves and no amount of beauty or hotness can cover that up. We take a quick glimpse to make sure we don't have spinach in our teeth or our hair isn't a wild mess, and we look away as soon as possible. We never really LOOK at ourselves.

Try this. Stand before a mirror with a timer. Start the timer. Gaze into your own eyes and see how long you can go before you feel so uncomfortable you look away. Chances are you won't last more than a minute, which can feel like forever when you are doing this (try this naked and you probably won't last more than 30 seconds, no matter how good you look). Self-examination is not easy. The trick is to really look deep into your own eyes and try to connect with that person in there looking back at you. Try saying "I love you" three or four times and see how you feel.

Most likely you will feel foolish, embarrassed, inauthentic, and fraudulent—if you feel anything at all. Many of us are so detached from ourselves, it's a wonder we can love anyone else at all. And magic? Forget it. Detachment from our own inner being is not conducive to experiencing the magic life has to offer. It's not conducive to much of anything except unhappiness and disappointment.

With time and practice you will learn to start saying "I love you" and smiling, laughing, feeling a sense of joy and pride and happiness as you come to first like, then love, those eyes staring back at you. Then you can start telling yourself how proud you are, how cool you are, and how you are such a great best friend to yourself. This is how you reconnect to self.

The mirror exercise isn't as simple as it looks. Regarding yourself deeply for more than 30 seconds is hard for most people. What do you feel when you look into your eyes and say "I love you" several times?

In her seminal book *Happy for No Reason*, author Marci Shimoff wrote about the mirror exercise and how it can raise our happiness "set point," which governs just how much happiness and joy we feel. "If you're like most people, consciously recognizing the positive about yourself may feel conceited. After all, we're raised not to toot our own horns. So, we end up not giving ourselves credit or acknowledgement, or, even worse, we beat ourselves up, which shuts down our hearts, contracts our energy, and–you guessed it–lowers our happiness set point."

By appreciating and giving props to ourselves, we become capable of greater levels of happiness and self-love. Our focus shifts, and soon we are more inclined to see the positive in life, including the magic, instead of everything that is wrong.

Childhood Inventory Quiz

In this book we talk about moving beyond our past to live in the present and feel more self-confident and genuine. Where can you start? Try a childhood inventory. Ask yourself the following questions as a baseline for where you are right now in this journey. Take time to answer these questions by going as deep as you can.

1. What is your earliest childhood memory? Was it pleasant? If so, why? If not, why?

2. What was most enjoyable to you as a child? What activities did you enjoy the most?

3. Can you recall a moment or experience in child-hood when you felt truly loved, appreciated, and valued—an experience so memorable that it has never left you? Can you bring it to your mind's eye now and fully feel it?

4. Of the activities you enjoyed the most as a child, were you allowed to continue those activities later into your life? If not, were you given a reason at the time for why you weren't allowed to continue these activities?

5. What messages did you feel you received as a child about who you could be and couldn't be? Are you still following those old rules? If so, why do you believe you are? If you're following those old rules, do you think they are still working for you?

6. If you could change one thing about yourself, what would it be? Why?

The idea behind this quiz is to bring to light some things in your childhood that might be holding over to your adulthood. These can be good things or not so helpful things. They are only for reference as we move forward.

Journal Exercise

We know. Not everyone likes to journal. Sometimes that is because we have a box around what journaling is supposed to look like. Or we may think back to childhood and think of diaries—those little pink things with locks on them that only girls used. Men, journaling is for you, too.

Your journal can be as simple or elaborate as you want it. Lock or no lock. Leatherbound. A college–or wide–ruled notebook. Journals can be electronic, too. Whatever feels good is fine. As we go through this book there will be periodic journal exercises to explore.

Therapists often recommend to their clients that they take up journaling. Writing down your thoughts each day can help you get in touch with your feelings and think through challenges you are facing more clearly.

For the exercise in this chapter, get your journal (if you don't have one yet you can type it out on the computer or write it on random sheets of paper) and answer the following question in as much depth as possible. As you continue reading the book you might find you can add more to this journal entry, but try to be as detailed as you can this time around. The idea is to get clear in your mind the questions you want answered and how you want to feel once you complete the reading of this book. Okay, let's go.

1. What insights do you hope to gain from reading this book and completing these exercises?

That's it for now. By examining where you were and where you want to go, you can find the path to moving into your magical, authentic self.

The Magic of Relationships

Treasure your relationships, not your possessions.

Anthony J. D'Angelo

The beginning of love is to let those we love be perfectly themselves, and not to twist them to fit our own image. Otherwise we love only the reflection of ourselves we find in them.

Thomas Merton

Don't smother each other. No one can grow in the shade.

Leo Buscaglia

British poet John Donne wrote his seminal poem, "No Man Is an Island," about the human need for relationship.

NO MAN IS AN ISLAND

No man is an island,
Entire of itself;
Every man is a piece of the continent,
A part of the main.
If a clod be washed away by the sea,
Europe is the less,
As well as if a promontory were,

As well as if a manor of thy friend's
Or of thine own were.
Any man's death diminishes me,
Because I am involved in mankind,
And therefore never send to know for whom the bell tolls;
It tolls for thee.

Though we must first grow to respect and love ourselves, there is little magic to be found in life unless we take the next step and seek to cultivate and nourish relationships. We may feel as though we are islands, with separate boundaries and clear borders, but the truth is, we are all a part of the vast ocean of life that those islands exist within. Like blades of grass in a field, we are both individual blade and part of the collective field.

Relationships are an essential need for humans to thrive. We don't do well all by ourselves unless we are monks or hermits who have disavowed all connection to others. Even those who need little social interaction and would classify themselves as introverts are still in need of human engagement on some level to thrive and grow. Many people who isolate too much for extended periods may find their world narrowing so much that they may suffer depression or other mental illness as a result. Total isolation is not a very magical way to live in a world brimming with people who can add to our lives in untold ways, and we to theirs.

Many people who isolate too much for extended periods may find their world narrowing so much that they may suffer depression or other mental illness as a result.

Relationships are good for the mind, the body, the spirit, and the soul, and they can come in many forms. Lovers, friends, families, pets, colleagues, fellow companions on the trails of life. Do we need to have a deep connection with all of the people we know to thrive? Absolutely not. We can have relationships with people based only on a shared hobby, passion, or place of worship. We can have relationships with people we don't even know, such as a favorite poet, writer, or singer who truly speaks to us through their art. We can even establish a relationship with the manager of our bank, the cashier of our favorite store, or the person who does our taxes every year. Good interactions, no matter how long or deep, add to our well–being.

As long as it involves a connection between two or more people, it's a relationship.

MASLOW'S HIERARCHY OF NEEDS

American psychologist Abraham Maslow wrote about the "hierarchy of needs" in his seminal 1943 paper, "A Theory of Human Motivation." It was published in the journal *Psychological Review* and generated a storm of debate about his ideas and observations. His hierarchy has often been symbolized by a pyramid, with the type of needs listed from bottom to top. At the bottom are physiological needs such as food, water, and shelter. As we move up the pyramid, we have things such as security/safety, self–esteem, self–actualization, and at the very top, transcendence. Midway up the pyramid are social needs such as belonging and love. These needs, Maslow wrote, motivate human actions and behaviors.

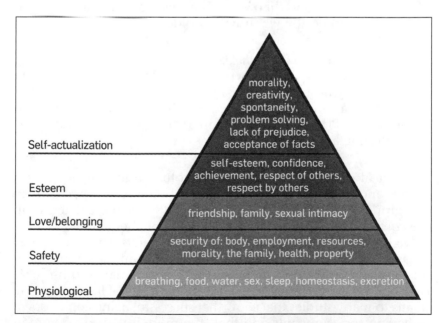

Abraham Maslow's "hierarchy of needs" shows our most basic needs at the base of the pyramid and then works its way up to the higher needs regarding self-actualization.

How to Live a Mindful, Meaningful, Magical Life

The social needs include friendships, social groups, work colleagues, families, romantic attachments, churches and religious organizations, and other types of relationships humans are motivated to form to avoid loneliness, depression, anxiety, isolation, and lack of love and connection. Even being involved in something like a book club, sports team fan club, knitting circle, coffee klatch, or group that hikes different trails each month provides the type of connection so vital to human thriving.

Our primitive ancestors knew the importance of the tribe or clan, and that searching alone for food and shelter was dangerous. It made sense to band together, but it also provided them with other people to share stories and experiences with. A lone wolf may travel faster, but it is a lot safer to travel with a pack that keeps you company and has your back. For as long as humans have walked the Earth, they have joined together in groups and in creating the first villages and neighborhoods.

In today's high-tech world of social media we have the ability to connect with far more people all over the globe, but we also often feel more alone than ever. The best relationships happen face-to-face, especially when we get older.

In a March 9, 2021, *Psychology Today* blog post, "The Power of Relationships as We Age," Wayne Jonas, M.D., wrote that as more Americans live past the age of 65 than ever before, the later years can become a time of depression, isolation, and ill health when we are alone. Prioritizing social connections helps ward off cognitive decline and combats loneliness.

Social connections can include volunteering, meeting with friends and family, and taking on a new hobby. Older people may join groups of like-minded individuals at local senior centers or in the communities they live in, and this keeps them active and involved at a time when it's easy to feel alone and isolated. "To some," Jonas wrote, "it feels that this time of life is a time of endings. But it shouldn't be. Because the more active you remain—both physically and mentally—the more successful this time of life will be." He points to many studies that show that successful aging comes down to having social pursuits and that "the more involved you are in social activities, the better your overall health and cognition."

It's long been established that people in their later years are much healthier intellectually, emotionally, and physically when they have active social lives. Living for today and looking forward to the future can dramatically benefit our lives.

This goes for anyone of any age. Relationships that are reciprocal, nurturing, honest, and supportive are a healing balm for the soul, especially during challenging times, but it's also important to find people to laugh and be silly with. Close friendships are those where both parties can "let it all hang out" and be themselves.

Throughout our lives we connect with people for a short time, a season, or forever, and all those types of relationships have gifts and blessings and help us grow and expand our horizons. These connections can be positive or negative, but these situations teach us important things about ourselves we need to know. According to "6 Types of Relationships and Their Effect on Your Life" by Kendra Cherry, posted on *Verywell Mind* on September 21, 2022, there are many ways of relating, including romantically, platonically, and situationally, and there must be caring, respect, and closeness for positive friendships to form.

However, many of us only know how to relate on a codependent level, where we rely on someone else for our emotional needs when we should be relying on ourselves. Codependents put others before themselves and will sacrifice their own health, money, time, and happiness to please those around them. Dr. Sharon Martin, an expert on the topic, wrote in "How to Stop Being Codependent," a piece posted on her website on January 14, 2021, "Essentially, codependents consistently prioritize others over themselves which leads to exhaustion, resentment, feeling responsible for other adults, inappropriate guilt, physical and emotional health problems, unsatisfying relationships, feeling inferior, unloved, or unimportant." Yet so many of us have these types of relationships in our lives at any given time and it saps all the magic out of how we connect to those around us.

Dr. Martin explains that codependent behaviors include things like perfectionism, enabling others, self-sacrifice to the point of martyrdom, being passive or passive-aggressive, fixing and rescuing others, and never addressing one's own issues.

Codependency can be toxic when one person gives much more, expecting something in return, and the relationship feels more like an obligation to the other person. Cherry wrote in the *Verywell Mind* article, "Co-dependent relationships are co-constructed. While one partner might seem more 'needy,' the other partner might feel more comfortable being needed." Codependent relationships are conditional and not just between lovers or spouses, but between friends, families, and even coworkers.

Without self-worth and boundaries, we will accommodate many people to the complete detriment of ourselves.

Dysfunctional relationships abound when we don't value ourselves and construct boundaries. Without self-worth and boundaries, we will accommodate many people to the complete detriment of ourselves.

How do we feel when we interact with someone? People are mirrors in which we see ourselves reflected back, the good, the bad, and the ugly. This is the gift of any relationship, but it's the more challenging ones that seem to teach us the most about how we see ourselves and where we might be flawed or imperfect.

When relationships become too toxic, either because of lack of support, need to control, jealousy, abuse, lack of communication, or passive-aggressive behaviors, we might need to look at why we are contributing to an unhealthy connection that does not bring us joy and add more magic to our lives. Just as there is a plethora of research showing the positive benefits of relationships, there is research indicating toxic relationships can wreak havoc on your mental and physical health.

NURTURING HEALTHY RELATIONSHIPS

The ideal relationships are unconditional, but we humans are flawed creatures. We can aspire to getting as close to this as possible for the benefit of all concerned. When all parties involved are invested in the relationship and on equal footing, that's where the magic happens.

Some tips for strengthening our relationships include:

- Show appreciation for the other person.
- Listen when they talk and don't just rehearse our response in our heads.
- Respect each other.
- Show interest in the other person's hobbies and interests.
- Be honest, open, and vulnerable, which allows the other person to do the same.
- Support and encourage the other person's dreams and goals.
- Show compassion and empathy.
- Give the relationship the gift of time and undivided attention.
- Trust each other.
- Be there in bad times as well as in good times.

Healthy relationships come about when people *listen* to one another, take an interest in their lives, and act supportive, empathetic, and encouraging.

How to Live a Mindful, Meaningful, Magical Life

The American spiritual leader Baba Ram Dass (1931–2019) was a psychologist, yoga guru, and educator often credited with helping to popularize Eastern spiritual practices in the United States.

Ram Dass is famously quoted as saying "We are all just walking each other home." What this means is that our time on Earth is about our journeys and who we meet along the way, for whatever time we walk beside them. We are all headed home, to the place from where we came, and we have the honor of getting to walk with so many people along the way there–some for a day, some for a season, some for a lifetime.

This means walking beside others in times of ease and times of challenge, supporting each other, learning from one another, comparing experiences and sharing perspectives, for whatever time we have together. Connection with others is what we are about; it's the foundation of our humanity. Yes, we should have our personal and individual goals and dreams, but life is so much richer and deeper when we share ourselves with others, and they with us. We need each other, and we are at our best when we relate to others and share ourselves with them in ways that expand our capacity to experience life's magic.

FURRY FRIENDSHIPS COUNT, TOO!

Nobody can fully understand the meaning of love unless he's owned a dog. A dog can show you more honest affection with a flick of his tail than a man can gather through a lifetime of handshakes.

Gene Hill, author of *A Hunter's Fireside Book* and *Hill Country*

If it's the magic of unconditional love within a relationship you want, it might behoove you to get a dog, cat, horse, or other pet you can love! While many will say there is no greater love than that of a dog for its human parent, other pets can certainly provide us with the well-being that comes from caring and loving a pet and being loved by them in return. No matter what happens in our human relationships, our fur babies will be there to comfort us.

Pets provide us with love, laughter, comfort, joy, exercise, and a lot of magic. Amy Sedaris was right when she said, "Sometimes losing a pet is more painful than losing a human because in the case of the pet, you were not pretending to love it." They give us so much, and we often give them back so little. Yet our devoted pets are always there to brighten our day and lift our spirits.

As related in "The Benefits of Owning a Pet–and the Surprising Science Behind It" by Sandee LaMotte, posted February 20, 2020, on *CNN.com*, a study from Indiana University showed that just watching cat videos boosted energy and positive emotions in the viewers. Psychologist Harold Herzog of Western Carolina University has studied the human–animal connection for years and stated some of the benefits of pet ownership: "Higher survival rates, fewer heart attacks, less loneliness, better blood pressure, better psychological well-being, lower rates of depression and stress levels, fewer doctor visits, increased self-esteem, better sleep and more physical exercise are just some of the recorded benefits...."

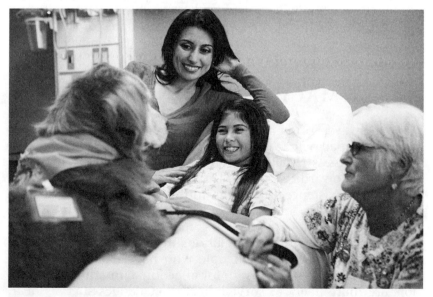

Dogs are widely used as therapy animals for people in hospitals, senior homes, rehabilitation centers, and even in prisons. Outside of such therapy work, dogs have been shown to help people lead healthier, happier lives in general.

How to Live a Mindful, Meaningful, Magical Life

Wow! He also said people's good moods increased around pets. Pets can also help lift the spirits of children in hospitals and people in Alzheimer's special care units. They are even used in some prison rehabilitation programs that allow inmates to bond with a dog and train them during their incarceration.

Matthew Wilson writes in "15 Reasons Why Having a Pet Is Good for You and Your Family," posted June 2, 2020, on *Insider.com*, that owning a pet does more than improve health; it can improve your lifestyle, help children learn about empathy and responsibility, and even boost their literacy skills. "While people who adopt an animal usually think they're changing its life for the better, pets have just as much of a positive impact on the lives of their owners." Spending time with a pet triggers the release of the love hormone, oxytocin, and makes you feel close and bonded with your pet.

Pets are also great conversation starters when making new friends, and people who own pets are more likely to date other people who own pets, so pets can help your love life, too.

No matter what kinds of relationships you have, they can become sources of pure magic and joy if properly cultivated, just like seeds planted in a garden. With enough attention, patience, and nurturing, they become our greatest sources of connection in our daily lives and remind us that we are truly never alone.

INTIMACY AND VULNERABILITY

One way to bring more magic into our relationships is to expand our capacity for vulnerability, honesty, and intimacy. In *The Art of Happiness: A Handbook for Living* (1998), written by the Dalai Lama and Howard C. Cutler, M.D., intimacy is said to be at the heart of our existence as humans. Intimacy, the ability to be open with and close to another, promotes well-being of body and mind. The book documents many medical studies showing the health benefits of intimate relationships, stating: "Medical researchers have found that people who have close friendships, people whom they can turn to for affection, empathy, and affection, are more likely to survive health challenges such as heart attacks and major surgery and are less likely to develop diseases such as cancer and respiratory infections."

Intimacy helps us maintain emotional health and well-being. Erich Fromm, the psychoanalyst and philosopher, claimed that humanity's most basic fear is the threat of being separated from other humans. We need each other, but even more important, we enjoy each other and find magic in spending time with those we love, trust, and feel close to.

If you're feeling skeptical about how much we need human connection, there is strong evidence of our need to bond and to belong playing out in the fiction we create. Don't believe it?

Think of it this way: A fear of being separated from other humans is often depicted in books, plays, movies, music, and other art. The

The current Dalai Lama has often spoken of the benefits of compassion, and in his book cowritten with Dr. Howard C. Cutler, *The Art of Happiness*, he talks about the importance of intimate relationships in our lives.

creators may have experienced and internalized this situation and be able to vividly depict this greatest fear in their work.

A television series like *The Walking Dead* skillfully illustrates the innate fear we have of being alone, abandoned, set adrift, and attacked by assumed or perceived enemies. Each episode has examples of humans from all walks of life either coming together to bond and support each other through horrible times or allowing the worst sides of themselves to come through. Most encouraging, however, are those moments in the series when people who may not have been friends before the apocalypse are now bonded deeply—more deeply in some cases than they could ever have experienced with their own families. Even some enemies have become allies against the biggest threat: death by zombies.

The Dalai Lama suggests that to strengthen and improve our relationships, we use the approach of "basing our relationship on the qualities of affection, compassion and mutual respect as human beings. Basing a relationship on these qualities enables us to achieve a deep and meaningful bond not only with our lover or spouse, but also with friends, acquaintances, or strangers–virtually any human being."

We might also add that unless you come into a relationship as your authentic self, it is not an authentic relationship. Being vulnerable means letting it all hang out, despite what others might think, and allowing them to do the same in your presence. This is the magic of real, honest, true relating that builds bonds that can last a lifetime.

In Brené Brown's book *Daring Greatly*, she takes a deep dive into why being vulnerable is so difficult for humans. To most of us, being vulnerable is the absolute last thing we wish to do. In some societies vulnerability of any kind can be looked upon as weakness and as a risk. We are taught from childhood that being vulnerable can mean all sorts of nasty consequences up to and including death. If we aren't taught that being vulnerable can lead to fantastic, close interactions of all kinds, we may create the most superficial and fragile relationships. Even when you are vulnerable enough to create what you perceive as a good friendship or "besties" with someone, if that person doesn't know the genuine you, the connection won't be as deep and fulfilling as it could be. You aren't being accepted for being 100 percent who you are but rather on a construct you have made and that someone else accepts.

A professor at the University of Houston's Graduate School of Social Work, Brené Brown has become a popular speaker and writer in her field.

It is important to note that most of us don't start off with the idea of being disingenuous with others. We create superficial relationships without even realizing that is what we're doing. How vulnerable and open we are to other people is a complex psychological and sometimes spiritual situation. Vulnerability and authenticity can help us build lasting and satisfying relationships, but first we must be aware of what it means to be authentic and vulnerable, and then take steps toward these ideals. How can we connect genuinely with others and take those baby steps toward authenticity?

It is not our purpose to become each other, it is to recognize each other; to learn to see the other and respect him for what he is.

Hermann Hesse

THE MAGIC OF COMMUNITY AND TRIBE

Being a part of a community, whether it's our own neighborhood or a meeting of like-minded people in our general area, goes a long way toward building a sense of belonging. A community is like an interconnected web linked by shared and common goals and interests, and we feel at home with people who have much in common with us or live nearby. Community knows no borders, though, and can be as much a global thing as local.

On a global scale, we might find community in shared religious or political beliefs, bonding in groups and organizations or on social media. We might come together over our love of travel or gardening or collecting seashells. On a local scale it can be all about getting together to play Bunco or pickleball or do a park or beach clean-up. Any activity or situation that brings us into "communion" with others adds to our sense of being a part of something and wards off feelings of isolation.

Community spirit engulfs anyone who loves where they live and wants to take care of their neighborhood. You can see this when a community holds a craft fair or a multi-family block party, or when they come together to help one another after a disaster strikes. Knowing you are surrounded by good neighbors makes everyday life a lot more magical and a lot less lonely.

This is especially important for older people because they are retired and don't meet others through a workplace. They can be cut off from human interaction other than family members who live close enough to visit unless they are living in a retirement home or facility. Children and young people have the benefit of building bonds with others through school and work. Seniors lack this and truly benefit from finding nearby meetups, groups, and activities that allow them to make new friends and bond with others. Senior centers are located in just about every neighborhood and are a great resource.

How to Live a Mindful, Meaningful, Magical Life

Your "tribe" of people can comprise almost any type of community so long as they work together toward some common goal and support one another.

"Find your tribe" has become a common catchphrase today on social media and in self-help books and means making close friends and contacts that relate to each other on many levels, not just shared beliefs and having kids in the same schools. A tribe is a group, big or small, of intertwined souls that get each other, support each other, and inspire each other and become like a real family. Your tribe may not share a drop of blood in common, but they share a common spirit. A tribe also shares interests that bring them together for camaraderie, laughs, and adventures, whether it be world travel or doggy playdates.

It is important to have yourself to lean on and to have close relationships with family and loved ones, but don't leave out the blessings and magic of being part of a bigger group of people that love you for who you are and support your goals and purpose. Individuals within the community or tribe may come and go as some pass on or move away, but the bonding spirit remains strong for all involved, and many lifelong friendships are forged among tribes you belong to throughout your life.

HUG SOMEBODY

Humans crave touch. A pat on the shoulder, a caring hug, a hand placed over ours when we are scared. Touch is healing to the body, mind, and spirit, and there is plenty of scientific research showing this to be true. Touch conveys caring, compassion, empathy, love, and understanding.

Touch benefits the giver and the receiver. We are not talking about anything sexual here, although that, too, has its benefits. Just a simple act of reaching out and showing someone that we care, especially in a society that often tells us not to touch and to keep our hands to ourselves, can boost feel-good hormones such as oxytocin for both parties involved. Holding a hug for a few moments releases serotonin and elevates mood. Hugs and touch also help strengthen the immune system. Massage therapy has been shown to reduce pain in pregnant women and alleviate prenatal depression, and our primate ancestors spent a lot of time grooming each other as a way to stay physically connected.

Researchers at Carnegie Mellon University, in a December 2014 article titled "Hugs Help Protect Against Stress and Infection," described a study that concluded that hugs serve as important methods of social support, and the more hugs one got, the more one was protected from severe illness and stress symptoms.

Touch includes petting a dog or cat, too. Make it a habit to hug the ones you love more often and see if it doesn't improve your level of well-being, and theirs, too.

FORGIVE

Just as we can only love ourselves when we forgive ourselves for the pain and suffering we brought upon ourselves, the same applies to our relationships. We must learn to forgive others, even if we don't agree

Hugs aren't just fun and comforting; they can actually benefit your health by reducing stress and even help prevent infections.

with or condone their actions, because until we do, we relate to them from a past transgression. They may have changed completely, but we are still holding them to a time and place out of a sense of self-righteousness so we can feel right and justified.

"Forgiving a person who has wronged you is never easy, but dwelling on those events and reliving them over and over can fill your mind with negative thoughts and suppressed anger," stated Dr. Tyler VanderWeele, co-director of the Initiative on Health, Religion, and Spirituality at the Harvard T.H. Chan School of Public Health. When we learn to forgive, he continued, "we are no longer trapped by past actions of others and can finally be free."

It's not just about freeing the other person but all parties involved. He suggests starting with small acts of forgiveness in everyday life. An example might be forgiving someone for being rude to you in a grocery store. You are not saying their behavior is okay, but instead recognizing they might have just gotten some bad news or be having a troubling day, and forgiving them their actions on the spot. "This way you can also learn to immediately stop the negative reaction and the feelings that come with it."

The closest relationships we have are with people who probably do dumb things now and then, often things that hurt or offend us, and if we hold onto the resentment and anger, it can eat away at our spirit. Practicing forgiveness is a challenge, but the more we do it, the easier it comes, and we find that we are enjoying the other person a lot more because we are not getting hung up on the dumb things they might do. We also recognize that we do dumb things to them, too, and by forgiving them, we inspire them to do the same to us.

Forgiveness is about accepting responsibility for your own role in what happened, as well as about accepting the behaviors of those who have wronged you. Acceptance does not mean you like what happened or think it was justified, but that you are choosing to let it go so you can feel better. Everyone makes mistakes in life, and sometimes those mistakes will be doozies, such as betrayals, crimes, abuses, and other indiscretions. We are not asking you to forgive someone right away or not to process the pain they put you through, but at some point you may feel like you just cannot drag the dead weight of the past behind you anymore. It is holding you back, and it is possibly also causing suffering to someone who has made amends and asked for forgiveness.

The act of forgiveness and having compassion for others who often screw up and make mistakes is like both parties finally letting go of the ends of the rope in an exhausting game of tug-of-war. It is also the acknowledgment that you know better and will do better, and that the relationship means enough to you to look forward, not backward. You might also forgive someone and never wish to see them again because of what they did, and that is okay, too. Some relationships are better left in the past if the situation was too horrible to ever trust them again, but don't take the emotional baggage with you as you venture out into the future. If you need to, work with a therapist or counselor who can help you process grief and anger and learn how to forgive so that you can live your life to the fullest again.

Perhaps do a "Forgiveness Inventory" of all the people, including yourself, that need your forgiveness. Write down their names, what happened, when they happened, how you felt about it then, and how you feel about it now. Then forgive them. It

It is okay to both forgive someone and say goodbye to them in your life. Don't let the emotional baggage weigh you down, but put the past where it belongs: in the past.

doesn't need to be in person. Making amends can happen in your own heart as long as it is genuine. For those people you feel you just cannot forgive, write that down and why. Just doing that can help alleviate some of the heaviness associated with that person and help you begin to detach so that you can possibly forgive them at a later date. Again, it's never about telling the other person that what they did was okay, but about telling yourself that you don't need to live in the past pain anymore.

We've all heard the stories in the news of incredible acts of forgiveness such as the mother who forgave the man who accidentally killed her child in a drunk driving accident, or the man who forgave the business partner who took everything he had and left him penniless. We think there is no way we could ever reach that level of compassion and understanding or forgive such heinous acts against us, but if they can, we can. It may take a lot of time and a lot of self-searching, but it is possible to get to the point where we understand what Lewis B. Smedes meant when he said, "To forgive is to set a prisoner free and discover that the prisoner was you."

You may still get triggered now and again, so just repeat the process and purge your spirit of any newly rising anger or resentment until you can think of the person and/or situation with a strong sense of distance and detachment. This leads to healing for the most important person involved: yourself. When you heal, your relationships will heal, too.

Forgiveness is a funny thing. It warms the heart and cools the sting.
William Arthur Ward

AUTHOR INSIGHTS

Marie's Story

Years of codependency and addiction taught me that until you love yourself, you cannot really love another person. That love will always be need-based and incomplete, or a seeking of something to make you whole. Remember the famous line in the movie *Jerry Maguire* starring Tom Cruise: "You complete me." Nope. That's codependency. Two halves may make what looks like a whole person, but if something happens to one of them, you are still only half a person.

I learned my lessons over and over again with relationships that were generally one-sided, never in my favor, and involving people who were addicts, codependents, or highly dysfunctional. Once I saw how this pattern was showing up for me again and again, not just in romantic relationships but in friendships and work relationships, I was finally able to break out of the behaviors on my part that drew these types to me. Yes, we draw to us the

People who do not recognize their own value may get caught up in dysfunctional relationships, such as with alcoholics, drug addicts, codependents, users, gaslighters, and even violent personalities.

people who are at our level of self-love, self-worth, and understanding, so when we keep finding the same types of people showing up with different faces, we know it is us, not them, that we need to work on.

I still work on self-love on a daily basis, but I have little to no desire or patience for codependent relationships of any kind now that I know how exhausting and self-sabotaging they can be to our happiness and well-being. Relationships are a mirror of who we are inside projected outward. I still have issues with certain people in my life, as I am a work in progress, but the awareness is there where it wasn't before.

If I don't love myself first, I can't love others without conditions. And they can't love me because they can't even see or know the real me. How could they unless I know myself?

Denise's Story

Creatives aren't just writers, painters, dancers, sculptors, or actors. They're anyone who dares to draw outside the lines. Anyone who creates on any level. An inventor and/or scientist who allows their mind to (pardon the *Star Trek* reference) boldly go where no one has gone before. Or are they? Are creatives unrestrained? Do they *never* play the games others do around relationships and lack of authenticity? On the contrary, creatives can be either the most authentic people you've ever met or the least.

One thing I learned over many years of writing is that most creatives struggle as much as or more than anyone else with individuality and genuineness. I discovered this when I was 14 years old and writing my first short story.

When I was 14, my school gave me a test to decipher why my math skills were far below my grade level (I mentioned this in another chapter). After I took the test, they still had no clue what my problem was. One thing to remember is that this was in 1976, and back then they didn't have some of the tests or understanding they do now about the math learning disability called dyscalculia. They didn't inform my parents that that was my issue, because most likely they didn't even understand that it was the problem. They put me in a class full of kids with reading problems, even though I read at a college level. They didn't know what to do with me. I was an enigma (a word they literally used to describe me).

The teacher included me on an exercise where I had to complete a short story that was already started. It was sci-fi, and as I created the rest of the story, I quickly discovered I loved this stuff called writing fiction. From that point forward I wrote and wrote and wrote. It was my bliss.

Dyscalculia is rather like dyslexia, but instead of having a problem reading words, the person with this condition has a hard time understanding numbers, equations, and spatial relationships.

Race forward many years into adulthood. Once I decided to write for publication in the romance novel world, I discovered conformity was the name of the game if someone wanted to become published and do things "the right way." Writing to "market" was sometimes even more important than it was to be a skillful writer. An eccentric like me, who didn't want to stick in one lane (why couldn't I write a historical one time and a contemporary the next?), was considered "wrong" for not falling in line. Believe me, I tried conforming. I studied the market until I was blue in the face. Tried to write "not too different but fresh." It took me a while to acknowledge what was apparent to me right away. I was miserable staying in a lane. I wanted to write all the things. Romance, science fiction, thrillers, gothics, historical, horror … you name it. If I had a story idea for it, I would usually write it. I didn't want to be the oddball because conforming meant success, or what I thought was success at the time. Money. Opportunities. Accolades. More money. Best-seller lists.

For many years I tried to be someone I wasn't for the writing world. Finally, I ripped the bandage off and let it all hang out. Boom! I wrote in any genre I wanted and, to use another popular phrase, damned the torpedoes. Second to all of that, I didn't have a pen name. Everyone in the writing world, especially publishers, said that authors should have a pen name if they wrote in more than one genre. Well, because I wrote in so many genres, it would be difficult to have pen names. People knew I wrote in many different categories, including things like romance and horror (tricky genres to admit to writing if you don't want to receive odd looks).

I was eventually true to who I am and found a deeper lesson and a genuine happiness that could never have happened if I had totally conformed.

Did being the oddball mean that I never received money, opportunities, accolades, or landed on best-seller lists? I'm being authentic here when I say that not conforming did, in some ways, inhibit my ability to make money and make best-seller lists. It doesn't mean I *never* landed on a best-seller list, received awards and accolades, or garnered some cash.

What's the takeaway? I was eventually true to who I am and found a deeper lesson and a genuine happiness that could never have happened if I had totally conformed. Being who you are is paramount to authenticity, and it brought me closer to relating to others in the most genuine way possible. People have told me that I have inspired them to be who they are instead of following the crowd. If I can inspire someone else to find their bliss, that is one of the best gifts I've ever received.

How to Live a Mindful, Meaningful, Magical Life

MAGICAL TIPS

Take an Inventory

Because most of us are socialized not to be vulnerable or different from our cultural norms, we may make false assumptions about our own propensity to be vulnerable, or even fail to understand why we are acting defensive or unapproachable. We build armor around ourselves trying to make sure nothing bad gets through. We play–act our way through life. Believe it when we tell you that many people can detect when others are not genuine. Even if they are not aware of why, they react subliminally to the messages their intuition is giving them about you. They may feel uneasy around you, distrustful and unsure. That's not a good recipe for building a friendship. This is not to say that someone can't misjudge you based on their own inability to be genuine and their personal bias. This is a complex subject. However, if you as an individual aren't starting off genuine and from the heart, you've made it that much easier for people to judge you based on a false image you project onto the world.

Not sure you're being true to yourself? The questions below may help you see if you are ditching your authenticity and twist-

Overly concerned about first impressions? You might be losing your true self if you try too hard to put a good face on in front of other people.

ing yourself into a pretzel to fit. This is not a comprehensive quiz. It gives you some parameters on how you might be presenting yourself to the world.

1. When you first meet someone in a social situation, are you concerned with making a good first impression, no matter the circumstance?

2. Are you prepped to make only small talk, and if the other person goes deeper you automatically back off?

3. Do you worry excessively over your physical appearance? This would include spending extraordinary amounts of time planning your wardrobe for a social situation.

4. Do you feel you must be "on trend" all the time?

5. Are you afraid to wear clothing that you "vibe" with and love?

6. Are you always taking advice on what type of music you should listen to or books to read? If you are criticized for enjoying certain books and music, do you comply and pretend you don't like them or hide the fact that you like them?

7. Are you always afraid of speaking your mind (even in an unassertive, respectful way)?

These starter questions are the tip of the iceberg, but they give perspective on your level of conformity or authenticity.

Your life blooms by cultivating love for yourself and others, from the inside out. Life's sweetest, most meaningful moments are savored together, when deeply connecting to others and by loving beyond yourself.

Dean and Anne Ornish, authors of *UnDo It! How Simple Lifestyle Changes Can Reverse Most Chronic Diseases*

Just Say No

Adding more magic to relationships often involves strong boundaries when it comes to time and energy. When we can learn to say no to the things we don't want to do, it allows us to say yes and be more joyful to what we do want to do.

How are you saying yes to others when you want to say no? Is this helping or hindering your relationships? What do you get out of saying yes to something you'd rather not do?

Asking yourself these questions is rather enlightening because it often reveals how you get some kind of payoff for putting yourself last.

Now come up with ways you will start to create more boundaries and enforce them. What will you say no to? How will you make it stick? Are you willing to have a relationship end if someone refuses to respect your boundaries?

Can you look at where you have been trying to "buy" love by giving way too much, or chasing after unavailable people by sacrificing your own soul?

Saying "no" is uncomfortable at first, until you get used to putting yourself first and foremost. You cannot be there for others if you are never there for yourself! As Dr. Martin says in "How to Stop Being Codependent," you need to stop acting like a martyr and a people-pleaser and put an end to "denying, avoiding, and minimizing your feelings." You count.

People can say "yes" too much for fear of looking selfish, so it can take a bit of strength to stand up for yourself and say "no." But sometimes it is necessary so as to not let others take advantage of your good heart.

Reflections Of...

Divide a few pieces of paper into two sections. Make a list of all your major relationships, past and present, on the left column. On the right, list whether the relationship was positive or negative and why.

Review the list and mark each relationship with KEEP, CHANGE, or END. For those that you mark CHANGE or END, journal on the back of the paper or in your personal journal how you can change your role in the relationship, or how you will compassionately and respectfully end the relationship if needed.

Meditate, then journal, on how you see yourself in each of your major relationships. What role do you always seem to play? What patterns always seem to emerge over the duration of the relationship? Is what you see worth keeping, or is there something you now see you must change within yourself to change the relationship?

The Magic of Connecting to Source

Intuition is seeing with the soul.

Dean Koontz

I believe in intuitions and inspirations ... I sometimes feel that I am right. I do not know that I am.

Albert Einstein

But if we see ourselves as connected to God, or as reconnecting to our Source through meditation, then we can attract anything we want into our lives.

Dr. Wayne Dyer

Esther Hicks, who channels the entity Abraham, said, "Who you really are is Non–Physical Energy focused in a physical body, knowing full well that all is well and always has been, and always will be. You are here to experience the supreme pleasure of concluding new desires, and then bringing yourself into vibrational alignment with the new desires that you've concluded, for the purpose of taking thought beyond that which is has been before." By getting into vibrational alignment with the source of all that is, whether we call it Spirit, Universe, God, or something else, we then have the power to manifest our dreams and live a life filled with magic.

First we have to identify what "Source" means to us, and then we must learn how to connect with it. We are born connected to

Source, and as children, while often deeply intuitive, we can live immersed in the awe and magic of the grandeur of the world around us. Our spirits soar and our hearts sing at every new experience, and we have a sense of trust in the universe. We allow Source energy to flow in and out of us with ease. It's only as we get older and more jaded and cynical that we cut off that flow or even pretend it doesn't exist.

Once we cut off Source, Spirit, God ... the Universe ... we lose the connection to the source of our magic.

Connecting to an inner Source is a concept so enormous it can seem overwhelming. As children we are sometimes brought up with the doctrine or "religion" of our parents and other adults who defined what we must believe in and practice when connecting to a higher power. Over time we either rebel against these ideas, question them, or continue to believe in the concepts wholeheartedly. Using our religious faith (no matter what religion it is) may assist us in making life decisions and finding our way through the stormy weather of life. Even if we do not have this foundation, knowing there are ways to connect to Source can bolster our concept of self-worth and self-love.

So why should we bother to connect to a higher power or Source? What do we even mean by Source? Is Source an external higher power completely separate from us as a person? Is it a god, goddess, or other divine being? Or is it simply connecting to the power that already resides within every human being, such as the higher self or internal GPS? Because there are so many ideas about what Source is, we will stick most closely to the idea of Source being within yourself. After all, all the other names for this Source indicate that it is in us, of us, all around us, that we are a part of it and it is a part of us. Even a traditional religion such as Christianity states that the Kingdom of Heaven is within us and all around us, like some invisible force field from which all physical manifestation springs.

Source is like a field of all possibility, and we possess the tools to plant our dreams and desires into that field to make them grow, and, in turn, make ourselves grow and expand. To be all that we can be.

Everyday Magic

Infinite riches are all around you if you will open your mental eyes and behold the treasure house of infinity within you. There is a gold mine within you from which you can extract everything you need to live life gloriously, joyously, and abundantly.

Joseph Murphy

Source can be equated with spirit, which along with body and mind completes the triumvirate of human experience. Source can also mean all that is, which we are a part of and immersed in, and the same creative and generative energies that allow Source to make our reality are present within us, too. The problem is that most of us were raised to believe that this Source was some anthropomorphic being outside of us that judged us or oversaw our actions and behaviors like a parent in the sky. Or we were raised to not even think about Source or spirit and to focus entirely on making money, building a career, and finding a mate, all external things.

If only we could all understand that the power to create magic exists within us, too, and teach this to children at an early age. What amazing lives of abundant good we might live! Eckhart Tolle summed it up beautifully when he said, "On a deeper level you are already complete. When you realize that, there is a joyous energy behind what you do."

Instead, we are governed by subconscious programming that was instilled in us by other people and institutions, and we rarely get off the hamster wheel long enough to ask if we even believe in this dogma or not! We rarely stop and assess our lives and where we got derailed from the inner knowing we had long ago, and that incredible connection to whatever it was that created us.

For some people, it's easier to think of Source as the spiritual dimension that is a part of us. Our spirit is that invisible force within that is totally tuned in to and locked onto the greater cosmic forces, and can work with them for good, or

Source energy isn't something that lies outside of us but is, rather, within us all.

How to Live a Mindful, Meaningful, Magical Life

against them for chaos and disruption. Our minds have their own jobs to do, as do our bodies, but it is the spirit's job to recognize it is part of the Source of all there is.

The good news is, we have a tool kit of concepts that come under an umbrella of connecting to Source, including intuition, alignment, spiritual practice, mindfulness, meditation, prayer, and ritual. Within each of these concepts is a variety of types to explore. All have the end goal of allowing us to access that Source energy within and find a way to work with it, not against it. It's like floating on a river and choosing to surrender and relax and go with the current and not keep up the exhausting struggle to go against it.

Not every tool in the toolbox will work for everyone, but if you have not dipped your toe into a variety of possibilities, you might be missing things that may assist you in bringing you closer to your own inner truth and closer to self-love.

INTUITION

Intuition.

For many people it's a loaded word. What do you think of when you hear the word *intuition*? Does it conjure images of someone throwing spaghetti against the wall and hoping it'll stick? Does it mean guessing and hoping the answer will be right? Or does it mean accessing a yet unquantifiable part of our brain that can assist us in making the right decisions?

Do only people such as painters, writers, and other creatives utilize their intuition to help them smooth out the path before them? As it turns out, no. There are scientifically minded individuals who also take the balanced approach to how their mind works. Albert Einstein is quoted as saying, "The intuitive mind is a sacred gift and the rational mind a faithful servant." As he was bringing his theory of relativity into the world, he was often maligned by other scientists who thought his theory was complete bunk. Dr. Einstein stuck with it despite the naysayers, believing with his intuition that the theory would prove right. He did the scientific work but made intuitive leaps that helped him get to the answer.

In the biography *Steve Jobs* by Walter Isaacson, Jobs is quoted as saying that intuition was a thing even more powerful than intellect. This has to make us wonder if there are scientists out there relying in part on their intuition without knowing it.

Of course, as with everything else in life, not all scientists will describe intuition the same way, nor will they think of it the same way even if they give credence to it.

Intuition and creativity are not limited to those who practice the fine arts such as painting, writing, and dancing.

The May 20, 2016, edition of online publication *Live Science* quoted research from the April 2016 journal *Psychological Science* that showed people can use their intuition to "make faster, more accurate and more confident decisions." Joel Pearson, associate professor of psychology at University of New South Wales in Australia and lead author of the study, said past studies didn't measure intuition because researchers had no way to quantify it. Intuition, according to these newer studies, was defined as "nonconscious emotional information" from the body or brain such as instinctual feeling or sensation. These studies suggested that if someone realizes their intuition is serving them well, they will discover that it improves the more they use it.

We aren't all genius scientists and inventors. Does that mean we shouldn't bother to work toward utilizing and increasing our intuition? Of course not. We can all benefit from using our intuition more frequently and putting in the work to bolster it.

Intuition is a powerful ability we all possess but often ignore. As

The late Steve Jobs was a noted expert and entrepreneur in the high-tech field of computers, someone you would suspect relied on logic, yet he was a strong believer in the value of intuition.

technology has grown in our everyday lives, some of the "magic" of our intuition has been pushed aside. This doesn't mean we must dump technology entirely, but it does mean we need to re-connect with that part of us that is instinctual, the part that helped save us from the lions, tigers, and bears hundreds and even thousands of years ago and can help us today.

Even if we don't believe in intuition as a viable Source to help us create the life we want, intuition will still come to us. We might not recognize it, and we might ignore it. The key to making our intuition work for us on a more optimal level is discovering methods to leverage it in a powerful way to make it work for us on an individual level.

While Einstein recognized he was tapping into his intuition, other logically oriented individuals might use their intuition but not recognize it when they see it. An example might be the police officer or firefighter who makes a split-second decision that saves their own life or that of someone else. Of course, they are using training, but they may also be using intuition. If they ignore their intuition entirely for training, or vice versa, there's a possibility they might make a mistake. Using our intuition isn't an all-or-nothing prospect. Combining it with logic is the ultimate magic.

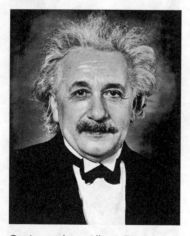

Part of the reason people may not utilize intuition is that as humans we tend to disbelieve anything that can't be quantified, labeled, and sci-entifically proven. We can overdo the details and think that if it can't be measured, it must not exist. Intuition is, in some scientists' opinions, unre-liable. While intuition may not be provable by the traditional scientific method, we know it is real through our own subjective, personal experi-ences with it. Cutting ourselves off from possibilities just because they cannot be duplicated in a lab is most certainly a way to short-circuit our chances of increasing our intuition.

Genius such as Albert Einstein's is not a wholly-owned subsidiary of logic and reason but has a generous dash of intuition, creativity, and even artistry. Thinking outside the box is vital when inventing new creations and groundbreaking theories about the world.

Everyday Magic

There's one thing you can do to remain moderate in your assessments. Call it becoming a skeptical believer. What is the difference between a skeptical believer and a cynic? Plenty. A cynic only believes in what he can see, touch, hear, taste, and smell. They may become so cynical that nothing can budge them off a set point that screams vociferously, "Never! It's not possible! I don't believe it!" While all of the senses can inform intuitive accuracy, utilizing only five senses can limit our ability to increase intuitive hits. A skeptical believer uses their first impression or hit to help inform whether they should be skeptical. There's an openness that says, "It's possible. It might be possible. It feels right or it doesn't feel right."

Proof is in the pudding, as the old saying goes. If you are still skeptical of your own ability to use intuition to your advantage, consider the following things.

We have all made a split-second decision to take a different driving route one day. We may have heard later that an accident occurred on our old route at the exact time we'd decided to divert to another route. We all remember those lucky dodges that saved us from inconvenience or maybe danger and death. We have all had feelings that someone we have met should not be trusted and either ignored that initial caution to our chagrin or were relieved we followed that hunch when we learned it was right. Some may believe it was dumb luck, but we would like to think that developing our intuition can only help, not hinder.

Yet intuition is more than avoiding danger. It is in taking those small chances or leaps of faith when our fear is bigger than our dreams. Many times, as children, before cynicism got a hold on us, we followed our intuition almost more than our logic.

As children we dreamed of enjoying careers that sounded cool, and we were often drawn to those career ideas with fierce longing. Firefighter, nurse, teacher, astronaut, fighter pilot, movie star. Did those dreams last into our teenage years? If not, was it because practicality and other people's visions of what we should be overtook our dreams? Did pragmatism convince us we could not do at least some of the things we dreamed of accomplishing? Are the people who accomplish these dreams just lucky? Not at all. Many of them followed their intuition to get there, even if they didn't realize that was what they were doing.

Young kids typically dream of glamorous or dangerous careers to achieve in adulthood such as becoming firefighters, but just because those dreams may later be abandoned doesn't mean pragmatism won the day.

Cultivating intuition is a vital step toward becoming more aware of your magic and growing self-love and self-worth. We all owe it to ourselves to give ourselves this gift.

Make your mind one-pointed in meditation, and your heart will be purified.
The Bhagavad Gita

The man who has no inner life is a slave of his surroundings.
Henri Frederic Amiel

MINDFULNESS, MEDITATION, AND ALIGNMENT

Mindfulness is everywhere, but at the same time it is sorely lacking. How can it be both? Stick around and we will tell you. Mindfulness is not anything new, but our awareness of it as a "thing" or a state to be desired is relatively new in our social awareness in many modern societies. It is a buzzword that is brought up in New Age circles, but it is moving into the mainstream and seems to be catching fire even in the corporate boardroom and everyday workplace. Initial skepticism in even hard-core disbelievers (we are generalizing here) has started to loosen. Many people are learning how mindfulness can increase their effectiveness on the job and have health benefits.

Most of us would have to be living under a rock if we had not heard of mindfulness, and maybe the same could be said of meditation. Most of us do not understand what it is to be aligned within ourselves, aware of our own divine purpose and energy. Let us explore the elements of mindfulness, meditation, and alignment and see how they relate to each other.

Mindfulness is the ability to focus on the here and now, to be aware of our current condition, to bring ourselves into the present. Wait … that sounds like meditation. It really is. While most people might not think of it as meditation, there is significant overlap between the two concepts and a huge variety of techniques we can try in order to accomplish a state of mindfulness. Alignment with our feelings, goals, and spirituality can be accomplished within a mindfulness and meditation practice.

When we participate in mindfulness, we are intensely aware of everything we are feeling, hearing, and sensing. This is not to be confused with sensory processing disorder or the overload some empaths can feel. Often when we are stressed, we are fearful, perhaps experiencing physical discomfort, ruminating, and worrying about the past, present, and future in one big jumble. The idea behind mindfulness is to reduce that rattled, scattered feeling and bring us into harmony.

Practicing mindfulness can include using guided imagery, doing breathing exercises, and basking in the moment without judging the experience or attaching ourselves to the emotions within our thoughts. This awakening to what is really going on in our current state should be a calming if not an ecstatic condition that can bring us into alignment with ourselves, and hopefully make us more likely to experience the magic of loving our current state.

Most people, when thinking of mindfulness, picture someone meditating in a natural setting, but you don't have to be doing meditation to practice mindfulness. Mindfulness is about being present in the moment, allowing yourself to appreciate and absorb what you are doing in the here and now and to be aware of the world around you and all of its senstations.

Putting on our skeptical believer hat for a moment, is mindfulness and meditation just woo-woo bunk? Scientists say no. Your ability to participate in mindfulness and meditation could be affected, though, by the level of skepticism you bring to the table. As with most things, if we do not believe we can do something, we may be guaranteeing we will not be able to do it. Keeping an open mind is our best bet. Many of us believe we cannot meditate, so we never try. Or perhaps we tried it once and failed. Or maybe we thought we were doing it wrong when we were not, and therefore, we dumped the idea into the woodchipper.

Still not convinced? If first responders can learn mindfulness and meditation, you can, too.

According to *The Daily Meditation*, the University of Miami conducted two studies that showed that by using meditation, firefighters and police officers can reduce or alleviate stress and therefore perform far better at their jobs. The first responders engaged in a course that taught them principles called Mindfulness-

Based Attention Training (MBAT). This training consists of concentration, body awareness, connection, and open monitoring (a
continual state of being aware of what is happening around you–
situational awareness). For the purposes of first responders needing an awareness of more than one thing going on at a time, the
course makes an emphasis on how to be open to the entirety of
the responder's environment and not concentrating on one thing.
If that sounds overwhelming, practice makes perfect. Even people
who are easily overstimulated by crowds and/or find their empathic abilities frequently overwhelmed can benefit from mindfulness training.

Are you afraid of missing out?

Much of our scattered feeling from time to time can evolve
from FOMO, fear of missing out. FOMO can come from being dis-
engaged from our present and lack of mindfulness, but it is also
from a fear that what we are doing now, in this moment, simply
is not good enough. We have all had FOMO. We settle on the
couch reading a book that we have been trying to get to for days

Have you ever settled in for a relaxing evening only to be interrupted by a text or phone
call from a friend inviting you to go out? Do you stay and enjoy some "me time," or do
you accept because you fear missing out on something?

How to Live a Mindful, Meaningful, Magical Life

or maybe weeks. We have our beverage, a cozy blanket, and maybe music. We are content with our situation and enjoying ourselves. We feel great. Suddenly the phone buzzes with a text or a voice mail from a friend asking us if we want to do XYZ event with them, but we have to choose ASAP because the event is to-night. Feelings of *what if* and *why not* hit us. What if we miss out on the best concert ever? What if our friend gets mad because we say no? Maybe we say yes, even though we do not want to. We were perfectly happy to read a book and were really enjoying it. Yet we threw that over for a fear of missing out. Discontent sud-denly bursts our bubble, and the what ifs, wherefores, and maybes explode. A prattle has overtaken our brain. What we were enjoying moments ago is popped like a water balloon.

When we fall victim to FOMO, we miss what is happening in the present, what was happening before things jumped the shark and our mind convinced us we could or should do some-thing else that might be more exciting. What if we focused on what is happening right now? The favorite song we're enjoying. The book we're reading. The sounds of birds or the wind.

This is not to say that we should never be spontaneous and leap on something even more exciting to us. But if we are hon-estly finding genuine gratification in that moment, there is no need to upset it for another.

When caught up in FOMO, we forget we have control over what we do and how full we make our lives. We forget it does not feel good for us to be insanely busy.

Is your life one frenzied, stressful jump to another do, do, do, do, do?

Stress is a badge of honor in modern society. You know that lady you see on Instagram or Facebook posting about how busy she is, how incredibly overwhelmed she is? It is probably true. But should we admire that? Because sometimes we do admire the do-it-all facade. We praise that person for being busy. Busy and always talking about being stressed and overwhelmed is the "ex-pected" and "honorable" way to exist. We are productive, success-ful, accomplished, and worthy. That might be true.

It also might not be true.

"Busy" can hide disappointment, anger, peer pressure, I'm–not–good–enough feelings, societal expectations, and a whole lot of depressing things that drain energy and enjoyment out of our lives.

Realistically, daily life means our schedules may be busy, especially if we are working in a high–pressure field. But then there is our own time, when we have control of how insane we decide to make our schedule.

Is there something you are doing because you think you "should"? Because other people expect it, but you do not want to do it? There is a great deal of value in assessing these questions. You will find there are many things you can chuck to the side. This leaves room for more of what you want to do. In that crazy schedule you've created, ask yourself what really blows your skirt up. What do you crave to do but keep jettisoning because of other expectations?

Do it and watch the magic happen. You will love yourself for it.

PRAYER AND OTHER TECHNIQUES

There is nothing mysterious about prayer. It is simply the opposite of meditation. Think about it. When we pray, we talk to our concept of Source or God. When we meditate, we listen for the response.

But many people who claim to believe in God equate prayer with rules and regulations, believing that in order to "please" God, prayer must be done perfectly or in a state of total submission and surrender. We believe we must do everything just so, and use all the correct words and phrases, in order to make our prayer work. Otherwise, God will turn His back on us and ignore our pleas for divine intervention.

Some people pray because they feel it is expected of them because of their religious faith and that God will disapprove if they don't, but one should look at prayer in the same manner as talking with a good and caring friend.

How to Live a Mindful, Meaningful, Magical Life

It's so much simpler than that, which is probably why we complicated humans can't seem to grasp it. Praying is just talking to God or Goddess or Source or Universe. How do you talk to your best friend? Talk in that way to whatever it is you believe this Source to be. How do you talk to your beloved dog? Talk to Source that same way. How do you talk to your favorite Boston fern? Talk to God that way.

Source is far more loyal, loving, and true than any friend or dog or leafy fern, so don't be afraid to just talk, in your own way and style. You can beg, but you really don't have to. You can cry, plead, jump up and down, bargain, and bully, but you don't have to. You can speak in hushed tones or yell at the top of your lungs, but you don't have to. If you want to sing your prayer, go for it. Just as long as you open up the lines of communication.

Many of us used to pray when we were children, but we gave it up when we got older and wiser, especially after years of unanswered prayers. Why bother? What a waste of time! Who needs it? We wondered why many of our prayers didn't work, but rarely did we examine just what it was we were asking God for, or how we were asking for it. And now we are so sure God won't listen or care, we don't even make the attempt.

It's not only our loss, it's God's. Because, you see, God loves to answer prayers, if they are the right prayers to answer. God doesn't like to be told what to do or how to do it. God works in God's ways, in God's time, according to God's will. And that will might not be your will.

That is why the world's major religions are all based upon submitting to the will of God, because it is a higher will than ours. In other words, God knows best what's best for us.

Children probably have an easier time talking with God than adults because they have fewer hangups, anxieties, and preconceptions. They are more likely to see God as a friend and comforter than as an intimidating, all-powerful being.

Which is why sometimes the best way to pray is to just say, "Hi, God. Thy will be done." But you don't have to.

Say anything. Just say something. And mean it.

If you want to pray with a hundred other people praying, God would love it all the same. As long as you mean it in your heart, which is really where your personal closet is anyway.

St. Paul instructed his followers to pray without ceasing. What he meant was that our life should be as a prayer, lived in awe and reverence of the powerful Spirit that moves in and through us at all times. To pray without ceasing is to exist in a constant state of awareness of the Higher Power at work in our lives. To pray without ceasing could also be defined simply as living our lives with love for everything and everyone we meet.

The power of prayer is only recently being examined by scientists and medical researchers as a potent form of healing. There are tons of research studies at Harvard, Duke, and other notable universities and hospitals indicating that prayer promotes healing in patients who may not even know they are being prayed for, and the growing body of evidence shows that thoughts have energy and that energy can be used to save lives and improve the well-being of others. If a prayer from a stranger can help cure a sick patient, imagine what your own prayer can do for your own life, when offered to God with love and sincerity.

In Kent Ingle's "The Power of Prayer: Science Proves It Works, Has Positive Physiological Effects," published on February 12, 2019, on FoxNews.com, author Ingle quotes Marilyn Schlitz, Ph.D. and lecturer at Harvard, who says, "It's clear from the correlational studies within the epidemiology data that positive relationships exist between religious and spiritual practice and health outcomes on a variety of different conditions." Moreover, she says that in a study and confirmation study on intercessory prayer, "the prayer groups had statistically significant improvements in outcome, suggesting that the intervention has clinical relevance."

Ingle also references researchers at the Heritage Foundation who said, "We have a logical reason why religion might influence physical health through mental health, through enhancing social support, through influencing health behaviors, all affecting physical health outcomes." So, at the very least, prayer is beneficial. It works. In fact, "Today, 101 medical schools incorporate patient

spirituality in their curriculum, up from 17 in 1995. This fact suggests that these principles are being incorporated into medical
education...."

> *Prayer ... is engaging in a conversation
> between who we really are aside from our
> personality and image and the very Source that
> created us to be who we are.*

Prayer isn't just about healing, though. It's a way of getting
quiet and connected to the very power within and all around us
that can heal. It is engaging in a conversation between who we
really are aside from our personality and image and the very
Source that created us to be who we are. It's conversing in the
purest, most powerful form.

It's important to speak from the heart and tell Source what
you want in prayer, for yourself, for others, for the world. But
don't forget to say thank you. In fact, sometimes you can even
just pray to say thank you without asking for anything. Alice
Walker is quoted as saying, "'Thank you' is the best prayer that
anyone could say. I say that one a lot. Thank you expresses extreme gratitude, humility, understanding." So, if words fail you,
just say thank you.

TURN ON, TUNE IN

Think of yourself as a toaster or a blender, and Source is the
electricity. The electrical current is always there, ready to be tapped
into. It never goes away, not at night, not while you are upset or
hurt, not even during the Super Bowl. But you can't get the benefits of electricity without taking one small action yourself first.

Plug in!

All you need to do is plug yourself in, turn yourself on, and
let the force flow through you. Even a lamp doesn't work until
it's plugged in. Imagine you are a radio, and the Source is the

ever-present broadcast floating through the ether, waiting for you to turn on, tune in, and pick up the radio waves that are present everywhere. But until you tune in your personal dial to the Divine, nothing happens.

It's so simple. That inner divine knowing is always there, ready and waiting for us to make contact. But without any action on our part, without either turning on or tuning in, we remain silent and in the dark. In order to truly feel the presence of Source in our lives, we must consciously become aware of it by keeping all channels open to receiving our good. This means keeping

Imagine you are an electrical plug and the Source or God is the source of power. The power is always there, and all you need to do is plug into it.

conscious contact through meditation, prayer, a moment of silence, or any other technique that reminds us to direct our attention inward. When we feel tight or frustrated or things don't seem to be going smoothly, that means we've blocked the flow of Source energy in our lives. We've either unplugged ourselves completely or just forgotten to turn ourselves on to the constant Source of energy and substance that is always at hand.

We are human appliances forever plugged into the Divine outlet, just waiting for the current to flood us with life juice. But we have to do our part. We have to flick the switch.

Let's try it right now. Turn off the TV, the computer, the radio. Shut down that cell phone that is glued to your hand. Close the door and sit on the bed or a chair. Just sit and be quiet. Listen to the natural sounds of life going on around you. Now go within, breathing deeply as you do. Turn your attention inward, deeper and deeper, until you find a silence inside that calms you.

Now listen. Listen to what the silence is telling you. This is your heart and soul speaking. This is the sound of Source within, urging and prompting and inspiring you. Can you hear it? It starts off as a whisper, but it's there.

How to Live a Mindful, Meaningful, Magical Life

*Listen to what the silence is telling you. This is
your heart and soul speaking.*

Tuning into the divine is easy. It's the getting quiet part that trips most of us up. But until we learn to plug ourselves in—and that requires continual practice—we will forever feel depleted of the life force. Start today to take even five or ten minutes to just connect. Those five to ten minutes will soon become the most important part of your day, and hopefully expand into 20 or 30 minutes, thus changing your entire life in the process.

Source is always home. All you have to do is go up to the door and ring the bell. Then stand there and wait for the door to open. Don't let impatience or fear send you running in a game of Ding Dong Ditch. In a short time the door will open, and you will be answered with a wink and a smile and a hug for an old friend. You'll be invited in for a nice cool drink and a long, heartfelt talk.

Go in, sit down, kick up your feet, and relax. You can afford to take the time, even if the phone is ringing, work is calling to you, and the kids demand your attention. Those things will wait. Your life, and your connection to Source energy within, should not. Make this your priority each day.

Start off with short, five-minute meditations and gradually work your way up to longer ones. The great thing about meditating is you can do it almost anywhere.

Then be prepared for a wonderful, awesome, inspiring visit. Source is a great host, and an even better friend.

After a while, you may want to add journaling to the mix. Write down any thoughts, ideas, or inspirations that come to you during your quiet times, or any questions you would like to share with your Higher Power next time you pray. Keep a record of your prayer requests and any solutions you've been given during meditative moments or flashes of intuition.

Everyday Magic

When you've managed to master three five-minute mini-meditations, begin to extend the amount of time you spend in silence until you are ideally doing two 20-minute sessions, one in the morning and one in the evening. If you can only do one, pick a time that is best for you, and try to do no less than 20 minutes. It may seem boring or unproductive at first, and you probably won't get any brilliant flashes of insight or inspiration right away, but if you stick to it, you will notice several things start to happen. You will begin to experience a sense of well-being and inner strength you never felt before. You will be more in tune with your instinct and intuition. You will be kinder and more loving and tolerant to those around you. You will improve your health. And, yes, occasionally you will get brilliant flashes of insight or inspiration. Write them down as soon as you finish meditating! These are messages from Source within, answering your earlier prayers. Ignore them at your own loss and risk that it will next speak to you with a stronger method, perhaps the old "two-by-four to the head."

If you want to give it a try on your own, the only things you need to remember to do are:

1. Talk to Source/God/Whatever.

2. Be quiet.

3. Listen for Source/God/Whatever.

4. Repeat when necessary.

5. And breathe!

Any other details are negotiable. Do whatever turns you on and tunes you in.

TRUST YOURSELF

We live in a world where other people's opinions often seem to matter more than our own, thanks to social media and peer pressure. Truth is, everyone has an opinion, and those opinions are usually

If you get a flash of inspiration during meditation, pause and write it down as quickly as you can before you forget it, then reread it later.

How to Live a Mindful, Meaningful, Magical Life

based on limited knowledge or personal experience (or both) and are shaded by individual fears, biases, and flawed thinking. Yes, ours as well.

We will never be able to please every person we meet. We can't even please those close to us on a consistent basis. We get lied to and let down by those we know as much as we do those we barely know.

Trust yourself. Have faith in yourself and your dreams. Focus on what brings you happiness, joy, and magic. Take the time you would ordinarily spend trying to twist yourself into a pretzel and focus on your own inner guidance system. This is not to say you always ignore helpful or constructive criticism or that you shouldn't listen to the opinions and beliefs of others, but don't try to force yourself to fit those beliefs if they don't resonate within.

Trusting yourself may feel foreign at first, but the more you do it, the more you come to realize how you've been living in the past through the eyes of other people.

Stop doing that! There is no magic to be found there. The magic is found when you can be honest with yourself, true to yourself, and loving of yourself.

·

FRIEND OR FOE?

Albert Einstein is quoted as saying, "The most important question a person can ask is 'Is the Universe a friendly place?'" We can look at Source/God/Universe as something benevolent that works in our favor, or as something punishing that makes us pay for our mistakes. Thing is, we will get evidence of whichever one we are focusing on. We may not always understand the mysterious workings of source energy or the divine in our lives, and often it may seem that we are cursed with challenges, obstacles, and tragedies.

Perspective shifts can go a long way toward seeing magic where before we only saw boulders in the road. If we judge what happens to us based on our own reactions, which usually come from a place of fear, it can indeed look as though the Universe has an unfriendly face. What happens if we respond out of love, even when it's the last thing we feel like doing?

There is also magic in seeing Source as neutral and allowing of everything, including the things we label as bad or tragic. We may be right, but what if the possibility existed that the things that we judge negatively are blessings in disguise, or that there is so much more to the rhyme and reason that we cannot see, like the part of the iceberg that lies below the waterline?

Just like an iceberg that has most of its substance beneath the surface of the ocean, we only see a part of the picture when it comes to the Universe. What might seem like a hostile or impersonal existence might have much more to it beneath the waves.

Whatever created us and molded each of us into the amazing and unique individuals we are had to have had a reason, whether for the purpose of natural selection or because everything is made of the energy of love. What you choose to believe about this will color the world you see and how you feel connected to something greater than yourself through your own lenses of perception.

AUTHOR INSIGHTS

Denise's Story

Intuition can happen accidentally. In my case it was both an accident and intuition that helped me achieve some dream–come–true scenarios in my life.

As a kid I wanted to be an archaeologist, a psychologist, a paranormal investigator, a television and movie writer, a museum worker, and maybe even a librarian. Those are the things I remember most vividly in my fantasy wheelhouse. When I mentioned this to adults and other kids, they'd look at me like I was nuts. After all, we can't be all the things, can we? At least that's what I thought and what they believed. Because everyone told them when they were kids that they couldn't be everything they wanted.

So, I went along with that self–limiting idea. I couldn't be all the things I wanted, I said to myself. But because I was a child, I could still play with all of these ideas because play is what children do.

By the time I reached my teen years I was writing full gothic novels by pen and paper. One contemporary romantic suspense I wrote was set in a library. In these stories the heroine often went to Britain or Ireland and had adventures in a castle. And, of course, there was her hero. Everything was happily ever after.

I was reading and watching horror movies and loving every moment of it. I watched my favorite television shows and invented and wrote blurbs/log lines for the episodes. Then I enacted episodes in my head. No one knew I was doing this. I figured they'd say I was silly and/or stupid. As my British friends might say, "You are a nutter, Denise." As a kid I also watched tons of archaeology–related shows and read books about Pompeii and Herculaneum, wishing I was the archaeologist working on these sites.

Because my mother was a practical woman (she was born in 1921 and experienced the Great Depression and World War II), she wanted me to be something practical like a secretary.

I took creative writing classes in high school and loved it. I also excelled in it and never received lower than an A in the classes. Because my mother was a practical woman (she was born in 1921 and experienced the Great Depression and World War II), she wanted me to be something practical like a secretary. With that in mind I trained to become a secretary because I knew I could always make money doing that. The kicker? I never liked being a secretary. To me it was boring on every level, but I did it to earn a living.

Skip ahead. In the mid–1980s I had this feeling I called "something is missing." I was incredibly bored and unsatisfied with my life. Had the situation continued I might have developed clinical depression. One day the lightbulb went on. I asked myself a crucial question. Why wasn't I doing some of the things I dreamed about?

What was stopping me? I didn't know, but looking back, I can see it was fear. My innate shyness, empathic abilities, and anxiety kept me from venturing into the very things I'd longed to do since childhood. I had to decide. Would I stay in that fear that was holding me back? Or would I realize the only way to have those dreams come true was to face the fear and take a plunge?

I researched. There was a local amateur archaeology group I could join, and I could volunteer at the local museum. I jumped into both and loved every minute of it. In secret I continued to write romance and paranormal type novels I figured no one would ever see. Fast forward. In 1991 I decided to write novels for publication. In 1999 my first novel was published.

All of that alone would have been great. But there's more.

In 1996 a military move sent us to England for three years. I was ecstatic because I'd always wanted to go to Britain and Ireland (by that time I'd been to Ireland once). One day I was sitting in the military guest quarters before we found our rental house, and I was writing in my journal. Then it hit me like a ton of bricks, the most amazing feeling. A peak experience. I realized that all those things I'd dreamed of wanting as a child had come true to a large extent.

- Married to a great guy. Check.
- Writing books. Check.
- Visiting England. Check. And I'd done one better. I
  lived in England.
- Archaeology and museum time. Check.
- Psychology. Check. Well, I was one course short of a bachelor's in psychology.

It was a profound experience and incredible high.

It wasn't until a few years ago that this realization expanded to show me something else profound. I was writing horror movies, television series, and novels. Plus, I'd squeezed in paranormal investigation and recognized my own psychic and mediumship abilities.

The dreams I'd had as a kid had come true.

Years later, when I started enjoying doing archery, I discovered another way to find focus. At the time I did not perceive it as a mindfulness exercise, but looking back on it, I see that is exactly what I was doing.

When I did archery, I had a bow with a sight that I could look through. That certainly helped me focus. Could I make bull's-eyes? Sometimes. Not often. People emphasized holding my bow the proper way, etc., which certainly helps. Yet there is more than one way to hold a compound bow, which is what I used ... it depends on who you talk to. Did my shot accuracy improve just because I held the bow the right way? No.

Then my coach told me to concentrate on where I wanted to hit and just think about that spot exclusively.

Then my coach told me to concentrate on where I wanted to hit and just think about that spot exclusively. Not on where my arm was aiming. He contradicted the experts and said, "Don't aim. Your arm will follow where you look." I would see the spot I wanted to hit, then the color of where I wanted to hit. If the color was red, I'd say to myself "red, red, red, red" and BOOM, that's about when I'd let the arrow go. My ability to hit closer to the bull's-eye and to get bull's-eyes increased tremendously. Because I'd picked a spot and said the color to force myself to concentrate. I was telling the arrow where it was going to hit, and the arrow often did as it was told.

All the preparation I did with training with my coach and equipment wasn't worth squat until I could find a way to concentrate that worked for me.

And the fact that I'd accomplished so many of the things I'd longed to do as a child was because I decided to follow my intuition and do things that made me happy and not just what I thought I should do or what others might want me to do.

Not until you surrender does the spiritual dimension become a
living reality in your life. When you do, the energy you emanate
and that then runs your life is of a much higher vibrational
frequency than the mind energy that still runs the world.

Eckhart Tolle

Marie's Story

It's hard to pick just one time in my life when listening or connecting to Source, especially via intuition, played a huge role in the trajectory of my dreams and goals. The sad thing is, I wasn't adept at listening to my intuition once I became an "adult" and was instead focused on listening to everyone else and following guidance that was not my own. When I was young, I felt the presence of something grander and greater in me and all around me and spent a lot of time in nature feeling a powerful, spiritual connection to God or the Universe. I cannot even recall what name I gave it at the time, but I was really tuned in. As I got older, though, it seemed to fade into the background noise of my life, and I often ignored it, was way more focused on external voices, opinions, and validation, and lost my spiritual foundation in favor of the world at large.

That loss was palpable, especially when it came to listening to my inner voice. I couldn't hear it much at all, and I paid the price again and again. There is one really intriguing time when intuition told me not to do something that I ended up doing anyway, and I paid a harrowing price. I ventured out to see a lecture by Carl Sagan at the Jet Propulsion Laboratory in Pasadena, despite my inner voice screaming at me not to go. I had difficulty opening the doors in my apartment and one doorknob refused to turn, before I forced it open. My husband at the time even said, "Maybe you aren't meant to go," but I ignored it. No way in hell I wasn't seeing Mr. Sagan speak! So I got out of the apartment and into my car and drove off ... and

The late Dr. Carl Sagan (shown here posing with the Viking spacecraft) was an astronomer who helped popularize space exploration and a curiosity for the stars for people worldwide.

How to Live a Mindful, Meaningful, Magical Life

ended up having what many people would call "missing time" while driving on the freeway from Burbank to Pasadena.

I was on the 134 East when I somehow ended up missing two hours and ending up on a different freeway heading far to the north. This was in the days of those massive cell phones and no GPS or even internet access, and I pulled over in a panic, blubbering like a baby, called my husband at the time, and he told me what to do. I managed to find my way back to the right freeway and hightailed it home.

To this day I have no idea how that happened or how I managed to stay alive and not kill myself or anyone else in my zoned-out state, but it truly brought home to me that I must always listen to the inner voice and to the external signs it presents when I don't.

MAGICAL TIPS

Alignment Inventory Journal Exercise

Time to whip out that journal. Remember things you dreamed of doing as a child. Rejoice if you are doing them now. Are there other things you wish to do that you once only dreamed about? Maybe it is time to revisit these dreams and see how you can make them come true. Using a journal (this can be electronic or paper), write down the things you said you wanted to be when you reached adulthood. List hobbies you have dreamed about but never seem to find time to do. They don't have to be career-related. Have you accomplished or participated in any of them? If not, in what way can you bring some if not all of those things into reality in some form, no matter how small? It does not have to be all at once. Invest in your alignment with self-love and magic by giving yourself these gifts.

Intuition Inventory

Now make a list of the times in your life when you listened to your intuition and benefited from it. How did the voice or message come to you? What did it say? Why were you receptive to it at the time? What was the end result?

Make a second list of the times when you did not listen to that inner voice. Answer the same questions, this time thinking about why you were *not* receptive to it.

Compare the two lists and jot down the patterns you notice, as well as how you can, in the future, honor that voice more fully and frequently. Sometimes when you see the actual benefits and damages of listening and not listening to your intuition, it's quite eye-opening and shocks you into more awareness.

Frenetic Energy Assessment Exercise

See if you recognize any of what is described below. If you do not work from home, this scenario would be somewhat different. Yet if you look at the basic structure of the situations described, you could see how this sort of crazy jackrabbit energy could happen with an office job as well.

You walk into the laundry room, eager to start the laundry. You sort the laundry. Put in the first load. Walk away to finish a work assignment. Two hours later you have this nagging sense you have forgotten something. It bugs you. The phone rings. It is a call you have expected from a friend. You would really love to talk to them a long time, but your work requires completion, so you make it a short five-minute conversation.

During this entire time, you feel a sense of urgency, a low-key hum that feels almost like anxiety. Perhaps your heart is jumping around in your chest. An hour later you remember the laundry. You curse. Hurry to the laundry room, but halfway there you remember you should have put something in the mail. You charge back to your office, get the mail piece, run outside and put the piece in the mailbox. You hurry back to the laundry.

Getting overwhelmed by multitasking can cause you to lose focus, forget things, misplace stuff, and feel like you can't accomplish what you need to do.

There is a ton of laundry, but there is other work to finish, too.

How to Live a Mindful, Meaningful, Magical Life

You toss the washed laundry into the dryer and throw in a new wash load. You head back to the office. You look at the clock, and you are feeling wiped out already and wonder if you are losing it because you are forgetting stuff that needs accomplishing even when you have written it down in a meticulously detailed planner.

You hop back and forth, a relentless multitasking experience running your day. By the time you stop for the day, you are frazzled and probably experiencing a general sense of dissatisfaction. You might be exhausted, anxious, and cranky.

Feel and look familiar? Most of us can relate to that sense of spastic and frenetic energy running through many of our days. Most workers are praised for being able to multitask, and that praise can be addicting. Multitasking champion or not, eventually that hair-on-fire energy will bring you down and cause you to forget things and to make mistakes.

What can you do to slow down and get things done? Use your journal to ask yourself the following questions.

1. Are you forgetting and misplacing things?

2. Are you making a lot of mistakes?

3. Are there tasks at home or work or both that you can delegate? Give this some sincere thought.

4. If you cannot delegate, assess which things are life or death. You will find most of it is not life or death. There is a good chance some of it can wait until tomorrow or even later in the week.

5. Make a list of the most important tasks and stick with those. Secondary things will just need to wait.

6. Consider taking a deeper look into whether you have anxiety issues that are generating this sense of constant motion. Many people will find those issues are buried in their childhood where the message they received is that they were never good enough and/or could not get anything right. Sometimes secondary to that are messages we receive in

social media where we compete with others to be the most put together, look a certain way, say certain things … you name it. Remember that you are an adult now. There is no overlord adult. You are the master of your own ship.

Breathing and Grounding Meditation Exercise

This one is so easy it can be done anywhere and anytime. Whenever you feel that frenetic energy building, take a pause. Take one breath. That is it. One deep breath. Do the following:

1.   Notice one thing you hear.

2.   Notice one thing you see.

3.   Notice one thing you feel. If you are sitting in a chair, feel that structure under you.

Do this simple exercise whenever you catch yourself engaging in that jackrabbit energy.

As you have probably noted, there are many different types of meditations available to you. It can be difficult to decide which ones to try. The best way to pick a meditation method is to try as many different kinds as you can and keep at it until you find one that feels good and works well for you. Start with just 10 minutes and expand up to 20 minutes a day for the best effects.

Examples:

1.   Directed or narrated meditations with background music. These are some of the most common meditations, but you might find them distracting in some cases. It depends on your personality. "I found a meditation with gentle music where I was told I was lying on a giant lily pad floating

All it takes to relax yourself sometimes is to pause and take a single deep breath. You'll be surprised by the results of this simple exercise!

down a shallow, slow creek. It was one of the best meditations I've experienced. Absolute bliss!" *Denise*

2. Mindfulness based with music. One of the features of mindfulness meditations in particular is that they do not expect you to stop thinking. You are relaxed but you allow your thoughts to travel through your head without snagging on each one and ruminating. Just let those thoughts go through. Do not attach any extra emotion to the thought. Just let it float on by.

3. Take this one step further and listen for any intuitive "hits" you receive in terms of images, phrases, ideas, or thoughts and write them down as soon as you come out of the meditative state. Once you do this enough, these hits won't have to wait until you are meditating—they will happen all the time.

The Magic of Well-Being

Putting your well-being first—like putting your oxygen mask on before you help the person next to you—that really benefits all your relationships.

Gabrielle Bernstein

The acquirement and enjoyment of physical well-being, mental calm and spiritual peace are priceless to their possessors.

Joseph Pilates

Your health and well-being should be your number one priority, nothing else is more important.

Robert Cheeke

It's impossible to experience the magic of life if you're feeling bad. Feeling good is about "well-being," which means both "being well" and being a being who is well in body, mind, and spirit. See the difference? You can be "well" in the sense that you are currently not sick with a flu or dealing with a heart condition or recovering from throwing out your back, but your mind and heart and spirit may still be experiencing distress and unease. Well-being incorporates all levels of who you are so that you can enjoy your life and live it in the present and to the full.

Remember: the magic is in the present, so if you are worried, anxious, stressed, or sick, chances are excellent that you are not fo-

Negative emotions such as anger, anxiety, fear, jealousy, and sadness can have a negative impact on your physical health. Instead of indulging in irritation and upset, address what is causing these feelings and deal with them.

cusing on the golden gifts of the moment or seeing the good in your life. You might find you are grumbling and whining and biting people's heads off. An overall sense of irritation can invade your thoughts and emotions that can seem disconnected from what you are experiencing right in that moment. The thought "Why am I so angry?" may have invaded your thoughts, and you don't have an answer.

Older people who have wisdom and life experience will often say that without your health you have nothing, but what they often mean is that without your well-being you have nothing. It is certainly possible that you can be a miserable person and be healthy in a physical sense. At the same time, the more miserable you are mentally, the higher the chances that there will be physical ramifications. Stress is a huge contributor to the breakdown of our bodies physically, but we often ignore this fact over and over.

Well-being is often defined as the state of being happy, healthy, and prosperous. This can entail everything from robust physical health to fulfilling work, financial prosperity, enjoyable relationships, and a sense of having a purpose in the world. The World Health Organization defines it on its website as "a positive state experienced by individuals and societies. Similar to health, it is a resource for daily life and is determined by social, economic and environmental conditions. Well-being encompasses quality of life and the ability of people and societies to contribute to the world with a sense of meaning and purpose. Focusing on well-being supports the tracking of the equitable distribution of resources, overall thriving and sustainability. A society's well-being can be determined by the extent to which they are resilient, build capacity for action, and are prepared to transcend challenges."

A state of well-being means you are flourishing on every level, not just one or two. It all goes together to create the con-

Several factors play into a state of well-being, including physical, social, psychological, and financial aspects. Achieving balance in all these aspects can indeed be challenging, but it is certainly worthwhile!

ditions for magic to occur because you are open and tuned in to Source and at ease, focused on the moment at hand and the joyful gifts it contains.

We must feed our bodies with healthy foods to be healthy, and the same goes for our minds, our emotions, and our spirits. Taking care of ourselves is where it all begins, with finding time for self-reflection in meditation or prayer, moving our bodies, cultivating friendships and relationships, getting better quality sleep, sometimes engaging in spiritual or religious rituals and pursuits, and learning to look for life's silver linings. There are so many aspects to well-being, but the end result is always the same: a greater capacity for feeling strong, peaceful, balanced, and happy.

Total well-being can encompass many different levels, including emotional, physical, spiritual, social, career/purpose, and societal/life satisfaction.

The Centers for Disease Control and Prevention defines well-being as:

- Physical well-being
- Economic well-being
- Social well-being
- Development and activity
- Emotional well-being
- Psychological well-being
- Life satisfaction
- Domain-specific satisfaction
- Engaging activities and work

This list defines the areas we can focus on to increase our personal and collective levels of well-being.

CULTIVATING WELL-BEING

We know what well-being means and the parameters that define it, but can we learn and cultivate more well-being as a skill that, with practice, we could improve and excel at? According to Dr. Richard Davidson, neuroscientist and founder of the Center for Healthy Minds at University of Wisconsin–Madison, the answer is yes. In "The Four Keys to Well-Being," in the March 21, 2016, University of California–Berkeley *Greater Good*, Davidson states, "Based on our research, well-being has four constituents that have each received serious scientific attention. Each of these four is rooted in neural circuits, and each of these neural circuits exhibits plasticity–so we know that if we exercise these circuits, they will strengthen."

These four constituents or skills are:

1. Resilience–Looking at how we respond to the things that happen. We cannot always control what happens, but we can control how we respond to it.

2. Outlook–How we perceive things and our ability to see the positive in people, situations, and things.

3.   Attention–Focusing the mind on the present moment and improving the quality of attention.

4.   Generosity–Engaging in altruistic and generous behaviors that cultivate compassion and kindness to foster well–being in ourselves and others.

Well-being is not just about eating healthier foods, getting more exercise, or improving our sleeping patterns. It is about the brain's capacity to grow and expand in ways that promote a greater level of well–being. It is also about taking responsibility, Davidson states, for our minds.

This is good news because it means that achieving more well–being operates similar to learning a new habit, and we can all learn new habits. With practice and some repetition, our brains can literally become more happy–adapted.

Psychological well–being is often cast aside in favor of working on our physical and mental health, but it is equally important that we achieve emotional health. Our emotions drive our mental states and can affect our bodies in negative ways. In *Verywell Mind*'s "How to Improve Your Psychological Well–Being," updated February 10, 2022, Amy Morin, L.C.S.W., writes: "Studies have discovered that people with higher psychological well–being are more likely to live healthier and longer lives. They are also more likely to enjoy a better quality of life."

Morin states that high psychological well–being is about "feeling happy and doing well. People with high psychological well–being report feeling capable, happy, well–supported, and satisfied with life."

Morin suggests the following:

1.   Create a sense of purpose–"Living a life with meaning and purpose is the key to improving your psychological well–being," she says. And no, that purpose doesn't

Having a sense of purpose in your life is a vital part of obtaining a sense of psychological well-being.

How to Live a Mindful, Meaningful, Magical Life

have to involve something as big as changing the world, just whatever gives you a sense of meaning.

2. Positive thinking–Pretty self-explanatory, because people who think positive often feel more positive about their present and their future. While positive thinking might not cure all your ills, it goes a long way toward improving your chances of having a good outcome. Few people with poor outlooks on life have satisfactory results happen in their lives.

3. Acts of kindness–Again, giving of oneself even in small ways reminds us we have the power to change our world. Like the pebble thrown into the pond, we ripple outward!

4. Practice mindfulness–Life is so much easier to deal with and enjoy when we stay present to the moment at hand. Research shows mindfulness improves strength, helps us cope with illnesses, and reduces levels of anxiety and depression.

5. Express gratitude–Being grateful to the people and things in our lives opens us to more to be grateful for. It's a shift in focus and a way to find joy in the little things, like a beautiful sunset or a garden full of fresh tomatoes.

6. Identify your strengths–When we feel capable, we are capable and we can handle anything. Confidence builds character.

7. Practice forgiveness–Letting go of past hurts and resentments frees up our energy for magic and happiness. We are not saying what was done to us was acceptable, but instead are letting go of the negative energetic hold it has on us.

We might add sharing ourselves with others with honesty and authenticity, which is the fodder for solid and supportive relationships. Living from our truth allows others to do the same, and we become models for those seeking their own paths to well-being. Others want what we are having, and the great thing is they can have it, too.

Anyone can.

Everyday Magic

THE MAGIC OF LAUGHTER

We've all heard the quote "Laughter is good medicine," and there is a lot of science to back that up. Having a good sense of humor offers many health benefits, according to studies done by the University of St. Augustine Health Science and the Mayo Clinic, among others. Some of those benefits include:

- Laughter stimulates the internal organs, and as you laugh, you take in more oxygen to stimulate your heart, lungs, and muscles.

- Laughter increases feel-good endorphins.

- Laughter relaxes muscles and soothes tension in the body.

- Laughter increases the heart rate and improves cardiac health.

- Laughter boosts the immune system and releases disease-fighting antibodies and neuropeptides into the blood.

The simple act of laughter has many benefits, especially reducing stress. Surprisingly, it also boosts the immune system, blood circulation, and endorphins, while reducing pain and improving cardiac health.

How to Live a Mindful, Meaningful, Magical Life

- Laughter improves mood and relieves pain.
- Laughter reduces the amount of stress hormones in the body.
- Laughter stimulates blood circulation.
- Laughter creates bonds between people and helps us feel more connected.
- Laughter just plain feels good and lightens the spirit.

The great thing about finding more reasons to laugh is that it is cheap, if not free. You can peruse social media for funny cartoons and memes or look for a great comedy on television or a streaming service. You can get friends together for a fun game that will no doubt inspire giggles and snorts or listen to funny podcasts during your long work commute. Recall funny stories at the next family gathering. Tell someone a dumb joke you overheard or share a silly story on your Facebook page. You can even join "laughter yoga," a class that combines yoga positions with prolonged, voluntary laughter.

As long as you are not laughing at someone else's expense, finding the fun and the funny is a great way to feel a sense of well-being and that all is good in your world. Since laughter is contagious, sprinkle it around like the magic fairy dust it is because we can all use more of that kind of magic in our daily lives.

JUST LET IT BE

Many people think that well-being demands we feel great all of the time, but this is not true. That would put too much pressure on us when we don't feel good, thus adding to our lack of well-being. The key is to allow our feelings to just be what they are—the good, the bad, and the ugly—and to process them and let them go. What we resist persists, and it is not the feelings themselves that derail our happiness and well-being but our constant resistance to them.

Suppressing negative emotions has a nasty way of making them show up in another, more virulent form later, perhaps as rage, addiction, depression, anxiety, even violence. True well-being allows for all emotions to be "felt and dealt" with. The happiest folks on the planet are not those who never suffer (we all suffer), but those who have learned to accept things and not get bogged down into the dark depths of unprocessed and unacknowledged emotions. They know that "this too shall pass," and they allow it to do so.

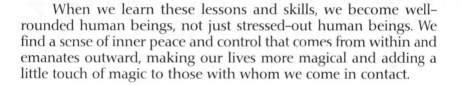

Suppressing negative emotions has a nasty way of making them show up in another, more virulent form later, perhaps as rage, addiction, depression, anxiety, even violence.

When we learn these lessons and skills, we become well-rounded human beings, not just stressed-out human beings. We find a sense of inner peace and control that comes from within and emanates outward, making our lives more magical and adding a little touch of magic to those with whom we come in contact.

MINDFULNESS

There is no shortage of books, seminars, websites, podcasts, YouTube videos, and TED Talks about well-being and mindfulness, because the two really do go together. Mindfulness asks that we live in the now, and well-being can only be achieved in the moment we are experiencing. Stressing over the past or being anxious about the future destroys well-being. It all happens in the NOW, right here, where we are.

Cultivating mindfulness might just be the greatest skill we can acquire to achieve a higher level of well-being. Mindfulness can come in so many forms:

- Meditation and walking meditation
- Prayer and chanting
- Journaling
- Dancing and movement

* Gardening
* Being with loved ones
* Unplugging from technology
* Cuddling a dog or cat

Yes, cuddling a beloved pet counts as one way to practice mindfulness, and a very comforting way it is, too!

This list can go on for pages, but you get the idea. Finding ways to get yourself into the moment is what mindfulness is all about. Whatever floats your boat is what will work best because you will do it, and when you do it enough times that repetition creates those new neural pathways in the brain discussed earlier. Even eating lunch can be a practice in mindfulness if you slow down long enough to savor every bite and taste your food instead of the usual gulping and shoving it down the gullet so you can go check your email again.

Anything can become a mindfulness practice if you are present, fully aware, and tuned in to what you are doing as you do it. There is ample research showing how mindfulness can help with depression and anxiety. It is considered a science–backed intervention for depression and can help regulate emotions and reduce symptoms. Much of the research involving mindfulness and depression focuses on what is called "mindfulness intervention." One form of this is Mindfulness–Based Stress Reduction, or MBSR, created as a therapeutic program in the 1970s by Jon Kabat–Zinn, Ph.D. MBSR research has been shown to also be helpful at reducing depression during a crisis such as the COVID–19 pandemic, as discovered in a study titled "The Benefits of Meditation and Mindfulness Practices during Times of Crisis Such as COVID–19," *Irish Journal of Psychological Medicine*, published online May 14, 2020 (provided to NIH by Cambridge University Press).

Another study, titled "Effects of Mindfulness Exercises as Stand–Alone Intervention on Symptoms of Anxiety and Depression: Systematic Review and Meta–Analysis" and published in the March 2018 issue of *Behavior Research and Therapy*, found that these exercises do alleviate symptoms of anxiety and depression in general even as a stand–alone therapy modality. The conclusion states, "This is the first meta-analysis to show that the mere regular performance of mindfulness exercises is beneficial, even without being integrated in larger therapeutic frameworks."

There is plenty more science where those studies came from, proving that just doing one thing alone, staying present, can have untold benefits on our bodies, our minds, and our spirits. Rushing through life while ruminating on the past or stressing over the future is no way to feel good. We cannot change the past, and we have no idea what the future holds. That much is obvious.

Living in the present is where we must begin our journey to well-being, because it is the only moment we have—and the great thing is, it's free! We don't have to buy anything or go live at an ashram for a month or pay anyone to teach us unless we feel moved to do so. We can start today taking small steps toward living more mindfully. Sounds easy, but it does ask us to commit to a practice on a regular basis to ensure mindfulness becomes our new habit and our new way of being in the world. That practice can be anything we want it to be, as long as we do it often, daily if possible. To those who have mastered this practice and experience the magical benefits of well-being, the dedication and commitment are worth every moment.

WHERE DO YOU LIVE?

We don't mean your street address or country of origin, but where you live your life and what that looks like. Is your home comfortable and airy, and a reflection of you? Do you have a room where you can meditate and sit in silence? Is your house cluttered with toys and clothes everywhere you look? How about your office or cubicle at work? Does it make you feel relaxed or agitated?

Where we live is where we spend our time, and if that environment is cluttered and messy or filled with reminders of things we should be doing, it makes us anxious and stressed. We should be able to walk through the front door after a long day's work or coming back from errands and exhale, feeling like we are home in body, mind, and spirit. No matter how big or small our living and working spaces might be, there are things we can do to make them homier and comfortable and offer a sense of flow and serenity.

Your home environment should be comfortable, peaceful, and reflect your unique personality.

Ever hear the expression "A cluttered mind is a cluttered life"? Too much stuff, whether physical or emotional, makes us feel tired and trapped. When we look around and see clutter, it constantly reminds us of things we should attend to one day, things that probably aren't all that important or we would have attended to them right away. Those reminders bog us down mentally as well as physically by taking up space that could be used for something we value and need more.

When we take some time to clear out the rooms we live in, we feel more alive in those rooms. Keeping areas clean and clutter free gives us the feeling of being able to breathe. Air circulates. Light comes in. We feel lighter, too.

It might be time to have a spring cleaning and go through things you no longer use in your home and workspace. It also might be time for a spring cleaning of the mind and spirit to free up some space and allow life to flow back through unblocked. It might be time to enlist the rest of the family to clean up their messes. It might be time to fix up that spare room and turn it into the home gym or craft room you've dreamed of. You don't have to spend a ton of money to turn your living space into a home you love. A minor makeover to just one room can add so much value to your life and create a sanctuary out of a stressor. Later, when finances allow, you can make over another room until your whole living space is a true reflection of who you are and what is important to you.

If you have the means to move somewhere more conducive to your individual spirit, by all means do so, but for many that is not possible. Going from the city to a cabin in the woods, or vice versa if you are more of an urban spirit, may be the dream, but until it's an affordable dream, you can bring some of the elements you love into your existing home. Paint a mural on one wall of

Can't afford to move? Perhaps you can change your current surroundings to give you a new sense of place. Little tricks like scenery wallpaper or changing furniture to set the mood can do a lot.

a cityscape or a wooded lake, and design according to your vision of your dream home. Do this enough, and your existing home might just become your dream home.

So, take what you have and make it better, but better for you, regardless of the size or location. Paint the walls a serene color, replace old flooring with something fresh and modern, put some inspiring pictures on the wall by your desk, or add fresh flowers to every room.

If you don't feel good about where you spend most of your time, your well-being suffers. Being comfortable and at peace in a welcoming, cozy, and uniquely-you space does wonders for the soul and adds magic where before there were only four non-descript walls surrounding you.

AUTHOR INSIGHTS

Marie's Story

A few years after I had my son, I was on a plane traveling to another city to attend a conference. Like so many times before, I heard the flight attendant go through the safety procedures and pretty much ignored them. I knew what to do. But this time, I heard

Airplane safety procedures dictate that in an emergency adults put oxygen masks on themselves before placing the masks on their children. Adults who are incapacitated cannot help children.

her say that I should put my own oxygen mask on first and then put my child's mask on because I could not help my child if I passed out.

My son was not with me, but this struck me hard, because I had been burning the candle at both ends for years. My initial reaction was to say to myself, "Hell, no. Those masks drop down, I'd put my child's on first. I'm a good mom!" But the more I thought about it, the more I realized she was right. I could not, and cannot, help anyone else if I am not helping myself first.

I was always too much more concerned with the well-being of others to realize that mine was slipping away and fast approaching burnout. It took a few crashes and burns for me to understand that my well-being had to be high priority. My physical, emotional, mental, and spiritual well-being had to come first, not in a selfish way but in a self-preserving way, if I was ever to be a great mom or friend or daughter or anything else.

That simple airline procedure woke me up to the realization that I was not healthy and that this was affecting those I claimed to love and care for. I won't say I immediately went home and made a self-care list or that my well-being skyrocketed in the coming months, even years. It was a slow process, allowing myself to take care of number one first and not feel guilty about it.

If I ever do travel on a plane with my son, I will put my own mask on first if needed. He is old enough now to put on his own, but even if he weren't, I understand that I am no good to him unless I am living in a state of my own well-being, and hopefully being an example of how he can learn to live the same way when he is a father one day.

Denise's Story

When we talk about well-being, two thoughts come to mind. Cynicism or optimism? Which is better? Am I an optimist or a cynic? Both, actually. On certain days I can be the most cynical person in the room. What?

That isn't something most people in the spiritual/healing industry will admit to out loud. There's no denying that many people in the spiritual community are incredible and have a wealth of positivity to share. Thank goodness. Because people engage with mediums, psychics, and others in this field to look for hope, answers, and healing.

> *Many of us also have that shadow side that battles with us on a daily basis. It's real. It's normal. It's human.*

Many of us also have that shadow side that battles with us on a daily basis. It's real. It's normal. It's human.

There are also many people telling you to look at the world as difficult. That you have to work pedal-to-the-metal all the time to get anywhere and be anybody and succeed. So, yes, this bombardment can create that minute or hour or day of cynicism. It took me awhile, though, to understand that it is natural to be a cynic on certain days.

My goal as a medium and psychic is to show people that our loved ones in spirit are with us, love us, and support us. I also delight in helping people discover that "aha" moment. The moment in a reading where things that didn't make sense to people before suddenly become clear. Helping a client come to that lightbulb experience is exciting and lifts me up as well.

So which is best? A cynical, down-to-earth attitude toward life? Or a very optimistic attitude?

Optimism. To me that's where it is at. Where someone discovers the light at the end of the tunnel and has a sudden understanding and clarification. If I helped someone locate it … what a win for us both! I also want people to know that sometimes when they're feeling like that lightbulb has extinguished, there is a way out of darkness. There is always hope. Always light.

So, whatever you do ... hang in there. This world needs the unique and amazing you.

MAGICAL TIPS

Every Breath You Take

We gasp for breath, taking in shallow snippets of oxygen that barely do the job of feeding our brain cells with necessary nutrients. Caveat here. If you have physical issues with your lungs or heart, you might be a shallow breather. It has also been found that people who have experienced chronic stress (perhaps from childhood) could have learned to breathe this way in reaction to that stress. In any case, there can be physical reasons why you are a shallow breather. Trying deep-breathing techniques might benefit you. If it causes too much discomfort, of course you are free not to do it. It might also be wise to consult with a medical professional to make sure everything is medically the way it should be for you.

We should be practicing deep, diaphragmatic breathing until it becomes habit, like the Five-Second Breath. Take in a breath through the nose for five counts (unless you have a cold or just had a nose job, then use mouth), placing the hands upon the abdomen to feel it rise. If the belly isn't rising, you are breathing too shallowly! Fill the abdomen with as much air as you can get in and then hold for five counts. Exhale for five counts through your mouth. Repeat again and again until "belly breathing" becomes old hat.

For some, deep breathing can be difficult, such as those with asthma or COPD. Talk to a medical professional about what precautions to take during deep breathing.

Breath is awareness. Breath is life. We can't stress enough how "de-stressing" correct belly breathing is. When the body gets the oxygen it needs, it calms the nervous system, and far less adrenaline and cortisol get released into the bloodstream. Adrenaline and cortisol are the by-products of stress and anxiety, and they are two of the most taxing hormonal substances our bodies can deal with.

Now that you know how to breathe and why you should do it correctly, here is a quick meditation that you can try for one week. It will introduce you to the art of being quiet and give you a starting point for more extensive meditation periods involving breathwork should you wish to add them to your spiritual practice.

For the next seven days, three times a day, stop whatever you are doing and sit still for five minutes with your eyes closed. Breathe deeply from the diaphragm, just as we learned earlier. In through the nose, hold, out through the mouth, and feel that belly rise with each inhalation. If any thoughts enter your mind, gently escort them to the edges and push them over with love. They can always get up and come back later to bother you. For five minutes, let your mind go blank and just be in the moment, moment to moment. Do not listen but let yourself hear any sounds that come into your environment, acknowledging them but not focusing on them. If a cool breeze brushes across your body, just feel it, but then let it go and do not give it your concentration. The idea is to be totally present for five minutes, and totally aware of your "being" as you are being.

What will happen is that you will come out of it feeling refreshed, in touch with yourself, and more present in your own life. You'll also feel happier, more connected, and more at peace, which translates into a sense of well-being.

We need repetition, especially when we are trying to adopt healthy new habits like breathing correctly, meditation, exercise, prayer, and inner work.

Unplug!

Ever stop to look at how many electronics, gadgets, and devices you engage with in the course of one day? You get up in the morning and check email on your phone, then turn on the television to watch the news. You might commute to work and listen to the radio or a podcast, then get to work and sit at a computer for hours, answer emails and texts and private messages all day,

These days, we are overwhelmed by televisions, computers, smartphones, music, and even VR goggles. It's impossible to get in touch with yourself or the Source with all of these electronic distractions.

scroll social media on your lunch break at your desk, only to go home later that evening and turn the television back on or binge a streaming series on your cell phone. Sound familiar?

Our constantly plugged-in existence leaves little room for engaging in the present moment, noticing the sights and sounds and smells around us, or even connecting with others face-to-face (not over a screen). No wonder we feel stressed out all the time, as if we never have a moment to ourselves to just ... BREATHE.

Try this for one day. Chances are you may feel a lot of anxiety, but find just one day when you can totally and completely unplug from all electronics and devices. That means no television, no radio, no computer, no email or texting, no social media. Completely unplug and find other things to do such as walk in nature, go outside and tend to your garden (or plant some seeds and start one), visit a friend or neighbor, declutter your house for a charity pickup, volunteer at a neighborhood charity, play with your pet, sit by the pool if you have one, try a new recipe, or just do nothing at all.

This might best be done on a weekend day if you work during the week. You will probably feel awkward and strange not being able to connect to the World Wide Web, but we can guarantee you'll find peace instead by connecting to the real world, so much so you might just make this whole unplugging thing a regular part of your well-being goals.

We dare you!

5–3–1

The Center for Healthy Minds at the University of Wisconsin–Madison teaches a daily practice called "5–3–1." It's easy to do and cultivates greater well-being. The steps are:

- Meditate for five minutes.
- Write down three good things that happened that day.
- Complete one act of kindness.

As simple as the above may sound, doing them on a regular basis can lead to a greater sense of happiness and inner peace. The act of kindness doesn't have to be big and bold. Pay ahead for someone's coffee. Help an elderly neighbor carry in groceries. Send a supportive message to a friend going through a hard time.

Well-being begins with you but increases when you share of yourself with others.

Being Mindful in Ordinary Ways

Do you think that being mindful means pure meditation, or that sitting in the lotus position with incense burning and eyes closed is the only way to become mindful? Actually, you can be mindful doing everyday chores. Really.

Often we think of doing laundry, dishes, or vacuuming as something we hate and will avoid as long as possible. Few of us like completing these tasks, and we rush through them. Afterwards we can feel frazzled and maybe even slightly angsty, or even feel full-blown anger at having to do the chore in the first place. Listening to a podcast or music while doing chores might lighten the load, but there is something else you can do as an experiment. It takes a bit of practice, but don't despair.

Try this while vacuuming. Notice and feel your body in that moment. Are your shoulders tight? Any other muscles tight? Take a deep breath and purposefully relax these muscles while doing the task. Allow the flow of pushing the vacuum

You can actually practice mindfulness while doing chores such as dusting, vacuuming, dishes, and laundry.

back and forth to settle into a rhythm in your mind. Think of it as a meditation. A way to flow through that moment with ease. As you are pushing the vacuum you can even repeat in your head, "Back and forth." Or even, "I am in the flow." Use these sentences as a type of meditation as you build them into the rhythm.

You can also try this while washing dishes by hand. What are the sounds the dishes make as they come together? What does the water sound like? Notice each sound as you hear it and concentrate on each movement. Does the dishwashing liquid have a scent? Is that scent pleasant to you? If not, can you find a dishwashing liquid for next time that you like or at least isn't unpleasant to you? The dishwashing liquid thing might sound funny or insignificant, but if the scent of the dishwashing liquid is gagging you, you'll be less likely to want to do the chore. Even somewhat unconscious things like this make a difference.

Using this being–in–the–present approach, you may notice that instead of thinking of the 20 things you have to do next or being uptight and eager to finish, you may feel more relaxed as you complete a chore you normally want to escape or hurry to complete. Think of it as a "break" from chaos rather than a contributor to it. You cannot get much more in the moment than that.

The Magic of Nature

In nature, nothing is perfect and everything is perfect. Trees can be contorted, bent in weird ways, and they're still beautiful.

Alice Walker

Forget not that the earth delights to feel your bare feet and the winds long to play with your hair.

Khalil Gibran

In all things of nature there is something of the marvelous.

Aristotle

Ralph Waldo Emerson once said, "Nature always wears the colors of the spirit." Maybe that is why we feel so good, so connected to life and its magical forces, when we are in a natural setting away from the distractions of the intellect or the concerns of the body. Our spirits have a chance to come alive and dance to the music that can only be heard by the spirit, the soul, out in nature.

According to a 2022 study by the Environmental Protection Agency (EPA), the average American spends 93% of their lives indoors. They spend 87% of their lives inside buildings, then another 6% in automobiles. That's only 7% of an entire life spent outdoors, which equates to one half of one day per week. Another study for Nature of Americans reported over 60% of adults spend

American philosopher and leader of the transcendental movement Ralph Waldo Emerson recognized the value of nature in our lives as a nurturing force.

five or fewer hours per week outdoors in nature. Even more concerning was that the majority of people surveyed claimed they were satisfied with that amount of contact with nature. Yet the study also showed that the more time people spent in nature, the higher level of satisfaction they reported, signifying that we have a major disconnect between ourselves and the positive aspects of spending time in nature that can only be "cured" when we spend more quality time outside.

We live inside, work inside, even exercise inside, preferring to walk or run for an hour three days a week on a treadmill in a stuffy gym. If we do take our walk or run outdoors, we usually have our noses in our phones or earbuds in our ears so we can look at and listen to anything other than the sights and sounds of the natural world around us.

We were not born to be locked up inside walls. Humans cannot thrive unless we get out into nature and commune with the sky and the sun, the sea and the trees, the birds and the butterflies and flowers. The sights and smells of nature lift us out of our intellects and into our spirits, reminding us of the beauty of creation in all its glory and our place within the web. We are not the web itself, but one strand, working in conjunction with all other strands.

We forget about that when we are stuck indoors, whether at home or in cubicles at work, cars during the commute, planes and trains during travel. We become closed off to the incredible and rejuvenating, life-giving and life-sustaining energies to be found in nature. Our skin grows pale from lack of sunlight, but so, too, do our souls. Our spirits long to flow along with the river's current or on the gentle summer breeze. Our minds ache to be free of everyday worries and concerns, and our bodies wish to feel the solid earth beneath our feet and the wind in our hair.

Instead, we tolerate the cold blow of air conditioners, the constant hum of televisions and people chattering, and the sight of solid walls where the only reminder we get of our wild child natural side is the occasional glimpse through a window of children playing in the grass at a park across the street or the sound of their laughter as they splash around in a neighbor's pool, the way we once did.

Nature has healing magic for the mind, body, and spirit. An article titled "Spending at Least 120 Minutes a Week in Nature Is Associated with Good Health and Well-Being," published June 13, 2019, in the journal *Scientific Reports*, states: "A growing body of epidemiological evidence indicates that greater exposure to, or 'contact with,' natural environments (such as parks, woodlands and beaches) is associated with better health and well-being, at least among populations in high income, largely urbanized, societies. While the quantity and quality of evidence varies across outcomes, living in greener urban areas is associated with lower probabilities of cardiovascular disease, obesity, diabetes, asthma hospitalisation, mental distress, and ultimately mortality, among adults; and lower risks of obesity and myopia in children. Greater quantities of neighbourhood nature are also associated with better self-reported health, and subjective well-being in adults, and improved birth outcomes, and cognitive development, in children."

The modern world has disconnected many people from nature. Reconnecting to the beauty and spirit of the natural world has great benefits to our sense of well-being.

How to Live a Mindful, Meaningful, Magical Life

Time magazine's July 14, 2016, article "The Healing Power of Nature" documents numerous scientific studies about the benefits of nature for our bodies and minds. These include a 2015 study by Paul Piff at the University of California–Irvine that found that people who spend just 60 seconds outside looking up at towering trees were more likely to report feeling awe, and afterwards were more likely to help a stranger, than people who spent the same time looking up at a building or skyscraper.

Another study done in 2016 showed that urban areas with more parks scored higher on measures of community well-being than those that had fewer or no parks. This was most likely a combination of exposure to nature and to social interaction and a sense of community, both of which have been found to improve health and well-being, especially when it came to depression and anxiety. Urban dwellers, according to the *Time* article, were "far more likely to experience anxiety and mood disorders than people who live in rural areas. That's the bad news, since about 80% of Americans live in cities." The study also found that "Accessible natural areas may be vital for mental health in our rapidly urbanizing world."

We don't have to live in the great outdoors as our primitive ancestors once did to reap the benefits, but we do have to venture into it now and then. There is a reason why most vacation destinations involve "getting away" from the hustle and bustle to a cabin in the woods or a beachfront resort. Just going outside for a few minutes fills our senses with nature's magical wonders. The sight of birds flying high in the blue sky, the smell of freshly cut grass or spring flowers, the feel of warm sun on our bare arms and legs–our senses come alive and delight in nature in ways they simply cannot when we are indoors.

NATURE'S GIFTS: FORAGING AND GARDENING

Spend an hour in a garden and you can see visible proof of the magic of nature. Flowers of every size and shape astound the eyes with variety and bursts of bold color. Vegetables and fruits grow on vines and trees to sustain and nourish life, including us. The sights, scents, and sounds abound. Birds chirp in trees, flitting from branch to branch before taking flight into azure skies. The buzz and hum of pollenating bees fill the air as they flit from flower to flower.

We are usually too engrossed in our indoor activities to notice any of this. Gardening and foraging are two ways we can spend time in nature. Foraging merges the serenity of mindful walking or hiking through the woods or brush with looking for what grows in our local and regional environments. When we forage, we look specifically for edible roots, branches, berries, and leaves, which means doing a little research beforehand, or at least not eating anything until you have!

When we forage, we become hyperaware of our surroundings, from the trees overhead to the soil beneath our feet. The sounds we hear in the woods or wherever we choose to forage provide us clues to where wildlife is hiding out or to the proximity of a creek or river. We get down and get dirty touching the soil, picking things off branches, feeling the joy of finding something extraordinary like edible mushrooms. Foraging allows us to take part in the circle of life that occurs when nature is left alone to do her thing. We take only what we need, and nature restores with more growth, more harvest for the next time.

Wildcrafting and gardening allow us to take what we have learned in nature and plant our own bounty, our own harvest. We learn about seeds and what plants work best in our location and weather conditions, and we plant seeds and seedlings. We tend to our gardens by watering them and naturally getting rid of pests. We remove pesky weeds and watch as the seeds sprout or the plants begin to bloom and reveal their herbs, flowers, veggies, and fruits.

Perhaps we do some research or take a class in healing and cooking with herbs, and we plant whatever we need for what ails us. We reap what we have sown, and we use the harvest to eat and cook with,

You need to know what you are doing when it comes to picking food. For example, many types of mushrooms are dangerous or even lethal to eat.

to make teas and tinctures with, to replant for next year's harvest. A garden is our own private and personal connection to nature and all it has to offer, a microcosm of the macrocosm.

A garden can be a huge tract of land or a small patch of ground in a tiny backyard. Potted plants and vegetables can adorn a balcony of a condo or apartment, and window boxes can grow flowers and herbs for those who have no balconies or yards. There is a garden for every type of gardener.

One great benefit of having a flower garden is the attraction of pollinators. Planting nectar and pollen–rich flowers will attract bees, butterflies, and hummingbirds, who then spread that nectar and pollen to other plants. Should you choose a pollinating garden, be careful to keep it pesticide–free so as not to spread toxins. There are hundreds of books and videos available to teach you how to plan out a pollinating garden according to which pollinators you want to attract (there are many plants that attract all three) and which plants grow best in your location.

Getting children involved in gardening is a wonderful way to keep them outdoors and exposed to the natural world and its magical wonders. Most children today have gadgets and cell phones and are becoming indoor hermits compared with past generations. Kids used to play outdoors every chance they got, but now their attention is on computer screens. A garden of their own is a great way to give them something to connect them back to nature and show them the importance of being responsible. They can learn about the cycle of life and how important it is to tend to their gardens, because neglect will result in dead plants. Allowing children to pick and choose what they want to grow invests them even more in the outcome, especially when they can eat the fruits and veggies of their choice and feel proud to have taken part in growing them from the ground up.

Get the kids involved with your gardening. Not only will it help them appreciate what they eat more, but it is definitely a nice bonding practice.

BRINGING NATURE INDOORS

There is no excuse for anyone who wants a garden not to have one. Even if you have no yard or balcony or window boxes, you can have your own indoor garden where you can grow flowers, herbs, and some veggies. Indoor gardens can be anything from a few potted plants on a kitchen counter to a sunroom filled with flowers and herbs. The only requirement is a little research into the proper temperatures and conditions needed for growing what you want with the space and sunlight you have.

Certain flowers and herbs may need more sun than others, and depending on the space you have, you may be limited to what veggies you can grow indoors (think sprouts!), but the basics needed for a successful indoor garden are sun, plenty of fresh air, and the right amount of water. Once plants start to grow bigger, you may need to swap out pots for a bigger size and up the watering frequency. All indoor pots should have proper drainage, including decorative trays for excess water. You can even use a saucer for smaller pots.

Once you get some solid growth, you can harvest the herbs or veggies and use them in teas, cooking, salads, tinctures, sachets, or salves or give them as gifts to friends and neighbors. And who doesn't like the scent of fresh flowers every day? Growing them as opposed to buying them at the store already cut allows you to enjoy their beauty and aroma on a much longer basis.

Some plants such as mint and basil allow you to take cuttings of the original plant without harming it and put them in some water to root before replanting them in new pots. Again, there are numerous books and online videos to direct you on how to create your own little indoor slice of natural magic.

Don't forget to talk to your plants! Bless them for what they offer you. Lovingly water them and tend to them. Many studies have

If you live in an apartment or don't otherwise have access to an outside space for gardening, try an indoor garden!

shown plants react to music and emotions, so shower your plants with some positive vibes to help them flourish.

Indoor gardens remind us that outside our windows is a world of amazing wonders that we may not have access to on a daily basis. We can, however, experience those wonders on a smaller scale by bringing nature to us, even if we are stuck at a computer five days a week.

SUNLIGHT AND WATER

The sun gives us life. Without the sun, nothing could survive, yet we spend so much time indoors our bodies are crying out for a good dose of natural vitamin D and the healing benefits only the sun's rays can give us. All it takes is about 20 minutes of exposure to the sun to offer us the benefits of improved sleep quality, boosted mood and libido, better eye health, stronger bones, reduced stress, regulated appetite and circadian rhythm, and increased energy and wakefulness.

Morning sun helps reset our internal sleep clock and tells the brain it's time to get up and get going. When we skimp on morning sunlight, our bodies might decide it's not yet time to wake up, and we feel sluggish all day. Without that first burst of natural light, our circadian rhythms are disrupted, and we end up not being sleepy later, when it's time to go to bed, because we have not exposed our brains to the natural change from dark to light to dark again.

So many of us are worried about getting skin cancer, so we "shun the sun," yet short periods of exposure are good for the skin and everything underneath it.

So many of us are worried about getting skin cancer, so we "shun the sun," yet short periods of exposure are good for the skin and everything underneath it. We are not suggesting lying in the hot sun for two hours, but a short walk or a 15-minute meditation session outdoors with arms and legs exposed provides health benefits without the sunburn or skin damage. There are a few exceptions to this, and the bottom line is to realize that one size does not fit all with anything related to your overall health. Consult with your doctor or dermatologist about how much sun they recommend for you personally. If you haven't had your vitamin D levels checked, now might be a good time to do it if you have never done so before. If you are deficient in vitamin D, your health care provider will no doubt make a recommendation on whether you need a vitamin D supplement. There are cases where someone can be deficient in vitamin D and yet for reasons of sensitive skin or a history of skin cancer is not advised to expose themselves to much sun without sunscreen and/or covering.

Water makes us come alive, too. Ever wonder why you feel so energized after a day at the beach or spending time on the river or exploring a waterfall? Why do thunderstorms make us feel so charged up? Blame it on the presence of negative ions, which are found in or near moving bodies of water. Ions are charged air particles, and negative ions, such as the ones released from a rushing waterfall, contain an extra negatively charged electron. These ions break apart when exposed to things like moving water, sunlight, or radiation. When they break apart, they clean the air of pollens, dust mites, allergens, viruses, and bacteria, and neutralize the more de-energizing positive ions they encounter.

Sunlight and water, the perfect combination of natural elements that uplift our mood and spirit.

How to Live a Mindful, Meaningful, Magical Life

We feel much better around negative ions, even though they are odorless, tasteless, and invisible, because our bodies are made of both positive and negative ions. We spend so much time in the presence of positive ions, indoors with our technology and gadgets that produce too many of them, affecting our bodies and our energy levels. When we get outdoors and near bodies of water or out in the middle of a thunderstorm, we are exposed to more negative ions by inhaling them in the air, and our bodies enjoy the plethora of biochemical reactions that occur, such as increased serotonin levels that boost our mood. Sure, you can buy a room ionizer, but that takes all the fun away from riding the rapids in a raft with friends, standing knee-deep in the waves on the beach, fishing off an ocean pier, or watching the thunder and lightning of a good storm from a porch swing.

In *WebMD*'s "Negative Ions Create Positive Vibes," Denise Mann writes that negative ions can make us feel "like we are walking on air." We experience this instant refreshment "the moment [we] open a window and breathe in fresh, humid air."

EARTHING AND FOREST BATHING

Remember as a child wanting to be barefoot outside? We would run through the grass with bare feet, getting wet in the sprinklers or dipping our toes in a rushing creek. Maybe we went to the beach a lot and loved running on the hot sand to the shoreline to cool off in the foamy water. Shoes felt cumbersome, and we kicked them off every chance we got.

As adults we barely go barefoot indoors, let alone outdoors. We miss that connection to the ground beneath our feet, forgetting that we are electrical beings and that there is an electrical energy beneath the Earth's surface that we can tap into and experience greater well-being. All living things are electrical, and our bodies hold positive charges. Our skin receives the Earth's limitless supply of negative-charged electrons, which help create a stable internal bioelectrical environment that allows our bodily organs and systems to fully function. But this can only happen when we are shoeless and nothing stands between us and the Earth like a brick or cement patio or thick socks.

Earthing, also known as grounding, means going barefoot in natural places outdoors where the bottoms of our feet can come in direct contact with grass, soil, sand, and dirt, and thus ground us. The energy that comes from the Earth can move into our bodies via our bare feet as our skin acts as a conductor to receive the natural and electrical charges. We cannot do this if our feet are covered with thick–soled shoes or if we are walking on cement or AstroTurf.

To get the benefits of earthing, go outside and find grass, soil, sand, or even moss and stand on it for at least 10 minutes with no shoes or socks on. The more time you spend doing this, the better the results will offset your hours standing and walking on carpeting, flooring, and cement, and you can even turn this into a type of walking meditation. You might try standing directly on the moist soil while you are gardening.

You don't even have to stand or walk. You can roll down a grassy hill like you did when you were a kid or put your palms directly onto the dirt or soil or lie on a patch of clover while gazing up at the clouds. Anything that gets your body in direct contact with the Earth will work.

Sleeping directly on grass or soil has been shown to improve sleep cycles and normalize cortisol rhythm, and the best results occur when there is nothing between us and the Earth. Think of sleeping outside on the grass naked if you are up for the challenge!

If a walk in the woods or a hike through a dense forest is more your style, you might try forest bathing, which comes from a Japanese practice that doesn't involve water or bubbles or bath toys. Forest bathing, or *shinrin-yoku*, was first introduced in 1982 by the Forest Agency of Japan to get people outside and into the beauty of nature. It means to stand or walk in the forest in a state of mindfulness, engaging all five senses in the beauty of

Grounding is when you walk barefoot on the sand, soil, and grass of the Earth, giving you a direct, intimate connection with nature.

How to Live a Mindful, Meaningful, Magical Life

nature around you. It's literally taking a bath for the body, mind, and spirit.

Any wooded area will do, as long as you use your five senses to connect with the environment. Let go of the worries and anxieties of the day and lose yourself in the trees, the brush, the smell and taste of clean air, the sounds of birds and rushing water and buzzing insects. Enjoy the feel of moss or rugged tree bark, the crunch of leaves and twigs beneath your feet, and the sights galore of green, lush life surrounding you.

There is ample science behind the benefits of forest bathing, notably the work of Dr. Qing Li, president of the Japanese Society of Forest Medicine. Li has done studies into the positive benefits of forest bathing on the immune system and its effects on mood, stress, anger, and depression. Spending time in the woods isn't just for characters in horror movies. It's a magical place where we connect with life in all its glorious forms and allow ourselves to get lost in the beauty of our environment, even as we lower our heart rate, blood pressure, and cortisol levels.

According to "Forest Bathing: What It Is and Why You Should Try It," a December 19, 2022, posting on the KaiserPermanente.org website: "A good rule of thumb is to practice forest bathing for at least 20 minutes a day. If you don't have that much time to spare, that's okay. You can start with a shorter amount of time. Plus, the goal of forest bathing is to relax and detach–the practice shouldn't feel like a chore. It should be an activity you look forward to and enjoy." A key point is to look for the "moments of wonder," and the article mentions a study of the positive impacts of taking "awe walks," where you look at life around you with fresh eyes, seeing everything as new as a child might.

LEARNING NATURE'S WISDOM

Nature has so much to teach us. The cycles of birth, life, death, and rebirth help us to understand the course of our own lives and how everything continues on in some form after we die. Dust to dust, ashes to ashes. The seasons show us that there can be cold, dim winters when all that was green is now brown and dead, but springtime is always right around the corner, with new growth bursting forth, an increase of sunshine, and a return to warmer days. We plant our seeds in the spring so that we can harvest them in the fall, just as we plant the seeds of our goals and dreams so that one day we can reap the benefits of our effort, seeing them unfold before our eyes.

Everything operates according to natural laws that have more to teach us than just the science of the natural world.

We watch the stars and constellations change overhead, and we note that the angle of the sun is different in the fall than it is in the summer. Everything operates according to natural laws that have more to teach us than just the science of the natural world. They teach us lessons about life itself and how we can glean wisdom from everything happening around us.

Just as a foggy morning soon gives way to clear skies and sunshine, life may feel foggy and unfocused at times. Nothing seems clear, and we cannot seem to move forward. Our vision fails us. We can't see two steps in front of us, but we can see enough to take one step forward. When driving, a thick fog slows us down because our visibility is limited, and we don't want to crash into a car ahead of us. We creep along, hoping and waiting for some clarity of vision, until the fog dissipates and lifts and we move forward again at full speed. Yes, even fog can teach us about patience and inner examination and seeing the obstacles and blocks that keep us from a clear vision for our lives.

The waves of the mighty ocean have wisdom for us. If you have spent time near the ocean, you know that the tide comes in and goes out throughout the course of a 24-hour period. During high tide, the water is up to the shoreline, leaving little sand exposed, and we look at life as full and overflowing. Then, during low tide, the tide recedes for a while, and things feel bare and lacking. Then the tide comes back in again because it's all cyclical. What goes out always comes back in. That is nature's way.

During a low tide cycle in our lives, we might feel anxious because so much of the beach is exposed now, and there is no water unless we walk much farther out. We might feel nervous about being in a state of lack as opposed to the abundance of high tide. We see the water way out there, and it almost seems unreachable. Low-tide points in life can feel like they will last forever.

Sometimes life gets really tough, and we go into a major downward spin. In nature, there is something called a negative low tide. This is when the water recedes even further than a typical low tide and a larger area of the sandy ocean floor is now revealed. We freak out during negative low tide because the water goes out farther than usual. We might not even see where the water meets the shore without straining.

Then the tide begins creeping back in and we sigh with relief. "Ahhhhh, there it is." There is the water rising up to our knees, our thighs, our waists. Abundance returns (it never left, it just left our field of vision).

We love high tide. It's full of blessings. It's a time of prosperity and success. The water of life flows freely around us, and we can dive in and swim in it.

We might prefer the high tides in life, but low tides can often reveal the unexpected and the amazing.

Everyday Magic

Yet it is during the low tides when the gifts that lie just below the surface of the water are revealed to us. During low and negative low tides, seashell collectors often find a bounty of shells they would not be able to reach when the tide is high and they can't wade out too far. Some of that sea life is just not visible when the water is so close to shore. Negative low tides can feel scary and bare because of the lack of water, but to the sheller it's the best time to find those rare wonders of the sea that make us feel like children again, discovering some magical hidden treasure.

Life's greatest blessings often occur when we think we are in a negative low tide. It's just that without the water to cover them, we now get to see those blessings. They were always there, like the sun is always present when it goes behind a cloud. Just hidden for a while from our view.

The tides come in and the tides go out, but they always come back in. It's part of the cycle of nature and of life itself. And even when the tide is so far out that we think it might never make its way back to shore, there is magic to be revealed hidden in the sand if we open our eyes and look down at our feet.

CLOUD WISDOM

Like the ebb and flow of the ocean tides, clouds have much to teach us about life. The vast expanse of sky is like a blank canvas upon which we paint our daily hopes and expectations, and nature often matches our moods. Thick dark clouds that erupt in terrible storms can be terrifying and destructive. We cower in fear from their intensity and think they will drown us or wash away everything we love and care about. These big, unstable storms of our lives make us feel powerless and afraid. We want to hide until they pass.

The most destructive storms such as tornadoes and hurricanes represent the times in our lives when things are so unstable, we can't even see the clouds. As things grow quieter, we dare to peek through our fingers and note a chunk of blue sky peeking out from steel-gray clouds. The sun's rays penetrate the thick clouds and illuminate the sky like an angelic announcement that all is well and all will be well again. As time goes on, our lives re-

Cloud wisdom is a good metaphor for our emotional and psychological states, and rainstorms can be perceived as anything from threatening to nurturing in nature.

turn to normalcy and calm once our biggest challenges abate and vanish. We can breathe again, even as we pick up the pieces of the damage the storm left behind. Storms often teach us where our weaknesses are and what we need to work on, and they test our resilience and adaptability. They also teach us that life, like nature, is never static.

Then there are times when the sky is so overcast that we fret and worry that the sun may never return to brighten our day again. But then the grey skies burn off to reveal blue skies and warm sun again. Our mood lifts when we realize things are not as bad as they appear.

NATURAL AWE AND WONDER

Nothing makes us feel a stronger sense of magic and wonder than contemplating our presence in the natural world, whether we are standing before the ocean marveling at its grandeur or sitting under a starry night sky pondering our tiny place in the limitless

Take a few moments and pause to observe and appreciate the magnificence of nature in all its glory and mystery and wonder.

expanse of galaxies and nebulae and star systems and planets. Aside from the many health benefits of spending time in nature, there is the sheer awe that permeates every cell of our being when we witness a cocoon reveal a butterfly or an eagle soaring in the sky. We lose our sense of boundaries and separateness when we stand amidst a rich green forest lush with life or walk along a rocky path that overlooks a massive and grand canyon below.

Nature is filled with magic, and all we have to do is go outside to experience it in some form. It doesn't have to cost anything, and what we get in return is truly priceless.

WRITING A PRESCRIPTION FOR NATURE

If you're still doubtful, many medical experts have weighed in more often recently about the huge benefits of nature. If you think about it, noise created by the mechanical world such as car and bus and truck traffic (a big deal in big cities), demolition and repair and construction, the crush of so many people on the street or in a subway train at once ... well, all of it puts pressure even on the most unflappable human beings. Many people say they thrive in the big city, and perhaps they do. At the same time, many of those same people are overrun by ailments such as clinical depression, chronic stress, and other physical issues exacerbated by the noise, bustle, and hustle of the big city.

The American Heart Association noted that several distressing symptoms can be eased by involvement with nature, includ-

Yes, there have been scientific studies of the effects of the natural world on our well-being, and they conclude that being in nature is wonderful for reducing the effects of stress, fatigue, depression, and anxiety.

ing depression, stress, ruminating, fatigue, feeling antisocial, and feeling disconnected.

Even universities have studied the veracity of these claims. The University of Minnesota noted that even viewing scenes of nature can go a long way to soothing what ails you and can distract from pain and discomfort. Nurses observed that patients in rooms where nature scenes were shown tolerated pain better and spent less time in the hospital. When people are shown nature scenes it can trigger the parts of the brain that feel empathy and love. For people shown urban scenes, the parts of the brain that feel anxiety and fear were more likely to light up.

So if you can't be in nature at the moment, watching it artificially by screen can help you in the short term.

AUTHOR INSIGHTS

Marie's Story

Growing up in the 1960s and early 1970s meant spending more time playing outside than inside. As kids in the small New York town I grew up in, we had a schedule that began with knocking on each other's doors to see who could come out to play and not going home until the streetlights came on and the 7:00 P.M. all–clear siren sounded.

I recall spending hours alone in our big backyard with my book bag full of field guides to trees, flowers, leaves, and birds, collecting feathers off the ground and searching the tree branches for birds to identify. I had dozens of notebooks I wrote in about my nature studies and even got a bird caller from a cereal box offer. I had notebooks on the types of plants and flowers in our yard, the wildlife just beyond the fence to the woods, the birds that visited the treetops, and the stars and planets overhead.

Nature was a place of pure magic and discovery, where under every rock and between every blade of grass was a new surprise to delight the senses. Whether I was playing ball in the street with friends, playing flashlight tag at night when our parents were on the lawn chatting with neighbors, or walking through the woods behind our house to the lake, it was so much more natural to be outside than inside. Summer vacations lasted forever because we were not indoors unless it rained (and even then we might be out dancing in the puddles) and our eyes weren't locked on cell phones and computer screens. We were engaged with nature, with each other, or with ourselves in quiet times of contemplation while watching an inchworm move slowly up a wall.

> *We were engaged with nature, with each other, or with ourselves in quiet times of contemplation while watching an inchworm move slowly up a wall.*

My son's generation grew up playing outside, but already the writing was on the wall, as cell phones and computers were already a normal part of their existence. Luckily, school field trips still involved going to nature parks and museums, aquariums, and local lakes, so kids got a good dose of the natural world. But as they got older, there were fewer and fewer of them outside riding bikes or walking around in groups giggling and joking.

During the early months of the COVID 19 pandemic, that ceased altogether, but I noticed that as the restrictions lifted, the parks and lakes and beaches were suddenly filled with people again. Only this time, even more people were out and enjoying the fresh air and fun. It was as if they had finally realized what they had been missing not just during the brief lockdowns but for much of their young lives.

Today I smile when I see young kids playing across the street on the greenbelt, looking for frogs or tossing stones in the creek, or riding bikes in groups down the street like a scene out of a Steven Spielberg movie. I feel such joy when I see people outside again, without phones in hand. Sure, there are still the diehards that walk home from the local high school with their noses glued to a screen, but there are plenty of kids who walk without the necessity of a gadget to pass the time. They walk alone, in pairs, or groups, stopping along the way to check the creek for ducks or frogs or to visit with a neighbor's dog lounging on the lawn.

I miss playing outside and exploring the world around me. I am making sure I spend more time outdoors, whether it's playing

Children who spend time in nature versus in the concrete-paved world of urban America develop better physical coordination than their city counterparts.

with the puppy or smelling the roses that grow along the back patio. I live next to a golf course where I can step over my short brick wall right onto the 15th hole and there is an abundance of green grass, trees, animals and birds, and some little ponds and water features that, when not clogged with a steady stream of golf-ers, is incredibly peaceful. Just five minutes standing on my back patio is enough to remind me of the joys of being outside as a kid and how life–giving the sun and air are. I feel different outside.

I feel better. Happier. More tuned in to the Universe and God and spirit.

Here's the thing. The magic of nature doesn't desert us; we desert it. I think we all suffer because of it, and today's younger generations suffer most of all. We older folks need to be role models and show them the way.

Time to go outside. I'll be back when the streetlights come on.

Denise's Story

I have a love/hate relationship with nature. As a kid I wasn't into venturing outside despite the fact I grew up in a pine forest.

I was way more interested in sticking my nose in a book as often as possible. Before I even entered grade school and had recess outside twice a day (in both hot and freezing weather), I usually only went outside when my mom and/or dad was there or if I was at friend's house and there was some activity outdoors. Sometimes at home I'd play on my swing set, or I'd take a pine tree branch and use the needles to sweep away the dirt and fallen needles to construct hallways and rooms between trees. The trees were like the pillars that supported the imaginary roof. My burgeoning writer's imagination, I guess.

Doctors would see my extremely pale skin and think I was anemic. My mom explained it was because I didn't like to play outside much. They'd give me a blood test and discover I wasn't anemic. I never got many sunburns of any kind, especially not severe ones, and this was before the days of high SPF sunscreens.

When I was in my teens my parents and I would spend some time at a friend's cabin in the mountains where Dad and I would fish. I enjoyed it. I participated in a lot of sports (not very well, mind you) via physical education classes, and I loved to play tennis.

In my twenties and into my early forties I spent the most time outdoors when doing archaeology. I think it was the archaeology that made me feel even better while venturing outside. If you are doing something that truly inspires you while being in nature, you have the best of both worlds.

These days I'm still not much for extensive exploration of the great outdoors (that might have something to do with living in a high-altitude semi-arid environment that is hostile during the summer), but I do agree that connectedness with and experience of nature is a great thing.

In the last 20 years, one of my most profound experiences in nature occurred when I went to Crescent Moon Picnic Site in Sedona, Arizona. I sat on a bench near a large tree and listened to the creek running gently right in front of me. At that moment I felt transported, with a feeling of true connection to the Earth and amazing peace. I plan to go back again. Sometimes, when I close my eyes to rest, I imagine myself back there at the creek and sitting on the bench, and I find my pulse slowing down and get a sense of blissful peace. I highly recommend visiting Crescent Moon Picnic Site if you're in the area.

MAGICAL TIPS

Small Steps

Benefiting from nature's magic doesn't have to cost a lot or require a lot of time. Here are some simple ways to get outside in smaller doses while still increasing levels of well–being.

- Plant a garden. Small, big, flowers, veggies, what–ever you fancy. Get down into the soil and get your hands dirty. Plant seeds or seedlings, bulbs or grown plants, and focus on being mindful as you dig the holes, place the seeds or plants, then water them. Join a local gardening club and make new green–thumb friends.

- Visit a local park or take a nature hike alone, with a neighborhood group, or with your kids.

Bring the outdoors in with beautiful house plants, an easy way to bring some tranquility to your home. House plants also serve to improve air quality in the home.

- Shop at outdoor farmers' markets and street fairs. Get some sun while you peruse the goodies.

- Buy some plants to place around the house or at your office to green it up a little.

- Walk your dog(s) and enjoy your surroundings instead of just rushing to get back home to the computer. Leave your cell phone at home or put it in a pouch with your keys and doggie-doo bags.

- Install nature-based screensavers on your desktop, laptop, and cell phone to remind you to get outdoors more often.

- Meditate outdoors.

- Make an effort to visit the beach or woods or nearby lake once a month. Bring a picnic lunch.

- Join a stargazing or amateur astronomy club and get to know the night sky.

- Go to garage sales and look for treasures while enjoying the treasures of fresh air and sunshine.

Develop an "Outside Mindset"

In the April 13, 2023, *Sixty and Me* blog "Do You Know What an Outside Mindset Is?" Verla Fortier wrote about her diagnosis of a rare autoimmune disease as she was retiring from her career as a nursing professor. She was told to take her meds and avoid the sun, but she noticed that when she spent time in the woods, her spark for life returned and the thoughts of her disease drifted away. She stopped fighting her diagnosis and accepted what was, and she felt good again–even, as she describes it, "transformed."

Her simple choice to go outside every day made all the difference in her mindset and her well-being. She described it as "like someone giving you a helping hand out of that quicksand" of rumination and negative thinking.

Develop your own outside mindset. Get outdoors once a day, or as often as you can, and let the worries in your mind melt away in the warm sun or while walking under a canopy of green tree-tops. When you get stressed at home or at work, instead of reaching for an unhealthy snack or a glass of wine or beer, go outside and stand just for five minutes and remind yourself that there is so much life to be experienced, and magic, beyond the confines of four walls.

Hit the Road, Jack (or Jill)

The benefits of walking are manifold. You can hit the high road or take a leisurely stroll, power walk or lazy walk, do a walking meditation or walk to the corner store with a purpose in mind (milk and a loaf of bread). Walking does the mind, body, and spirit good via improved mood, better sleep, a bit of weight loss, toning the leg muscles, increased energy and stamina, stress relief, and better heart health. That's right, walking helps increase blood flow and blood circulation to the brain and the body's organs and cells.

Buy a pair of comfy walking shoes first. Create a walking routine and start out easy, gradually extending the time and dis-

You don't have to jog or run to get the benefits of movement outside. Studies show that briskly walking for a couple of miles each day has the same benefits as running for your cardiovascular system.

tance and building up duration and endurance if physical fitness is your desire and you want to tackle those 10,000 steps or train for a 5K or marathon. Or you can take daily strolls around the neighborhood to say hi to neighbors (and check out their yard landscaping), take in the fresh air and sunshine, and calm your nerves to boot. Walk alone or with a partner or walking group for the extra benefit of social interaction. If you know a lot of people in the area with dogs, start a dog-walking routine you and your Fidos and Rovers can all enjoy and benefit from.

Yes, you could go to the gym and get on the treadmill, but why walk in place for an hour staring at your phone when you can be outside on your very own "awe walk," taking in the sights and sounds of nature?

There are things you can do to connect to nature even if you aren't in it physically. If you want a taste of nature, especially the sounds, you can use any kind of nature sound generator and listen to it no matter where you are. There are various applications for phones, tablets, and computers you can purchase (and there are some free ones) that play a variety of nature sounds with or without music. Some feature categories such as rainstorms (including thunderstorms), waterfalls, various lake sounds (which usually include bird sounds, wind, etc.), wind, ocean waves, you name it. When you get the application, you might have to listen to several different types of sounds to discover the ones you like best and that give you those feel-good vibes. You might find that listening to a nature sound while you are working is actually calming and that even lowers your blood pressure and helps you concentrate on your work. These nature sounds can also be an excellent way to help you fall asleep. Give it a try. You might be surprised by how much you like it.

The Magic of Universal Laws

Change is the only universal law.

Ahmed Mostafa

You'll believe it when you see it.

Dr. Wayne W. Dyer

The happiness that we desire and the suffering that we shun come about as a result of causes and conditions. Understanding this causal mechanism of suffering and happiness is what the Four Noble Truths are all about.

His Holiness the 14th Dalai Lama

Do you think there is such a thing as Universal Law? Most of us believe in right action, in following the law and doing no harm to others. Religions may tell us that there is one right way or the highway to do things, and then we decide if we will follow whatever book of rules is presented to us as the "answer." But what if we thought outside the box? Looked wide and kept our minds open to all the definitions of Universal Law? We might find a treasure trove of possibilities we never thought of before. Our lives might be enriched immeasurably by broadening our horizons rather than restricting them.

You would think there would be a universal definition of Universal Law, right? Well, yes ... and no. According to the peer-reviewed *Internet Encyclopedia of Philosophy*, Immanuel Kant's categorical imperative (formulation of Universal Law) says that if you do an action, everyone else should be able to do the same. In other words, if it is morally right, then everyone should do the same universally. Kant further said we could make a distinction between things we can experience in the observable world in nature and things we cannot, which we might define as the soul and God. His philosophy also expounds on free will and says that we cannot know the entirety of the soul and God but that we can hope they exist. Kant had whole books full of this philosophy and the smaller parts of this much larger whole.

Certainly there are other characterizations of Universal Law that slant a little differently, such as British author Stuart Wilde's statement, "The Universal Law is impartial. It will give you anything you believe. It will throw you garbage or roses depending on the energy you put into it. You are the one in charge, and you must accept that and stand alone. If you think God is coming down to fix things for you, forget it. God is out playing golf." In a similar vein he also said, "Balance and good fortune can only come to a person who is balanced and feels fortunate."

There is a tale (in various forms) that perhaps illustrates Wilde's statement. A man is floating in a body of water after having survived some catastrophe that put him there in the first place. He fears he will drown. He prays to his god for help, asking that he be saved from drowning. A lifeboat drifts by, but the man ignores it. His god will help him survive. He doesn't need the lifeboat. The man, unfortunately, still drowns. When the man reaches the afterlife, his god is there. The man is angry and asks, "God why didn't you save me? I prayed." God says, "I sent you the lifeboat. Didn't you see it?"

The 18th-century German philosopher Immanuel Kant advocated for transcendental idealism, which reflects modern ideas that space and time are not real but merely appear to us as real to provide structure to our experiences.

The old adage that God helps those who help themselves also could be illustrated by this tale. We could venture the opinion that praying to be saved or for an answer only works if you take what is being offered right in front of you. In the case of Wilde, he mentions that Universal Law will do as you will it. So does Kant.

Perhaps the immediate moral of the story is that Universal Law is not universal; it is in the eyes and mind of the beholder, and only we as individuals can decide what our Universal Law is. Too much world-building, walls, assumptions, and rules can stifle the beauty of what makes us who we are and what makes us thrive. Conformity, in some cases, can be the enemy not only of personal authenticity but for living as a happy, healthy human being.

For example, one person may love romantic comedy movies while another abhors them and loves science fiction instead. For the person who dislikes romantic comedy, the universal truth could be that romantic comedies are unworthy and awful. Or the person who dislikes romantic comedy can open their eyes and realize that for someone else romantic comedies are the best things in the universe. The fact that one person loves one type of movie, but another person doesn't does not make either person's wants or desires incorrect or bad. Another example is the argument people have over what music is or is not, who is a good singer and who is not, what book is a good book and what is not. At the end of the day, it is all personal choice.

It also does not hurt for us to deepen our knowledge of the way many other people look at Universal Law. When we find something that resonates within us, we can decide whether to follow that "law" for ourselves. There is wisdom in remembering that as we grow in our lives and time goes by, we might benefit from staying flexible to the idea of learning new things and growing in our wisdom.

With all the philosophies and belief systems out there, where can we possibly start?

Over the last few centuries, a host of different techniques, philosophies, and belief systems have arisen about Universal Law and the varying degrees and offshoots of what Universal Law might mean.

> *Reality is a projection of your thoughts*
> *or the things you habitually think about.*
> **Stephen Richards**
> How to Live a Mindful, Meaningful, Magical Life

LAW OF ATTRACTION

Depending on which sources you read, one of the first mentions of Law of Attraction goes back to William Walker Atkinson (1862–1932), who wrote the book *Thought Vibration or The Law of Attraction*. This idea was also mentioned in the 19th century by Russian philosopher Helena Blavatsky.

Attorney and publisher William Walker Atkinson was one of the pioneers of the New Thought movement, which drew upon the wisdom of ancient Eastern and Western civilizations to build on beliefs about the human mind and consciousness.

Rhonda Byrne's book *The Secret*, first published in 2006, was a runaway bestseller. The main concept behind this book was the idea that like attracts like. Positive energy attracts equal positivity. Negative energy will attract equal negative energy. Positive attracts positive. It is based on the idea of positive affirmations and thinking of positive things in order to bring about those results. Other key beliefs in this system include:

1. Removing negative things from your life can make room for more positivity to move into your life.

2. The present is always perfection. There are things you can do to improve your immediate situation. When we focus on generating ways to feel good in the present moment rather than fixating on unhappiness, we make room in our lives for the positive to take root in that moment.

ABRAHAM–HICKS AND THE LAW OF ATTRACTION

Over the many years since *The Secret* first came out, people have criticized the idea that we can make anything we want to materialize in our lives. Yet this book was not the only source to present the idea of the Law of Attraction. In 1985 Esther Hicks, an American author and inspirational speaker, began to channel a group of entities called Abraham that are said to be from a non-physical dimension. Abraham is described as consisting of the heart of all religions. The essence of this belief system (the Abraham–Hicks teachings) is presented in the following ideas:

1. People exist in a physical form on Earth because they choose it.

2. As people, we are creators, and we create reality with our thoughts. This imagination creates a vibration that naturally finds an equal vibration, which will cause whatever that vibration is (positive or negative) to come into being.

3. Life is meant for ease and not struggle. Focusing on things like joy will bring manifestations such as money, good health, etc.

4. Souls are everlasting. Death only comes to the physical body.

The writings of Abraham as channeled by Esther Hicks are extensive and have produced several books, audiotapes, and videos.

One of the main focus points of the teachings of Abraham is to put your attention on what you want, not what is. If you focus on what is, you get more of what is, which is basically the culmination of all the thoughts you had before. This doesn't just apply to you as an individual pursuing your wants and dreams, but as a member of humanity at large. One of the teachings of Abraham tells us that if we want to see change in the world, we must put our attention on the change as if it is already manifested, because if we give our energy and focus to the problem, we continue to feed into the problem.

Esther Hicks (shown here in 2007 with her late husband and cowriter, Jerry) is a speaker and author who educates people on topics like the Law of Attraction, which says that positive thoughts attract positive results, negative ones attract negative results.

So much of these teachings are common sense. Fighting against something is never as effective as dreaming of a new world and staying laser-focused on what that would look and feel like for all concerned. The energy, and the vibrations, are just different.

We will never find magic in life if our attention is on all the things that are not magical.

LAW OF ASSUMPTION

In essence, Neville Goddard taught that we are all part of God, that our imaginations are God, and that God's consciousness is awakened in us through the power of Jesus Christ.

Another less-well-known idea is the Law of Assumption, first written about more widely by Neville Lancelot Goddard (1905–1972), a New Thought author and mystic. He believed the human being is his or her ultimate creator, rather than an external power or God. He said that if we act and feel as if our goals and aspirations have been met, they will manifest. If we assume something to be true, it will be true. For example, in his book *The Wealth Mindset* he says, "So you and I can be anything in this world we desire to be, if we'll clearly define our aim in life and constantly occupy that aim." He also said, "There's no power outside the mind of man to do anything to man, and he by the arrangement of his own mind–by consenting to these restrictions in his cradle and being conditioned slowly through his youth, walking into manhood believing himself set upon–would have to be set upon."

Old layers of karma can stick to you
only if you keep adding new layers of karma glue.

Sadhguru

KARMA AND LAW OF RECIPROCITY

In the case of karma, we can look at it from a religious stand-point or from an everyday layman's point of view. Karma is found in many forms of religion such as Buddhism and Hinduism. In Desmond Biddulph's *1001 Pearls of Buddhist Wisdom* there is a quote that sums it up well: "All that we are is a result of what we have thought." Again, when we look at other topics we have discussed such as the Law of Attraction, we see many intertwined and sim-ilar aspects to these laws.

Karma states that for every action there is an unavoidable reaction and result. With that law in mind, millions of people ac-ross the world do good to receive good. If life follows karma, why would you ever wish to do something bad to another human? The rub is ... you have to believe karma is a real thing, and per-haps need to see it in action to believe it exists.

The Law of Reciprocity is a part of karma in a way, though it is founded more on social psychology than religion. The Law of Reciprocity is simple. If you do something nice for me, I will do something nice for you. Treat me well, and I will treat you well. This reciprocity can extend to simply following the general rules of polite society: Please. Thank you. Opening doors for others. Treating others with respect no matter what.

By treating others well, you are automatically increasing the chances of them reciprocating in kind. Taking this in mind, it is easy to see how this law fits nicely with the Law of Attraction and the Law of Assumption. We have to remember, though, that within that Law of Reciprocity there is always the chance that what we say or do will not be returned in kind. With this knowl-edge, and if we make a point to have our genuine goal in mind, we can increase the chances that if we do unto others as we would like them to do unto us, we can expand the likelihood they will respond in kind to us and to others. We are spreading good will and kindness.

If there is no guarantee that acting within this law will result in others doing the same, what is the reason to do it? There is more than one way to look at it. We can feel the personal satis-faction of doing the "right" thing, regardless of whether it was reciprocated. We are living by values we sincerely hold as important to us. Some things we should consider if practicing this law: Are we doing it from a genuine desire to give and receive good results for all concerned? Are we trying to create a win–win situation? Is the idea to benefit others as much as it is to benefit us?

 We can feel the personal satisfaction of doing the "right" thing, regardless of whether it was reciprocated.

Within all of this is something else to consider when practicing the Law of Reciprocity. Even if you want to practice it, your upbringing and prior experiences can slant how you approach it. In an earlier chapter we mentioned CPTSD (Complex Post-Traumatic Stress Disorder). Within CPTSD there are coping mechanisms people with CPTSD have learned as "survival" techniques. They learned these coping skills as children and may be completely oblivious that they are falling back on one of these techniques. These reactions are flight, fight, freeze, and fawn. In the case of reciprocity, one of the more common features is fawning.

People choose to fawn because fawning was a technique that they learned in childhood that they believed would help them survive. As adults these people are often highly skilled at the Law of Reciprocity, but not always for a healthy reason. This comes in the form of people-pleasing to the extreme, lack of boundaries, and other actions that do not serve the person doing the fawning. When people-pleasers were children, they became highly skilled at disguising true feelings to prevent punishment and anger from others. A desire to be approved of is paramount. At the end of the day, a person who fawns may not know this is why they are doing it, and therefore their Law of Reciprocity is based more on the avoidance of bad outcomes than on achieving a mutually agreeable situation. Fawning, like many of our most primitive survival techniques, can be difficult to break unless someone realizes they are doing it and why.

If someone feels they may fall into this fawner category, it is worth the time to be evaluated by a mental health professional specializing in working with CPTSD. One thing to note: CPTSD is a learned survival state created most often in childhood, when we were vulnerable to the adults in our world and sometimes to other children and situations. Whatever you do, please do not shame yourself. In the life of someone suffering from CPTSD, self–shame happens frequently, if not every day. This is why it is important to find a mental health professional if you feel this is a part of your everyday experience in the world. Take heart, though. As the saying goes, you've got this.

ABUNDANCE, LACK, AND STAYING CENTERED IN THE PRESENT

Humans, in general, are experts at noticing what is wrong with anything and everything. We are far more centered on pointing out lack than we are abundance. What is wrong with the world is plastered all over the news every day. Given our obsession with noting tragedy, murder, political upheaval, war, and natural disasters, and our easy access to more information about

Tensions sometimes arise between the generations—Boomers, Gen X, Millennials, Gen Z—who seem to believe their peers are better than the older or younger generations.

How to Live a Mindful, Meaningful, Magical Life

more bad things happening in more places, we can be fooled into thinking everything is going to hell in a handbasket every second of every moment.

Watch any YouTube video featuring music from another decade or old films of another time. Reams of people will lament that those were the good ol' days and that music was so much better than it is now, and that people respected others, dressed right, acted right … and the list of why we should return to those ideals or situations runs on ad nauseam. "Kids these days!" "Boomers do this!" "Generation X does this wrong!" Who hasn't heard someone say things like this or been guilty of such sentiments themselves?

Particularly notable are commenters who say they wished they lived in another century. While people are entitled to their opinions and beliefs, many of those people who perceive another time as better than this one may not consider that in every time period in history there were unique challenges. There were wars, famines, disease, and many dire situations in any decade and any century. People who exalt the virtues of the recent past sometimes forget difficult situations in their own lives at the time and may not consider the problems others may have experienced in that same time period. The good ol' days are snapshots in most people's minds and memories of times they have *enjoyed* in their own situations.

Does this mean we cannot look back on certain time periods in our own lives or other centuries and appreciate the good things that did happen? Of course not. If we cannot use a way-back machine to physically return to the good ol' days, a healthier way to approach life could be to center on the present and notice the abundance that is around us now.

Abundance is a more recent concept that can be used to replace or be in tandem with the practice of gratitude. With gratitude we are told to look for the things in our life that we should feel grateful for. Abundance reframes this a little, and for some it makes the process more amenable. For example, telling someone they "should be grateful" for something can come across, even unconsciously, as criticism or shaming. This is not to say that being grateful for something is wrong.

Abundance allows you to recognize what is already profoundly good or even great in your life right now. Today. Maybe even this hour or this second. It does not have to be big things. We will suggest an exercise below that can help you recognize the abundance in your life and therefore increase the chances this abundance will expand and increase with time.

MONEY AND PROSPERITY

Think about money and prosperity. Who doesn't think about money and prosperity? Is the idea of living an abundant, prosperous life something that you think you deserve, or do you cringe at the thought of being rich and living a luxurious life when others around you live in lack? The idea of lack suggests there is not enough abundance to go around, yet if you go outside and look at one neighbor's lawn and try to count the blades of grass, you can easily see that is not the case.

Prosperity is not a bad thing, and it is not always about your bank account. It is about seeing the amazing bounty of blessings all around you and focusing on that, as well as knowing in your heart you are worthy of sharing in that bounty. There is no reason to ever believe you are less than the person who has a gorgeous

Even if they lose big time, financially successful people have a way of building back wealth because of their positive energy, optimism, and ability to tap back into the universal source of abundance.

How to Live a Mindful, Meaningful, Magical Life

house and money in the bank. There is enough to go around for everyone because the Universe is creative and generative, and because not everyone wants the same things.

But let's talk about money. It's a huge hot-button issue for so many people and thwarts a lot of magical living by keeping you feeling as though you are not one of the lucky ones. When you have enough, you feel great, and it tends to attract even more wealth. Notice that? When you are living in lack and feeling the pinch, it seems what you have is taken away from you. To those who have, more shall be given....

This is not to say that people who have a lot are more deserving. Rather, their positive energy attracts more of what they have. And if they lose it all, they know they have the ability to tap back into that universal source of abundance and prosperity to come up with new ideas, inventions, processes, or ways to help others that bring in money in return.

Ken Honda teaches about "happy money" in his seminal book *Happy Money: The Japanese Art of Making Peace with Your Money.* As Japan's most influential money master and personal development

guru, with 58 books and several courses on the art of healing money wounds and attracting happy money, Honda knows that money cannot buy happiness, but it can open your world up to so much more than you thought possible. His focus is on healing the relationship we have with money so it benefits us, rather than harm us or keep us in lack.

He also suggests being thankful for any money that comes your way, something he calls "arigato money." Arigato means "thank you" in Japanese. Saying thank you to money as it enters your life is a simple process that elevates your spirit and turns you into more of a positive money magnet.

Entrepreneur and bestselling author Ken Honda writes books that advise on a combination of building wealth and personal growth.

Honda suggests not only identifying beliefs you have about money without judging them, but listening to what money has to say to you. Is it angry, demanding, whining, sad, fearful? Or is it joyful, happy, and excited about life? You can, as Honda states, become a "happy magnet" by being appreciative of the money you have as well as the good in your life, and magnetize and multiply arigato energy to bring you more.

There will always be rich people and poor people and those in between, but you have so much more power to manifest prosperity than you think you do. The key is to stop seeking and striving for money and abundance in the external "hows" and focus instead on how good you are feeling inside. Let the Universe take care of the hows, as it knows better what is possible than you do from your limited human viewpoint. Your job is to believe, to do the legwork, and to keep the faith and always, always, be thankful.

Let the Universe take care of the hows, as it knows better what is possible than you do from your limited human viewpoint.

You hold the magnet that attracts anything, good or bad, into your life and it is all about your energy and vibration. You, friend, are a powerful creator when you align with the energy of the abundance all around you. So, vibrate at the level of "arigato money" and "happy energy" and you'll see an incredible shift occur. Where you once only saw "lack of," you will now see "more of."

EXECUTION OF THE DETAILS

We can look at both Law of Attraction and Law of Assumption and find examples in everyday life that could be pointed to as evidence that either could work for some people. Most of us know individuals who are constantly crabby, angry, disagreeable, and miserable, and bad fortune seems to follow them everywhere. Hence the old saying "If I didn't have bad luck, I wouldn't have any luck at all."

Is the person experiencing all of these things because they are truly cursed and unfortunate? Did they start off life with things stacked against them? Did an entire host of things such as poverty, accidents, natural disasters, divorces, deaths, and car crashes give them reason to believe that they cannot be anything but miserable? Given that, is it inevitable that a person brought up with any or many of these disadvantages or advantages is fated to succeed or fail?

No, it is not inevitable. There are many factors to take into consideration.

Does genetics have a factor in how we react to our circumstances and what we believe in those same circumstances? A psychologist or medical doctor might say that yes, if you are born with disadvantages such as poverty, genetic abnormalities, poor family dynamics, mental and physical abuse, additional physical ailments, and/or chronic physical disease, the deck is stacked against you from the get-go. All of those are disadvantages, especially if a child grows up with numerous problems on their plate.

Sociologists might say that birth order could determine how different members react in the same family and that parenting is not uniformly applied to each child. They may suggest that the neighborhood a person grows up in may affect their ability to get ahead in life.

Outside the family unit an individual will encounter a variety of people and circumstances that will guarantee some impact

on how they look at their life. If we are not exposed when we are children to different people, places, and things, we may be more likely to find differences intolerable. Because of this we might believe that life is stacked against us, and we have no control over how things turn out for us. It may be easier for us to blame other people, places, and things for our personal circumstances.

Yes, growing up poor and disadvantaged definitely poses some obstacles in obtaining a dream or even getting ahead at all, but that doesn't mean it is impossible.

If we look at the Law of Attraction and the Law of Assumption, we can see that the training we may have received from our society (including our family) would lead us to believe that our lot in life is just what it is and cannot be changed. Yet we have all seen people with numerous disadvantages go on to achieve great things. Why? The possibilities are endless, but we can say that there is one thing most of these people have in common.

> *If we look at the Law of Attraction and the Law of Assumption, we can see that the training we may have received from our society (including our family) would lead us to believe that our lot in life is just what it is and cannot be changed.*

At some point they had to believe that only they could do something about their situation. Some might say then, "What if said person were given something such as a handout or gift?" Doesn't that give them an advantage over someone who is not given a gift? Yes ... but there is a twist to this. The person receiving the gift still had to decide what to do with that gift. In the same way, a person with all of the advantages given to them from birth can squander those advantages until there is nothing left. A person with few advantages can decide to take some steps that make it more likely they will succeed. Given those possibilities, it seems likely that both the Law of Attraction and the Law of Assumption could be true. This is not to say that gifts or handouts should never be given in kindness and love. What it does say is that at the end of the day an individual can decide what reaction they will have to whatever their circumstances might be.

If we think about it ... that is a tremendous gift in itself. That we are endowed with the incredible power of free will.

VIKTOR FRANKL AND FREE WILL IN ACTION

We can study many philosophies and religions and look for guidance, comfort, and peace. Yet few things bring home the incredible power of free will and the search for meaning into sharp focus like the story of Viktor Frankl (1905–1997). Frankl was a Jew–

A survivor of the Holocaust, Austrian psychiatrist Viktor Frankl founded logotherapy, which posits that people are primarily motivated by the desire to find meaning in their lives.

ish Austrian psychiatrist born in 1905 Vienna. While he wrote 39 books in his lifetime, the book he is most famous for penning is *Man's Search for Meaning* (1946). In this international bestseller he recounts many of his experiences and his resulting reactions to those experiences as a prisoner in Nazi concentration camps during World War II. He noted why some people died and some people lived, even when placed in generally the same circumstances and under the same duress. He believed that people are motivated by a need to create meaning in their lives. He said that life can have meaning in even the most horrible of situations depending on what that person decides they will believe about said situation. Can we take that belief and decide what to do next, which increases our chances of success and survival? Does that choice give our life meaning in that moment? Does it give us a reason to continue the journey, whatever that journey might be? Is there a sacrifice we decide to make or not make that can increase our chance of survival or a better life?

We have all heard stories about people who lived through disasters, and many of those people survived because of a right time and right place situation and perhaps survival skills overall. Yet many of them increased their chances of living based on the things they chose to do or not do in order to live long enough for rescue ... or to rescue themselves.

AUTHOR INSIGHTS

Denise's Story

If there is anything I've learned at all in my many years of studying religions and philosophies, it's that believing in something with my whole heart does not make it universally the law for anyone else. It is this realization I have come back to again and again when I am frustrated either with how things are happening my own life or with other people. This doesn't mean I don't slip back into this frustration from time to time. I am a work in progress, a spiritual being learning this stuff like anyone else.

I didn't think, until the last 15 or so years, that I was good at surviving. In fact, I used to believe (as my British friends would say), that I was "utter rubbish" at life in general even when others would say, "Oh you've done these amazing things." Most of us are like that, stumbling our way through how to do things to "succeed" and to be what we want to be on our own terms and in our own time. We don't believe we are as capable as we are. And I, like everyone else, had to claw my way toward understanding any of this stuff.

Where did I learn to see the world through a more flexible lens? It didn't happen all at once.

I was fortunate enough to have parents who were liberal in what they allowed me to watch on TV, see at the movies, and choose for my reading. Perhaps they understood that I could handle the "incoming information." They didn't believe that just because I saw something on television, in a movie, or in a book that it would damage me. I believe this gave me the ability to sympathize and empathize with other human beings and perhaps understand them at a young age. It became a powerful tool in my "survival kit." Where did my parents get this attitude? Well, probably from their parents, or who knows where else. It isn't something they ever explained to me or talked about at all. I think, though, that enduring tough stuff was baked into their DNA and forged by the will to survive.

For my parents, life was at times tough growing up on the western slope of Colorado in a little community during the early part of the 20th century and through the Great Depression. My father was born in 1918 right before the Spanish flu emerged in the world, and my mother in 1921 when the disease had slowed but not vanished. When the COVID-19 pandemic showed up, I reminded myself that if my grandparents and parents and all my other relatives living at the time could survive the Spanish flu, maybe I could survive another pandemic.

How to Live a Mindful, Meaningful, Magical Life

My parents were not brought up with a religious background. Growing up in a family like this meant I could freely explore many belief systems. My mother would always say that people can believe what they want to believe, but she didn't want others imposing their belief systems on her. My father was probably an atheist. I say probably because I never asked him, and he never said. Yet he had core values that he followed to the letter, some of which I agreed with and inherited and some which I didn't agree with and didn't emulate. The very same could be said of my mother.

When the COVID-19 pandemic showed up, I reminded myself that if my grandparents and parents and all my other relatives living at the time could survive the Spanish flu, maybe I could survive another pandemic.

If there was a disadvantage to having no guiding religious foundation, it was that the majority of other children I knew didn't understand this concept at all. Some of this resulted in me being bullied because I was "different." From the time I was in grade school, I learned the concept of religious bigotry and how much damage it can impose on other people. As a result, I am sensitive to defending others against bigotry of any kind.

Studying other religions and philosophies, no matter what they are, also gives me the opportunity to meet people where they are. Their culture. Their psychology. I believe when people are exposed to a variety of philosophies and religions, the chances of them following a Universal Law that respects all people is more likely. With open-mindedness and education comes an opportunity for empathy, kindness, and understanding. It is a Golden Rule made easier by tolerance and the desire for humanity to be brought together by love and the ability to express freedom to be who we are as individuals without imposing on anyone else our personal values.

Are there things we can consider right now that increase our chances of a happy and fulfilling life? Yes. We certainly do not have to be thrown into dire circumstances to learn and use these tools.

Marie's Story

As a longtime student of Universal Laws, especially the Law of Attraction, I still marvel at how quickly I can go back to my default setting of ignoring them all. This despite seeing evidence that they work. Humans are silly creatures.

My favorite law is "what you focus on expands." When I look back at my life, I can readily and clearly see where my focus was by the life I led, and how it brought me to the present. I love the idea that we know what we believe and focus on when we look around at our lives in the present. That can be shocking, because nobody wants to take responsibility for their mess, myself included.

That simple law is like a motto for me because I do have evidence of experiences when I focused on something I wanted so hard, and yet in such a relaxed and joyful way, it couldn't help but manifest. Whether it was buying my first house or selling my first house, finishing my first book or my thirtieth book, or meeting my friends and giving birth to my incredible son, I have the hard evidence, the data, if you will, that shows it works. But as they say in A.A., it works if you work it.

> *I still fall prey to times when I doubt and fear and grow impatient if I am not seeing the results I want right away.*

Knowing this, I still fall prey to times when I doubt and fear and grow impatient if I am not seeing the results I want right away. I go back to default Marie, who complains and bitches and puts up a fuss because I want what I want and I want it now, and then I wonder why the things I want in life aren't manifesting. Where is my focus in this? Surely, not on the joys of having what I want, but on the angst and anxiety and disappointment of not seeing it on my timeline.

If you look at your own life, you will see these laws at work. Maybe the reason you don't want to look closely—and yes, I can relate—is because it all points to one thing: your focus. And you may not like the idea that everything you didn't want or didn't ever have could possibly be your responsibility or your fault, at least in part. Obviously, if you want to be an elephant, it ain't gonna happen, unless you buy an elephant costume. Universal laws have limits, too.

When we tumble down into our doubts and fears, we lose alignment with these laws. I remember feeling so elated when I was clear and focused, as if what I wanted was so sure to come to me. Then the fear would creep in and it would feel as though someone stuck a pin in my balloon. I learned that my faith had to be as strong as my focus and that was not going to happen overnight. These laws are not about getting it on an intellectual level. Until I got it on all levels, nothing ever seemed to go right.

I still struggle. I'm not perfect, but generally, when it comes to dreams and goals, passions and purposes, love and joy and the magic stuff of life, I know that where my attention goes, something grows, and I prefer flowers to weeds. I have the power and the choice of where to put my attention and to commit to keeping it focused there until I see it in my physical world.

What I focused on in the past expanded into my present. What I focus on now will become my future. As simple as this all seems, it's one of the hardest laws to master, but it's how we let the magic in.

MAGICAL TIPS

Sticks and Stones Exercise

As spiritual beings we're striving for ways to feel good, even-tempered, fulfilled, and peaceful. You know that moment when you hear or see certain words and something inside you turns on automatically? You react perhaps with anger. Fear. Discontent. Disgust. Frustration.

Words. They're messy. They can lift you up or pull you down. People say certain things and BOOM, we're off to the races being triggered. I'm not terribly fond of the word "triggered." If you think of it, though, it covers how we can feel if words are used against us or if we *perceive* they are being used against us or others. In fact, we can become habituated to the need for outrage. Eventually these emotions take up too much space in our everyday life. As spiritual beings we thrive when we feel good. If we are constantly irate it is more difficult to find headway in our spiritual life. Is there anything you can do to stop that trigger from taking you along for a ride every single time? Yes!

Don't allow yourself to give in to the anger of the moment as this can lead to things you will regret.

The next time you're ready to become angry, consider the following:

1. It's super easy to jump to conclusions about what someone meant. What do you know about that person? Do you consider them to be a reasonable and generally good-hearted person? There's a big possibility what they said wasn't intended to be harmful. Pause and think before you leap.

2. Take a deep breath and be mindful about what you're thinking. Write down your feelings around the subject that has you riled. Why does this person's choice of words set you off? What can you learn about yourself and your reaction?

3. Can you change whatever is making you angry? If so, then proceed. If not, pause and take a breath. On social media this is especially important. We may disagree with what someone says, and we're tempted to make a comment. Most of the time it serves no purpose to vent on that person's page, and the resulting verbal altercation is unlikely to solve anything or make you feel better or vindicated.

4. Ask yourself if you're trying to care about everything. Access to information in this 24-hour news cycle and the internet means there are more opportunities to feel sad, bad, or mad. You only have so much room in your life and heart to care about absolutely everything that crosses your path. Guard that space fiercely. This doesn't mean don't care

about anything. Just be a bit more selective and watch some of your stress disappear.

Next time words set you off, take a huge breath and wait. Slow down the sensation that says you must react right now with anger. I guarantee you'll feel better.

Intentions and Abundance Exercises

In these exercises you will want to grab something to write on, or if you have already started using a journal, consider adding the intentions and abundance exercises to your journaling on a daily basis.

First, let us start with intentions:

1. Each morning open your journal and decide how you would like to feel. Select anywhere from two to six intentions you have in mind (many more intentions than that can be a little too much). What would you like to feel and manifest in the day? The wording here is a bit important. Most of us write down intentions by saying something like "I intend to be energetic." Instead try saying, "I intend to feel energetic." A state of "being" is helpful, but what if we can more deeply anchor our intentions by using "feel" instead? Examples: "I intend to feel intelligent." "I intend to feel generous." "I intend to feel competent." No wish is outrageous. Suppose you have something challenging happening in your work environment that day and you have felt particularly vulnerable and maybe not that confident. Your intentions might be "I intend to feel confident," "I intend to feel safe," "I intend to feel at ease." Writing these intentions down in the morning before you plunge into your day is a good way to help manifest how you would like to feel. Does this guarantee that you will feel all of these things and that every intention for that day will come true? No. But it greatly increases the likelihood over having no intentions at all.

Second, end the day with noting your abundance with the following exercise:

2.   Many times when we think of abundance we envision wealth, a new car, something material. While this is definitely abundance, we tend to ignore simple abundance staring us in the face every day. Noting abundance is hugely important if we are fighting complications in our lives, not feeling at ease, valued, understood, or confident. Snag your journal at the end of the day. Begin thinking about any good things that happened, no matter how simple or insignificant they may seem. Again, wording here is important. Start by saying, "Abundance was with me today." Note what abundance occurred. Example: "Abundance was with me today. I received a compliment from my friend Sherry. She said my hair looked great." Or, "Today I got that new (insert whatever it is) in the mail and I'm really excited!" "I bought that new book I've been dying to read." "The clerk at the grocery store today was really kind and friendly." "I received an encouraging email from a friend." "People held the door open for me today." No matter how simple these things may be, noting them brings them into your reality and makes you aware of abundance in your life. This awareness can bring abundance into the forefront and prove to you there are more positives happening in your life than you realized. If you do this consistently you may find your mood improving, uplifted, and even more abundance flowing your way.

Be certain to note things that might seem ordinary or that you generally wouldn't think of as abundance such as: "I love this rose gold pen. It's my favorite pen. I love this rose gold journal I'm writing in." "These pants fit really well." "It's sunny outside and that made me

The smallest things in life can remind us of the abundance we enjoy, even simple things such as a smile or helpful hand at a grocery store.

feel good." Note even the most basic things such as "I have a roof over my head and plenty of food to eat. I am warm. I am safe." All of this is abundance that cannot be denied if it is true at that present moment. It is all worthy.

Do not be concerned about the order in which you do the abundance exercise or which things you write down first. Just write down whatever comes to mind in a free-flowing manner. After all, no one is going to see these journal entries but you unless you decide to share them.

Count the Grass

When you finish this section, grab a pad and pen, put down this book, and go outside. Find a nearby lawn or patch of grass and try to count the individual blades.

Imagine such patches of grass existing in all sizes all over the world (and they do) and you'll begin to see just how abundant life is.

Go on, we'll wait.

The Magic of Gratitude

*Acknowledging the good that you already have in your life
is the foundation for all abundance.*

Eckhart Tolle

Great acts are made up of small deeds.

Lao Tzu

Memories of our lives, our works and our deeds will continue in others.

Rosa Parks

Gratitude is something of a buzzword today in psychological and New Age circles. It is also at the heart of all Law of Attraction teachings. And yet it is not a new concept. Ancient texts such as the Bible are filled with proclamations of the power of gratitude and giving thanks. The holiday of Thanksgiving is built around giving thanks for shared gifts between two cultures. Our language is filled with references such as "Count your blessings" and "Be thankful for what you have and you'll have more to be thankful for." Gratitude today has become something of an industry of its own, with products and books, courses and seminars all focused on the art and practice of being grateful.

Even 30 years ago most people didn't think of gratitude in quite the same way as they might today. This doesn't mean that

Gratitude is not about just money and health and career. Remember to appreciate and be grateful for the people in your life who love you and are there for you.

gratitude wasn't talked about in various circles in the past. In fact, parents might tell their children to be grateful for the food on their table, toys, and a roof over their heads. When we are children, though, the concept isn't as clear-cut or concrete. Like many philosophies given to us when we are young, the idea of something can sound good, but it may not have quite the impact or meaning it does until we are older and more capable of grasping these complex ideas.

What exactly is gratitude? As quoted in Tiffany Sauber Millacci's article "What Is Gratitude and Why Is It Important?" (PositivePsychology.com, February 28, 2017), Dr. Robert Emmons, a researcher on the subject, concluded that there are three parts to gratitude:

1.   Noting those things in our life that are good.

2.   Acknowledging them.

3.   Appreciating them.

This encapsulates the main idea behind gratitude, but these concepts can be broken down even more. Gratitude is similar to appreciation, but it is essentially "a sense of happiness and thankfulness in response to a fortunate happenstance or tangible gift."

Knowing that is all well and good, but how to find gratitude in our hearts, especially if we haven't been in the habit before?

IT'S NOT JUST FLUFFY: THE SCIENCE OF GRATITUDE

Despite the fact that gratitude is something people hear about a lot, it isn't exactly fashionable to be filled with gratitude. Let's face it, we are a society that loves to complain. We are grouchy about our stress, our problems, our political views, the latest weather disaster, whatever the case might be. Complaining is all the rage. We've come to accept this peevishness so readily that we often do not realize we are doing it and enabling it in others.

It isn't, as they say, *de rigueur* to have deeper conversations about what is going right with our lives. Complaining is so insidious and embedded in our unconscious that people who don't complain much are frequently looked upon with suspicion by others. Of course, envy or jealousy between people can make this more complex. Sometimes individuals who mention good things happening in their lives (especially on social media) are likely to hear negative comments from others who want to express their own grievances and may be weary of hearing what is going right in the positive poster's life.

If we are honest with ourselves, our society looks at gratefulness as something relegated to people who talk about New Age topics or psychology.

In fact, if you get into a discussion with someone you know really well, you might still find it disconcerting if they express gratitude in even the most superficial of ways. The conversation in your head might run something like this: *Why is this person talking about stuff like this? This is really deep. In fact ... it sounds sorta namby-pamby. Why are they always bragging about the good things they are experiencing?*

Perhaps the person who weighs in and reports all the good stuff could be trying to make themselves look great. Or it could be they see no benefit in reporting the bad stuff. Maybe they are just grateful!

If we are honest with ourselves, our society looks at gratefulness as something relegated to people who talk about New Age topics or psychology. The average, everyday dude on the street may consider the subject too "woo–woo." But what if you understood that gratefulness could not only improve your outlook but possibly improve your heath more than you imagined? Wouldn't you try it?

The Arizona Heart Foundation published an article on their website on November 2, 2002, called *How Being Thankful Makes You Happier*. In the article they mention several key elements in appreciation and gratitude that have a multiple of mental and physical benefits.

1.   Improving the quality of your personal relationships. Hearing someone express gratitude can lead you to reflect on your own life and those things you may feel thankful for as well.

2.   Thankfulness can make you less likely to report aches and pains and spend more time exercising. The exercise alone can have mood–boosting effects.

3.   You may be more empathetic to other people's challenges and become more interested in helping others overcome them.

Mindful.org's article "The Science of Gratitude," first published February 17, 2022, discusses the real science behind gratitude and how and why it is good for our health. Gratitude helps us to consider all the parts of our lives–the good, the bad, and the ugly–that we may not think help to improve our ability to thrive.

The Mindful.org article noted that students who wrote out what they were grateful for a few times a week suffered less from things like headaches, stomach distress, sore muscles, and a host of other complaints. The control group who did not write out what they were grateful for continued to have many of the problems listed above. When heart failure patients were tested in an eight-week journaling study, it was learned that patients in the gratitude group showed a more parasympathetic heart rate, which is a sign of better heart health.

In the University of Minnesota online article *10 Ways to Be a More Thankful Person*, the authors highlighted ways to feel more thankful, which included things like:

Feeling and acknowledging your gratitude for all the people and things in your life that are *good* has measurable benefits to your health and can even impact your relationships in a positive way.

1. Express out loud three good things that happened to you that day. Come on. You know you can think of something. They point out that expressing gratitude even when we're alone can be a powerful thing. Do not worry about talking to yourself. It's all good.

2. Be of service and thank your boyfriend/girlfriend/partner/spouse for those things about them that you are grateful for and admire. Not only does it give them a boost, but it makes you aware of it and less likely to take their good qualities for granted.

3. If you're feeling angry, maybe now is a good time to take a mental inventory of what you are grateful for at this moment.

4. Whatever you do, do not forget to thank yourself for the progress you've made in your life. Really think about it.

5. If you are having difficulty feeling grateful, think of someone who is in a situation less fortunate than you. This doesn't mean you do not have sympathy or empathy for this person, but it brings things into perspective right here and now.

When we stop to smell the roses, as the old saying goes, we are more likely to find happiness in our lives and to bring forth a general sense of positivity.

If you see no reason for giving thanks, the fault lies in yourself.
Native American Proverb

Gratitude is riches. Complaint is poverty.
Doris Day

LOCATING GRATITUDE

As with most things in life, the concept and application of gratitude is often simplified down to a few buzzwords and pop psychology nuggets that make it sound as easy as saying (with requisite funny accent) "Snap out of it!"

If gratitude is so good for us, why aren't we all jumping on the bandwagon to do it right now? Because our brains are essentially hardwired to be alert for negativity over positivity. Think back to survival of the fittest when it might have been more about surviving a saber-toothed tiger attack or that guy with the rock you didn't see until the last minute. We talked about this in our chapter on intuition and its benefits. For our purposes here, though, think of how that has lingered in our minds in the most basic and primitive part of our brain. Instinctively we are often on the lookout for the next shoe to drop. This isn't to say we can't be oblivious and the saber-toothed tiger won't still get its meal. It does mean that if we are hardwired to look for danger, training our minds to notice the positive takes a bit more work.

As mentioned in previous chapters, humans are complex psychological beings with dozens of experiences that can't be reduced (usually) to one event defining how we react to everything. We are created by "soup of life" experiences all mixed in a bowl and finally completed into a recipe. Our genetics, our health, how we are parented, events that happen early in our lives, which country, city, state, or region we live in, the weather we experience (yeah even that), our wealth or lack thereof … all of these things can affect how we look upon the idea of gratitude. That's the rub.

Humanity's evolution geared us toward looking for danger and the negative in order to be safe, so if we struggle to see the good and positive in life, at least we have a legitimate reason why this can be so difficult. We are trying to overcome eons of programming.

Sometimes our approach toward gratitude can be colored in a way that does not serve us if it is overemphasized.

Being grateful should never be about denying or suppressing negative emotions or experiences. Rather, it is about focus. Focusing on the good things in life and finding the good in all situations, even the bad ones, because there is usually always something to be thankful for, even if it is just a harsh lesson learned. Because what we focus on expands, placing our awareness more on the good in life expands our awareness of even more good things to come, and it keeps us from putting on the blinders of cynicism, negativity, and defeat that prevent the recognition of positives in the presence of negatives.

That being said, if something tragic or awful happens, we don't need to stop what we are doing and find things to be grateful for. We need to feel the pain and emotions and allow ourselves to grieve. Later, when we feel more grounded, we can look at the situation for things to appreciate, for the blessings, including the grief itself, but never should we force ourselves to be or feel grate-

The media focuses on the awful news in the world, especially natural disasters, war, and international strife, rather than showing all the good going on, because that is what garners ratings.

ful in the midst of true tragedy. It is critical that we allow ourselves to be fully human. Too often at a funeral someone will say something like, "Oh, I know you feel bad, but you had some good years with her before she got sick," as if this takes away the pain of losing that person you loved so much. It doesn't. Those good years can be acknowledged and focused on later when you are ready and have gone through the grieving process. If it helps to find blessings at the time of a tragedy, by all means do so, but never feel as though you are some kind of failure or "not doing it right" if you cannot find a single good thing in a bad situation at the time it happens.

Someone might ask how it is possible to feel gratitude in a world full of violence and injustice, but we guarantee that the blessings are out there, and there is far more good than bad. There are stories everywhere of people rallying against violence and injustice all over the world that we don't always hear about. Sadly, the media likes to shove the bad down our throats, and we often feel miserable and hopeless because of it.

A great tip during times when bad news dominates the airwaves and we are reeling in fear and sorrow is to turn to what is right in front of us to be thankful for: our loved ones, our home, our clothing and food, fresh water, a bed to sleep in, friends, our pets. If that is too hard to fathom in the moment, just the realization that we are alive and breathing is enough to be thankful for.

ATTITUDE OF GRATITUDE

With enough practice, we can develop an attitude of gratitude where we more habitually and automatically look for things to be thankful for every day. It does take a while, because we do have powerful default mechanisms that kick in when life gets tough. New habits are possible; it might take a month or even a few months, but with consistency, a major attitude adjustment can and will occur. Life gets a lot better when we see it through grateful eyes. Marci Shimoff, author of *Happy for No Reason: 7 Steps to Being Happy from the Inside Out*, wrote that gratitude is "a way to incline your heart toward joy." You become much happier, she wrote, "by focusing your heart's energy on your blessings."

Shimoff wrote about a Benedictine monk she met when he was in his eighties. Brother David, as she called him, told her that gratefulness was experiencing "great fullness" and that we can find something to be grateful for in just about anything. "No matter how much or how little you have in life, you can still be grateful." That might equate to feeling thanks for no reason at all, too, or for just being alive. "Happiness is not what makes us grateful," he told Marci. "It is gratefulness that makes us happy." Brother David picked one "theme" a day to focus on, such as water—every time he washed up or did the dishes or watered plants, he noticed and appreciated water. This was an exercise not only in gratitude but in mindfulness and being in the present moment, which is where we truly see the things we can appreciate even in the most mundane of activities. When we can learn to be grateful for the pen we are taking notes with, the fact that we have extra toilet paper and don't need to buy more for the week, or the bills we get in the mail for services that help us live better lives, we are on the way to more joy and magic.

As Marci noted, "What we appreciate, appreciates" in much the same way that the value of certain things appreciates as time goes on. Think fine wine or antiques or an investment with a great return. Gratitude is like having "compounded interest happiness" because the more you cultivate and express it, the more it grows exponentially. We must first learn to be the gatekeepers of our own minds and thoughts and deny entry to anything that makes us feel lacking, unworthy, bitter, or undeserving of things to feel thankful for. We get to decide.

It was a monk named Brother David who explained to Marci Shimoff that gratitude leads to happiness, not the other way around.

Feeling grateful has a way of relaxing us and alleviating stress and anxiety. When we focus on and see the good in anything, the stress of the bad seems to diminish and melt away. When we feel full of life's gifts, it's harder to let worry and fear control us. There is plenty of scientific research to back this up, but who needs it when we know it works by how it makes us feel inside and out. We just plain feel better, happier, strong, more vibrant, more alive when we give thanks than we do when we feel like the world is against us and everything sucks.

Life is such a precious and fragile gift, there is so much to be grateful for just being able to breathe in air without having to think about it. What a miracle that is! Our bodies are a work of art, yet how often do we thank them for keeping us alive each day? How often do we thank the Earth for giving us food, or thank other people for the services they provide? We seem to be oblivious to so many things around us that keep us surviving and thriving, yet all are reasons to be so very thankful. We might even be oblivious to all the ways others are thankful for us and the gifts we bring to their lives and the world at large.

We live our lives so focused on what we want that we forget what we already have.

It behooves us to embrace gratitude, yet just as we might have a happiness set point that, once reached, we cannot seem to go beyond, we might also have a gratitude set point that pulls us back down into complaining, bitching, and moaning about all the things we don't have or wish we didn't have. Raising that set point is part of a consistent and ongoing gratitude practice and requires some effort, but the end result is a life of more "great fullness." We live our lives so focused on what we want that we forget what we already have. The only way to have more is to open our hearts and spirits with gratitude for what we have now.

The human brain loves pattern and order, and it takes direction from us when we focus on something. If we focus more on the good stuff that we are thankful for, our brains begin to seek more of that and to perceive more things to be grateful for, which could have been in front of us all along while we were busy focusing on something else. Being caught up in the worries of life is not a good way to feel good, is it? Being grateful for what is working in our lives pushes our brains to find even more things that are working, because that brings order and pattern out of a chaos of information the brain is being asked to perceive and process on a daily basis.

THE OPPOSITE OF GRATITUDE

You might think the opposite of gratitude is lack or having nothing, but the truth is, the opposite is taking things for granted. Think of all the things in your life right now, many right under your nose, that you take for granted and forget to be thankful for. Are you jaded and no longer noticing the good in your life, or are you just so focused on trying to find big things to be grateful for that you cannot see the smaller gifts?

Open your closet and look at all the clothes you have to wear. Open your pantry and marvel at the food you have inside. Look at your car, no matter how much you'd prefer a new one, and see how it still works and gets you where you need to go. Pinpoint the little things such as a cup of tea or a printer that works, stuff you normally overlook because it doesn't seem fancy or flashy. If you were to make a list of all the things in your life you take for granted, it would fill books.

Being grateful requires that we look at everything we have and not just the stuff that stands out, like a flashy new car or thousands of dollars in the bank account. When we start to overlook all the good that is already there, we become jaded with life, bored and disillusioned. You might want more out of life, but first you should want and appreciate what you already have. It's there. You just have to open your eyes and see it.

One thing you can be grateful for is that you're not going hungry, which is something to think about in a world where many are starving.

How to Live a Mindful, Meaningful, Magical Life

There is a direct link between our capacity for compassion and our level of gratitude. We can be grateful for the blessings we have without feeling guilt or shame because someone else has less. A compassionate person not only wants to help others but realizes how much others have helped them in return and is grateful for that. A compassionate heart has the ability to feel happy for the good things while also feeling the pain of those who don't have as much. Grateful people tend to be more caring, altruistic, and generous because they don't take all that they have for granted and they are more acutely aware of what it feels like to be without those things.

As adults, we also teach our children and other children we know to model our behaviors, so it behooves us to be more compassionate and more grateful. As with a pebble tossed into a pond, that ripple on the surface expands outward and other people feel the positivity in us. We can inspire them to learn to shift their own focus and find things in their lives to give thanks for, and to find lessons and blessings where they never imagined they would find them. It's like owning a treasure map and sharing it with others, but the treasure and the path to get there are different for everyone who reads the map.

AUTHOR INSIGHTS

Denise's Story

Stepping into my past a bit, I realize I was given as a kid the old party line of be grateful for what you have. While this wasn't a bad message, it was also overlaid by a larger concept of lack. As I mentioned in the chapter "The Magic of Universal Laws," my father was born in May 1918, a few months before the Spanish flu ravaged the world, and my mother was born in 1921, as the virus seemed to be losing its grip and had started its journey to mutating into one of our modern-day influenzas. As all of us have noted in recent years, you can't make it through a pandemic and have everything be quite the way it was before. The hardships and damage happen, and there are adjustments to make. There are a million and one factors that went into how the Spanish flu pandemic changed the lives of everyone on the planet, including my parents even though they were just babies.

My mother and father went through their teens and very early adulthood during the Great Depression of the 1930s. They weren't born into wealth, and things only got harder during that time period. As a child I heard many a story of the hardships they endured, but also the good stories of simple times and what they did to entertain themselves that didn't cost much or anything at all. Then came World War II. My parents married in April 1941, and to make a long story short, it brought a new round of hardships. I heard many of those stories over the years. Often more than once.

I wasn't born until 1962, when my mother was almost 41 and my dad was 44. Though not everything is roses when you have older parents, I can list things that I feel had a positive influence on me and that I'm grateful for.

1. I learned many things about history that kids my age didn't because their parents were often 20 years younger than mine.

2. It's going to sound weird, but my vocabulary was affected. My vocabulary is peppered with words my parents and grandparents used that almost no one my age uses. This has helped me when writing historical novels and screenplays because I am sometimes a walking encyclopedia of old words.

3. I am nosy about history and have a keen appreciation for it and how it has influenced us all to this day.

Gratefulness can have a ring of expectation and in some ways a bit of shame to it, whereas abundance asks you to note what is good in your moment.

These are just three examples of things I am grateful for to this day. Unfortunately, somewhere among all of that my young mind could only appreciate the fact that I wasn't starving at that moment even though I had never gone hungry. Oh, and that I had a lot of amazing books to read all the time. Still, the early and repetitive emphasis on "lack" negatively influenced my ability to experience genuine appreciation of the things I did have and gave me an overwhelming sense that privation was around every corner. This intense pinpoint on scarcity didn't emphasize the good things in my life, nor did it make me more grateful. Why is this? Well, my parents might have said be grateful for food on the table, clothes on your back, and roof over your head. They didn't extend that conversation to anything philosophical or psychological. It just wasn't in their sphere, and I doubt it even crossed their minds. This is where I think abundance is a more helpful concept than just gratefulness. Gratefulness can have a ring of expectation and in some ways a bit of shame to it, whereas abundance asks you to note what is good in your moment. Right here. Right now.

Marie's Story

When my son was little, he had a disability that required me to focus all of my time on him. I brought him to doctors and for therapies, treatments, and surgeries. Helping him and advocating for him for his entire childhood took an incredible amount of time, energy, and resources. I couldn't work full-time and had to make money as a writer because I had to be at home with him. There were good years and lean years, but we always had what we needed. Yet while it was happening, I remember being so anxious and afraid that he would never be happy and healthy or be able to walk like other kids. I didn't feel a lot of gratitude at the time and was pretty pissed off that other kids got to walk and that their parents took it for granted, although I was thankful for his doctors and surgeons and therapists. Because I was so focused on what other kids could do, I still did not see the big blessing in all of that. It felt unfair to me that my son had to go through it, and it felt like a punishment that I could not just blink my eyes and make him "all better."

There were some years that were filled with despair and times when I thought perhaps my son would never be okay, would never be able to find happiness because of the physical and emotional trauma everything was taking on him. I wondered if he would have the confidence in life to go after his dreams and be proud of who he was. Again, there was nothing much to be grateful for other than that we had supportive family nearby and we would never be homeless. You learned to hang on to the little things to get through to the next day, the next week, the next month, and that is what we did.

As he got older and all the treatments and surgeries paid off more and more, I remember feeling as if, in all the trauma, there were cracks that were allowing the light of the blessings to finally shine through. My son had developed a strong resilience that most people his age did not possess. We were close and knew we could always depend on each other. My son knew that I was his advocate and would always look out for him. I began to work more as he was able to be more independent, and I could earn more money so we could have a better life. My writing career was doing well.

> *We were close and knew we could always depend on each other. My son knew that I was his advocate and would always look out for him.*

That shift in focus was palpable. We were both thriving now, not just surviving, and we were proud and happy to have made it out of the tunnel back into the light. We could see the people who helped us with clear eyes and grateful hearts, and even the painful surgeries had blessings that were becoming obvious as time went on and he could walk and even run. We began to laugh over silly things that happened during hospital stays, or funny things my son said to the doctors. (Once during a muscle treatment requiring a calming sedative, my son, who was about 8 years old at the time, suddenly began talking like a hippie right out of the 1960s! He had the entire staff laughing hysterically, although once he came out of the sedative "high," he couldn't remember anything.)

The challenges did not completely end, but they did get smaller and lost a lot of their power because the little things I could be grateful for carried me over until I could see the bigger things, and I saw the same happening for my son. Once I saw those bigger things, I could never unsee them. I know now that my son was watching me and modeling my fears and anxieties and my gratitude and appreciation. Kids really do learn from us, and I am now very grateful I handled things as well as I did to avoid creating more trauma for him.

Today, my son is happy and thriving; most of what we both went though is just distant memory. My focus is on the now, and so is his. We both learned so much about ourselves and about the importance of keeping some small part of our focus on the good and on the future. Without that, we might not have made it out so easily. We are blessed now to have the resilience and per-spective we learned during the hard times.

MAGICAL TIPS

Focus, Focus, Focus

You've heard of the real estate slogan "location, location, lo-cation," no? In terms of gratitude, switch that out to "focus." When everything is going great, it's easy to find things to be thankful for, but how about making it a habit to write down three things that you are grateful for that happened during the most difficult and challenging times of your life? No doubt shifting the focus and reframing the perspective will help you identify some things that were positive or of benefit.

Do this exercise in writing and be ready to surprise yourself with the blessings in the lesson. They are always there. You just have to dig for them sometimes.

When You're Stumped

We've already touched on some things you can do to be grateful, but if you're feeling a little uncertain, we've got some ex-ercises that you may not have thought of trying.

1. Challenge yourself to be grateful even when per-sonal circumstances are rough–mentally, physically, or both. When times are difficult for you it can be tempting to fall into cynicism and negativity. Really reach for a reason to be grateful. If you have photos taken during a hard time in your life, remember how you got through those circumstances and write that down as a way of cementing the mem-ory. This can help you take note of current things you can be grateful for.

2. Chat with a trusted family member or friend and ask them how they access gratitude. Make certain

this is someone who has shown they are resilient and generally a happy and well–adjusted person. This doesn't mean they are perfect, but chances are they've accessed gratitude more than once. Their wisdom could give you inspiration.

Here's a tip: set an alarm on your phone to remind you to pause during the day and take a "Gratitude Moment."

3. Set a reminder on your phone to ring once a day and call it "Gratitude Moment." Immediately stop everything and think about what you are grateful for in that moment. If you're inspired, set this reminder on your phone for more than once a day. This will train the brain to be more responsive to this way of thinking. It's a great habit to start.

4. If you already have a journal, write down every day what you are grateful for. If you are writing down the abundance that is evident in your life that day, include it with gratitude statements. If you don't have a journal, now is a good time to start one, even if it is just to note abundance and gratitude. Snag the journal and write down what you are grateful for if you are using the "Gratitude Moment" mentioned above.

5. Start a gratitude/happiness jar or other container. If the ideas above sound like too much work, you can take a simpler route. Write down one thing you are grateful for at the end of the day. Or if something happy and fortunate happens during the day, write that down. Take the paper and toss it into a jar, container, pretty box, anything that sounds fun. You might have something like this on hand already, but if not, you can be creative and design, make, or purchase something with the intent of using it for this purpose. Whenever you have had a downer day or encounter a moment of unhappiness, open the container and retrieve one of the

papers and unfold it. Reflecting on this gratitude or something happy that occurred in the past can inspire you.

Just SAY It!

Not a lot of people have manners these days, have you noticed? Perhaps they are just so rushed they aren't even thinking about it. Can you remember the last time someone said "thank you" for holding a door open for them, or allowing them to get in line before you in the grocery store? Make sure you are not that person and start today to say the simple words "thank you" as often as you can throughout your day. If your child puts his dish in the sink, say it. If your dog poops outside instead of on the floor, say it! If someone at the bank smiles and holds the door open, be sure to say it. Even better, smile when you say it so they know it's genuine.

There are so many opportunities to acknowledge and be grateful for the big and small gestures of others. You can even thank yourself if you get a project done on time or refuse that handful of potato chips while on a healthy diet. Just speaking the words is a powerful affirmation of gratitude that makes you feel better, as well as those you direct the words to. That is what is called a win–win.

Take a few minutes out of your day to say "Thank You!" to someone. This is just good manners, even if it's just a quick text.

Meister Eckhart once said, "If the only prayer you ever said in your life was 'Thank you,' that would suffice."

By the way, we want to say "thank you" for reading this book!

The Magic of Giving and Service

Blessed is he who speaks a kindness; thrice blessed is he who repeats it.

Arabian Proverb

You cannot do a kindness too soon,
for you never know how soon it will be too late.

Ralph Waldo Emerson

Is there any one maxim which ought to be acted upon throughout one's whole life? Surely the maxim of loving kindness is such.

Confucius

There has never been a better time to offer the spirit of giving and service to others. Being of help to others is something many of us are taught from an early age when we are told that we must share our toys. This is a wonderful way to start off our giving from the beginning of our young lives. It cements the idea that others are valuable and a part of our tribe. Or even if they are not directly a part of our circle, they are still humans who need connection to others by mutual support and sharing.

Most of us have heard the Golden Rule of "Do unto others as you would have them do unto you." While some may interpret this as a purely Christian concept, it is found in all major religions. Bud–

The Golden Rule (or its equivalent, depending on your beliefs) is a concept that should be encouraged in children from a young age.

dhism says, "Whatever is disagreeable to yourself, do not do unto others." Confucianism says, "Do not do to others what you do not want them to do to you." In Islam the ethics of reciprocity also call upon people to treat others the way they would like to be treated. In Wicca the Wiccan Rede specifies, "As you harm none, do what you will." There are many other religions and philosophies with the same basic tenet.

Lest we think only the religiously based of us are charitable and giving, there is plenty of evidence to the contrary. In an online *Psychology Today* article dated July 14, 2016, author Gleb Tsipursky, Ph.D., talks about a group of secular humanists, atheists, and skeptical groups who came together in November 2013 to organize a fundraiser to raise money for Mid-Ohio Food Bank. Any group that wants to help others can make an amazing impact regardless of religious affiliation, or with no affiliation at all.

Given that most religions and philosophies ask us to treat others well, it should be easy to follow along with the idea. Most of us have given of our time, money, and kindness to others. Yet even those who are willing to help others might find it difficult to do so when our lives are overflowing with our own concerns. For many the effort is too much, either because of personal health challenges, a perception of lack of time, selfishness, indecision, or an inability to see the best way to help. In the case of selfishness, this thought process can come from many different avenues, including psychological reasons that are broad-reaching and complicated. How many of us, though, would give more of ourselves in service if we also understood that it benefits us?

In "Why Giving Is Good for Your Health," a December 7, 2022, article on Cleveland Clinic's website, the authors stated that the warm and fuzzy feeling you experience from assisting others is a component in what boosts your physical and mental health. There are three chemicals released:

1. Serotonin (Regulates mood)

2. Dopamine (Gives a sense of pleasure)

3. Oxytocin (Gives a sense of connection with others)

Other benefits can include lowering blood pressure, extending lifespan, lowering stress, and building a helper's high that can combat depression. With all these benefits floating around, who wouldn't want to help others?

Society pressures us to be on the go all the time, and if we are trying to keep our own ship sailing, we don't always think of others right away.

In the UC Berkeley Greater Good article "The Four Keys to Well-Being" by Richard J. Davidson, from University of California–Berkeley, the author points out that many of us are spending so much time attempting to build up achievements and logging in extra hours at work that we have become more detached from others. We simply have no time when we're trying to keep our heads above water. Society pressures us to be on the go all the time, and if we are trying to keep our own ship sailing, we don't always think of others right away. This study mentioned that, per a recent analysis by Roy Baumeister at Florida State University, there are two types of well-being: hedonic (a sense of happiness) and eudemonic (a sense of meaning and purpose). They suspected that helping others is a significant part of finding meaning in life. Baumeister noted that a meaningful life is defined in a different way by every individual. He also said that in this study of 400 people, those who were more altruistic reported a bigger sense of purpose and meaning in their lives in general regardless of what was happening in their lives, both good and bad.

In charity there is no excess;
neither can angel nor man come in danger by it.

Sir Francis Bacon

We make a living by what we get, but we make a life by what we give.

Winston Churchill

How to Live a Mindful, Meaningful, Magical Life

REASONS WHY PEOPLE DON'T GIVE OR SERVE

We would be remiss if we didn't mention that there are definitely reasons other than being busy, tired, or not healthy that people don't serve others. In a *Psychology Today* article dated October 3, 2013, "3 Reasons Why People Refuse to Help Others," author Bobby Hoffman, Ph.D., mentions factors that can motivate all of us at one time or another. "Individuals help more when the psychological cost of helping is low, and the need of the person needing help is considered to be substantial. We hesitate to help when we believe the person in distress could have prevented the problem through a proactive and decisive action of their own. Holding the person accountable for their circumstances often accounts for refusing to give contributions to panhandlers or to people we think 'put' themselves in the position of needing assistance."

The difference can come in if someone has chosen to continually put themselves into a situation—for example, someone who needs to learn skills yet refuses to learn them. We have to assess if that person's need is temporary or if they have decided someone will do it for them and therefore they will never need to take up this skill for him- or herself.

Even in this case we shouldn't lump everyone into one category. Sometimes people with low self-worth and low self-esteem will believe they cannot do something or cannot learn something because of childhood trauma that led them to believe they are incapable. An example would be someone who was emotionally abused by narcissistic individuals. This ill-treatment can also occur in adulthood. Regardless of when this mistreatment happened, it can set a pattern for individuals to feel insecure, incapable, dumb, or have any number of negative self-judgments that are not true. It can result in a type of "learned helplessness."

Psychological studies indicate—unsurprisingly—that if we consider a person's problems to be of their own making (i.e., e.g., we think they are lazy, unmotivated, or undeserving), we are much less likely to feel sympathy for them and try to help them.

Another reason people choose not to help others is something to which many of us never give a thought. People can fall into the psychology of seeking to feel "special" by virtue of association with groups. This is not saying that all groups that take pride in whatever makes them special or set apart dislike helping other people. There are many groups who may differentiate themselves but also heavily devote themselves to charitable works.

On the other side of this coin are people becoming enmeshed in the psychological mind game played by groups whose purpose is to demonize others in a way that makes those others seem less worthy. These can be family groups, clubs, organizations, and political entities. These groups can say they are for good and yet display behavior that specifically causes others harm.

This explains how individually or in groups, we can seek to elevate ourselves over other people. Sometimes we will say we have worked hard for what we have, and other people should do the same. We will latch on to this mindset without knowing individuals' circumstances. Dialogue might start with someone saying, "All people in this group are …" and it goes on from there. If you encounter this thought process in yourself and want to change it, what can you do?

1. Think about why you might *not* wish to help an individual or a group of people. Are you capable of using your empathy and imagination to put yourself in their shoes for a moment?

2. Given this scenario, would you want someone to help you?

3. Even if you have never experienced their challenges, would you be averse to someone showing you even the smallest kindness or assistance?

This type of assessment can go a long way toward helping you decide when, how, and if you want to help.

Lastly, we might simply feel we have nothing to give. If we don't have money to spare, we think we cannot help anyone else. We have so much more to offer than just dollar bills. We have wisdom, skills, talents, and our love and support, and we can always give of our time and energy where it is needed.

How to Live a Mindful, Meaningful, Magical Life

Don't have a lot of money to help others? Not a problem! Your time is just as valuable. Doing volunteer work is an excellent way to give to others and is extremely rewarding to your sense of being a worthwhile person.

In the August 4, 2017, online *Time* magazine article "The Secret to Happiness Is Helping Others," the author mentioned ways individuals can get started in being of service. One way is to find your passion. Essentially, how much we give isn't as important as the amount of love we put into giving. Who are you drawn to help? What do you resonate with the most? Does that mean only giving money? Time can be more valuable than money.

EVEN SMALL THINGS COUNT: USING OUR SKILLS

When people talk about giving and being of service, they sometimes don't consider small things. They might think of assistance for natural disasters and putting themselves in the thick of the rescue or gathering supplies to send to those who have lost everything. Grand gestures can be amazing. Large gestures can include money or hours spent and are sometimes directed toward helping big numbers of people at once, or maybe a single family that might have lost their home in a fire or some terrible weather disaster. At the same time, people can make a difference in one way that is sometimes overlooked.

Kindness. Simple everyday kindness can go a long way toward building community and making life better for all. It is easy to think small things don't matter or can't have an amazing effect on someone's life that echoes down through the years.

Who doesn't have perfectly good clothes lying around that you never wear? Donate them to a charity and do something good with them!

Examples include:

- Delivering meals to shut-ins, including the elderly.

- Volunteering to read to children at schools.

- Donating books to the library.

- Offering to walk a pet for a friend who is ill.

- Sending a card to someone who is ill or has suffered a loss.

- Thanking others for holding a door for you or holding a door for someone else.

- Thanking your restaurant server and the person at a fast-food drive-through.

- Paying for someone's lunch and/or drink at the drive-through.

- Helping to clean up without being asked.

- Asking someone how they are doing, and listening to the answer.

- Congratulating people on their accomplishments, even if they were a rival regarding particular goals.

- Volunteering with a group that is picking up trash along a street or highway.

- Volunteering at a hospital.

- Volunteering at a soup kitchen.

The possibilities are endless. Random acts of benevolence not only make the person performing the thoughtfulness feel better. Who knows what kind of wonderful thing will happen because they took a moment to show kindness?

As mentioned before, many of us are not that cognizant of which skills we could use to help others. The exceptions would be someone who is a first responder such as fire, police, or paramedic/EMT, or doctors, nurses, and other medical professions. These are some of the people we think about who have exceptional skills and who are in the business of saving lives.

With that in mind, the rest of us might devalue our ability to help. Of course, if we already have low self-worth and self-esteem, we might not believe we own valuable skills to help others in the first place. How do we bolster our self-worth and do good at the same time? Take that first step toward doing something ... anything that could help someone else. Take a step toward volunteering in a way that lets your skills be used to better a situation.

HELPING WITHOUT HINDERING

"God helps those who help themselves" is a spiritual principle we know to be true; that our intention, aligned with Source or Spirit, leads to manifestation through the principle within acting upon our words and thoughts. If this is the case, then how do we help someone who does not believe or understand that they have within them the power to change their lives by changing their thoughts? We cannot force them to change their thoughts, nor can we forcibly align them with a higher force or power that could help them. These are things they must learn to do on their own.

But what we can do is act as guardians, guides, and angels at their service, cheerleaders standing on the sidelines urging them on to the finish line. We can learn how to help them without hindering their own ability to discover their capacity to help themselves.

There is a fine line between helping another person and enabling them or making them dependent upon us. For example, a drug addict or alcoholic will benefit greatly from the care and

Don't think you're not being supportive and loving enough if you are not succeeding in helping a friend or family member with their struggles. You can't force change in a person who is not willing or able to change. All you can do is be there for them as much as possible.

concern of those around him or her, but those same caretakers cannot give up the addict's drug of choice and make the commitment to get sober for him or her. That decision, that commitment, is between the addict and his or her Higher Power. Sadly, some addicts never find their Higher Power and thus feel alone and unable to heal from their addiction, merely because they have never been able to experience the flow of Divine love from within. Instead, they continue to believe that they themselves have no power to help themselves and they become perpetual victims, blaming everyone and everything else for their problems. They go into full-on victim mode, which is a great excuse for never having to take responsibility for their lives.

We can help wrap an injured bird's broken wing, but we cannot heal it. We can even help unwrap their healed wing and urge them to the edge of the precipice, but we cannot make them take wing and fly. There is a delicate balance between helping others and hindering their mental, emotional, and spiritual growth by trying to live their lives for them, or "fix" them, and nowhere does this become more evident than in trying to help another person heal a negative life situation.

Although we can realize the truth about someone and their situation—that it is perfect and whole and prospering with good—we still cannot MAKE someone heal or change or grow until they are ready, willing, and able to do so.

> *Although we can realize the truth about someone and their situation ... we still cannot MAKE someone heal or change or grow until they are ready, willing, and able to do so.*

When the person we are trying to help is aligned with their own inner power and capability, the work is done easily and effortlessly. When they are not aligned with it, helping them becomes much more of an effort because of their resistance, whether it be conscious or subconscious. This is the point where we must gently assist them in getting to the root of the problem and do the necessary inner and outer work for change. As Ernest Holmes wrote in *The Science of Mind*, "We can hire others to work for us, to care for our physical needs, but no one can live for us. This we must do for ourselves."

Imagine trying to experience joy or happiness for another person. You cannot do it. You can try to verbally describe what it feels like, but it will all be lost on the other person if they have never experienced it themselves. Just as you can lead a horse to water but you cannot make it drink, you can guide a person closer to the Source, but you cannot make them "see" it. To do so would be tantamount to mind control or the cultlike enforcement rampant in organized religion, where few followers have ever actually experienced a divine force, but all are called to worship according to doctrine set down by other humans.

What does this all mean for those of us who wish to serve others? Only that we must do so in a loving and supportive way that does not interfere with the other person's own spiritual growth and development. We can encourage them, rather than enable them; support them, rather than hold them up altogether; walk beside them when they are weak, rather than carry them; inspire them to throw off the bushel that hides their light, rather than throw it off for them (they'll just run for cover back underneath it the moment we are not around!).

We can encourage and inspire, but we cannot do the work for them. They have to have the desire to do it for themselves. Then and only then will the change be permanent, and the healing be perfect. Then and only then will they have learned to help themselves.

AUTHOR INSIGHTS

Denise's Story

I may have belabored this point, but as a kid I wanted to be many things. Not too many of those things were skills that related to helping other people. Being an introvert made it a little harder (in my mind) to make connections with many people all at one time. Volunteering was emphasized as a good thing, but I was too in my own little world to do much about it. I think a lot of kids are, especially in our teen years when some of us can allow the massive changes in our world to turn us inward.

In an earlier chapter I mentioned volunteering at a history museum and doing amateur archaeology. It wasn't until a few short months ago that I looked back on that and realized that in some tiny way I was helping others. My work in all three of those avenues meant that I could help entertain people and myself at the same time. When I assisted the history museum registrar with everything she did to maintain artifacts and other items that were part of the museum (including things that weren't on display), I was helping take care of the past. I was also educating myself. In some ways, in doing the archaeology, I was helping others discover more history and satisfying that insatiable part of me that is incredibly nosy and wants to know all the things. Was it a grand gesture? No ... it was making me happy, and the benefits of that were tremendous. Yet these days I like to look back and think maybe, just maybe, I was helping some other people by bringing history to life.

Marie's Story

One of my favorite ways to give to others involves my greatest passion and my purpose. Writing. I do give money and volunteer at local food banks, and I am always giving donations of clothing and household goods I no longer need, but the one way that lights up my heart is by offering words of support and encouragement to those who feel as though they might never achieve a goal or a dream. I feel that it is my purpose, and I love seeing how just a kind word of support can have a huge influence on other people, which then inspires them to do the same for others in their lives.

> *... I love seeing how just a kind word of support can have a huge influence on other people, which then inspires them to do the same for others in their lives.*

Because writing involves too much rejection, I found early on that I felt so much better by taking the focus off the pain and encouraging others the way I wanted to be encouraged, to help remove the sting of rejection for them that I knew they were reeling from. I did not want the rejection of an agent or publisher or family member to deflate their dreams. I was totally into helping others achieve their dreams.

I was told over and over again that I inspired people to start writing their first book or screenplay or to follow their dreams of this or that, and it made me feel awesome and as if I mattered,

Meaning comes to some people when they feel they inspire others through their own creativity. This is one reason writers write, even though it is a difficult row to hoe, filled with potential rejection and setbacks. It is also a lonely pursuit at times.

but it also drove home the point that not everyone needs the same things. Some people need money or food or clothing, and others need someone to believe in them. Giving of ourselves can involve something physical or something emotional and spiritual. The best way we can give to others is from the heart, and finding what we are best at is a great place to start.

The biggest blessing of all is that when we give, we also benefit from the act of giving. Our hearts and spirits feel lighter, and life becomes more meaningful as we see the magic we create for others. We feel more inspired; others want what we have, so we inspire them, too. The ripple spreads into a giant wave of generosity of spirit.

There is magic all around us, and it multiplies when shared. Like a circle of people standing side by side, when we give a gift to the person next to us, and they do likewise, that gift eventually comes back around to us.

MAGICAL TIPS

First Steps:
What If You Can't Decide What to Do?

For some of us it can be difficult to decide right off how we want to help or where we might offer our time and effort. Here is a checklist to help you get started.

1. Are there groups, charities, or organizations you feel drawn to help? If they have a website, you can poke around there and see if they still sound interesting and a good fit for you. Can you see any skills within yourself that they could use? Even if you don't know if your skills would help but are still interested in them, you could call and ask about volunteering opportunities. Based on the vibe you get from that, you can decide whether to move forward. Another example: Perhaps you have veterans of the armed services in your family and wish to help. Reach out to your local Veterans' Affairs office and ask what you can do. Many VA hospitals take donations of money or needed items. You might also be a volunteer at the nearest veteran's center or VA hospital and give a few hours a month in an appropriate capacity.

2. Combined efforts. Many clubs have a variety of organizations they support. If you are already a part of these organizations, you might have a great reach to help several different groups at once that need assistance.

3. Local food bank. What if you could donate even one food item to your local food bank each month? Or perhaps once a week? Just one item is worth the effort.

As you can see, there are numerous ways you can bring the power of kindness and giving to others every day. Consider it. It will not only give you a sense of purpose and bolster your mental health, but it can change lives.

Start Where You Are

Giving can begin right where you are, right now. See where you can be more of service at home to your spouse or children, or perhaps your aging parents could benefit from your spirit of service. A neighbor who is disabled might benefit from you running an errand for them. Opportunities abound all around you for helping others.

At the workplace, can you find ways to share your generosity and start a new yearly trend of having everyone bring in a bag of

In this modern age of electronic communications, the bonds we used to share with neighbors have broken down. People often just stay at home, never even knowing their neighbors. You can enrich your life and theirs by helping others on your own block and getting to know them better as friends.

canned goods for a food bank? This can extend to your neigh-borhood and community, such as a multifamily garage sale or bake sale that will donate a percentage of profits to a local charity. A work contest can be fun when the prize involves picking a charitable donation.

Charity does begin at home, and it has a ripple effect. You might think what you are doing is somewhat meaningless in the grander scheme of things, but anything of value is like a seed that, when watered with attention and nurturing, bears abundant fruit.

The Kindness Jar

Take a large jar and repurpose it as a "kindness jar" for your home or office. Attach a note telling others how to contribute. Perhaps everyone in the office can put their change from their morning coffee run in the jar, or your kids can contribute with IOU notes of how they will offer one random act of kindness that week. Whatever you decide to put into the jar, make sure you don't "raid" it for money if you're a little short. This is a committed, dedicated place for the sharing of your blessings and should be honored as such.

You can be in charge of the jar and where the contributions will go, or let a colleague or a child pick the destination on a ro-tating basis. Maybe one month you can support an animal welfare organization and another month a local domestic violence shelter.

Money is important, and there are a million different char-ities that would appreciate any contributions, but you can get cre-ative and instead have people contribute a slip of paper describing how they will give of themselves and share those at the end of each month. This can be anything from volunteering to contributing money to an organization or collecting clothing for a homeless shelter. Someone night feel compelled to do taxes for the poor for free, or offer their landscaping services to one un-derprivileged family a month.

The sky is the limit when it comes to ways of giving and being of service. Hold each other accountable. Giving is mean-ingless unless it reaches those we seek to help.

We also will be helping ourselves in return.

The Magic of Passion and Purpose

Nothing great in the world has ever been accomplished without passion.

Georg Wilhelm Friedrich Hegel

Follow your passion, be prepared to work hard and sacrifice, and, above all, don't let anyone limit your dreams.

Donovan Bailey

The purpose of life is a life of purpose.

Robert Byrne

Passion and purpose are like the gas and oil that help us drive our lives. We don't need either one to survive, but we do if we hope to thrive and be happy. The magic of passion and purpose infuses our lives with joy and meaning and gives us a reason to jump out of bed in the morning with expectation and anticipation of what lies ahead.

Passion can be defined as anything that generates strong emotions within us. Those emotions can be negative or positive, so in the case of everyday magic, we obviously want to focus on the positive emotions. Passion is what we love, what we cherish, what we are obsessed with and cannot stop thinking about. It's our "what," and if there is no passion in our lives, we feel like we are basically going through the motions. Blahs–ville.

Purpose is meaning. It's our "why"–why we do things and why we support things. Why do we feel drawn to certain jobs or careers, vocations or hobbies? Purpose gives us reasons for the seasons and acts as the foundation for the trajectory of our lives, especially our goals and how we spend our time.

We live a life of passion and purpose when we are fully in the present, infused with love and excitement and joy, able to see the positive and overcome the negative, working toward a vision or a goal. Passion and purpose go together like chocolate and peanut butter or strawberries and cream. They complement each other and add value to each other yet are intertwined by a common thread that defines who we are and what we want out of life.

Again, you don't need to have either one, but life without either one is pretty dull. Diane Ackerman is quoted as saying "I do not want to get to the end of my life and find that I just lived the length of it. I want to have lived the width of it as well." Having passion and a purpose is what expands our life and gives it length, depth, and width, so that when we are on our deathbeds we feel full of life and have no regrets. A life without passion and purpose is a life not fully lived, but so many people are terrified to pursue their dreams and do the things that bring them meaning. We have a default mindset that tells us we are not good enough or that we don't matter in the grander scheme of things, among many other excuses for staying small and living a half–life.

"I'm too young, too old, too fat, too skinny, too dumb, too smart, too poor, too rich, too whatever." We "too" ourselves to death! It's as if there is some perfect state of being we have to first achieve in order to move toward our bliss, or a perfect time when we will feel whole and ready to rock and roll. There is no perfect state or time other than the one we are in right now. Time is passing so quickly and with it, our unfulfilled desires and dreams, until we wake up one day and find that we never went after what lit our inner flame and we failed to find a purpose that gave depth and meaning to our lives.

It's sad. No, it's tragic because the time we take to come up with excuses is time we could be living with meaning and magic.

We spend too much of our time feeling inadequate because we are trying to impress or gain acceptance from our peers and family. Stop trying to live up to other people's standards and focus on accepting who you are. When you do, you will find contentment and peace.

The goal is to set aside all self-doubt and fear of failure (or success) and move ahead one baby step at a time until those steps get bigger. Like a muscle on your arm or leg, with more use it gets stronger. Those excuses come from our fear of the unknown, and, sadly, we would rather stay stuck in the known we don't like than dare to venture forth into the shadowy realms of possibility. What if we fail?

THE MAGIC OF FAILURE

What if we succeed?

Hockey legend Wayne Gretzky once said, "You miss 100 percent of the shots you don't take." Another legend, computer pioneer Steve Jobs, said, "Your time is limited, so don't waste it living someone else's life." There is a lot of wisdom out there to guide and inspire you if you feel you can't live with passion and purpose. Maybe you don't even know what your passion or your purpose is. Now is the time to do some digging and find out. You have a purpose, and you feel passion. There are many ways to discover each in the Magical Tips at the end of this chapter.

How to Live a Mindful, Meaningful, Magical Life

Motivational speaker Mark Victor Hansen (pictured) created the *Chicken Soup for the Soul* book series with Jack Canfield.

Mark Victor Hansen is quoted as saying, "Don't wait until everything is just right. It will never be perfect. There will always be challenges, obstacles and less than perfect conditions. So what. Get started now. With each step you take, you will grow stronger and stronger, more and more skilled, more and more self-confident and more and more successful." In case you don't know who Mark Victor Hansen is, he's the multi-millionaire mastermind behind the *Chicken Soup for the Soul* franchise. Had he given in to his own doubts about his passion for the *Chicken Soup* concept, had he focused more on his excuses than on his purpose, we might never have been given the amazing gifts of those books and the many other products and courses developed around them.

Imagine all the amazing art, books, and useful things, services, and inventions that exist today and what life would be like if all of the people behind them had not moved toward what lit up their spirits and lifted their souls? Thankfully, they found the motivation and courage to pursue their individual passions and ended up living a life that had purpose.

Purpose doesn't have to mean saving the world, although if that is what sets your soul alight, go for it. Purpose can be something like raising happy children, or making jewelry to sell on Etsy, or helping clean litter off local beaches. It can be grand or small, big or tall … but it has to be yours, not someone else's.

It is crucial that you take a good look at your fear of failure when pursuing your passion and purpose, because it will derail you every time. Failure can be a huge gift with major life lessons. Whenever you do something that doesn't work, you learn what doesn't work so you can try something new the next time. Those failures are not meant to deter you from your dreams but to provide input and data, like clinical trials, as to what needs work and where.

Failure helps you to know who you are, what you like and dislike, what your values are, and what you really want for your life in a way success never can. It does require a thick skin and a strong resilience. You want to bounce back from failure, not stay down on the ground. Failing at something is never an end but a beginning of a new way of doing things or a new way of being. Roll up your sleeves, get off the pavement, and try, try again until you get it right or decide it isn't for you anymore. There is no shame in realizing that what you thought you wanted is not really what you wanted, just as there is no shame in screwing up or dropping the ball now and then. It's human.

Fearing failure is more about feeling rejected or being ashamed that others are judging you as a loser.

What does count is that you feel passionate and purposeful about what you are doing, because that will be what carries you through the hard times. Fearing failure is more about feeling rejected or being ashamed that others are judging you as a loser. Guess what? The vast majority of people judging you either haven't made one step toward their dreams and are jealous, or failed once or twice and gave up and now wish you would, too. Wallowing in negativity and feeling sorry for yourself only keep you stuck where you are, not moving toward where you want to be. It's impossible to see the blessings you have and what miracles may come when you hang your head in shame and look down. Look up! See the possibilities. Now you know what not to do and which path not to take! Don't give up just because it causes others discomfort. Feel the feelings when you fail. Regroup and replan. Then go for it.

You've got one magical life to live.

Let's start with passion.

The most common way people give up their power is by thinking they don't have any.
Alice Walker

FINDING YOUR PASSION

We all have things in our lives that turn on our switch, float our boat, make our hearts flutter and our spirits soar. Passion comes in many forms: other people, animals, events, traveling, moving the body, having a hobby or vocation or career, volunteer work, making stuff with our hands, creating stories and art and music. Passion is individual, meaning each of us will fall in love with something different. Some might love bowling so much they join a league, and others might hate bowling and prefer hockey. You might feel passionate about saving whales, and I might feel passionate about saving desert tortoises.

Not to mention that your passions might change over time. One year you might be obsessed with making wood crafts, and another year wine bottle art is your thing. You may have a passion for food trucks for 10 years, then suddenly turn into a passionate fan of sidewalk cafes. Books your thing? Maybe in a few years you'll have the same passion for jigsaw puzzles. Passions come and go, but one thing stays forever–the powerful and potent love of something that gives you the tingles and adds value and pleasure to your life.

It is easy to think we must stick with a passion forever. That's a myth. If you look at this philosophically, you may do one thing for a long time and yet something might keep you from doing it the next moment or the next year. Or you might find you only have time for two of the 10 things you'd love to do. That's okay. As long as you're doing as many of the things you love to do as you can, it's all good. Another myth is that passions are either good or bad. As long as you aren't harming anyone or anything, chances are your passion and purpose is good.

Passion can come from almost anywhere. Often, something that starts off as a hobby can become a lifetime passion. And feel free to experiment. It's okay if your passion switches from one thing to another, or if you have more than one passion. Have fun with it!

There is no right or wrong when it comes to finding your passion. Whatever makes your heart sing is the song you need to play more of. Like the old expression about marching to a different drummer, you might not even hear the drums because the tuba is your passion.

> *We are told to go out into the world and get a job and bring home a paycheck, but the happiest people seem to be the ones who also work at something that brings them happiness, not just a nice paycheck.*

Some people turn their passions into what they do for a living, their dream career. Remember the lyrics to the theme song from the movie *Flashdance*? "Take your passion, make it happen." We are told to go out into the world and get a job and bring home a paycheck, but the happiest people seem to be the ones who also work at something that brings them happiness, not just a nice paycheck. They often say they'd do the work even if they didn't get paid. Now that's the magic of finding your passion—when it's present you can't help but be drawn to it. It makes life worth living. It brings a lightness to your step and a real song to your heart.

Mo Seetubtim, founder and CEO of The Happiness Planner, stated in her June 6, 2015, post "7 Rules to Live by for Those Who Live with Passion" on *Huffpost.com* that there are many ways to live life, but living a life of passion means you never feel bored, stagnant or stuck. It's a life where "you're constantly excited and inspired." She also stated that without passion, "life seems meaningless and mundane." She listed seven ways to live with passion:

- Find out what your passion is—look at your childhood or things that you could spend hours doing.

- Get obsessed with your passion—give it all you've got.

- Be open-minded and curious—stay open to the field of passion possibilities.

- Be spontaneous—allow life to flow and go with the flow.

- Love fully and deeply—don't hold back on giving and receiving love.

- Be inspiring to others—do things that inspire others to find their passion.

- Travel—open yourself up to experience the world. (If you have traveled, you can travel within and journey into the mind!)

"You see the world through your passion—this is the only way you can live and the only way for you to really enjoy life," Seetubtim said.

Leo Babauta, creator of the *Zen Habits* blog, wrote his own suggestions in "9 Tips on How to Find Passion in Life," a November 2, 2022, *LifeHack.com* piece. He suggested beginning by asking "What are you passionate about?" Look to see what you already love doing or learning about or reading about. Brainstorm ideas and look for inspirations in your own environment that might give clues to your passion. Avoid negative thoughts, and know that your passion wants to find you as much as you want to find it, so don't give up if it isn't obvious right away.

Another interesting angle comes from *Oprah.com*'s "The Secret to Finding Your Passion (Hint: It's Not What You Think)" by motivational expert Marie Forleo. She points out how it can become torturous trying to find our passion and figure out what we feel passionate about when we read tons of books, take psychological tests, recall our childhood interests, and gaze at our navels, so to speak. "Here's the problem. Passion can't be found in your head because it lives in your heart. And the flames of passion are fanned by engagement, not thought. Juicy, right?" She goes on to advise that we try not to figure out our passions by thinking about them but rather by taking action and feeling our way to the truth from the inside out.

Marie Forleo is known for her series of advice books *Everything Is Figureoutable.*

We can also bring passion into whatever it is we are doing at the time. "No matter what task is in front of you, bring as much enthusiasm and energy to it as you possibly can." By being fully present we might realize we have a passion for just being alive, and the doors of opportunity open much wider than we ever imagined possible.

Passion is both a feeling and an action, then, and we have the ability to ignite our own flames just by fully engaging with life right where we are. If we can learn to love everything we do, passion will show itself, but that will not happen if we are negative, complaining, bored, or detached.

Forleo also suggests asking yourself what you love to talk about, learn about, and teach others about, because passion can be found there waiting for us to put it to work as a new purpose. We can even ask close friends and family members what they see that lights us up that we may not see ourselves.

Ultimately, we have to stop thinking and talking and start doing by acting on our passions and seeing where they lead us. By injecting love into our lives at every turn, we find the entire ride is so much more magical and enjoyable.

FINDING YOUR PURPOSE

Actor and comedian Eddie Cantor once said, "Slow down and enjoy life. It's not only the scenery you miss by going too fast—you also miss the sense of where you are going and why." We often feel we have no purpose because we are too busy going through the motions of living our lives. But the truth is, any purpose to life will be found in the stillness and quiet when our spirits have a chance to speak up because the busy-crazy mind chatter is taking a long break.

Passion is what lights us up, but purpose is what gives our lives meaning—and yes, the two can be the same or totally different. People who have a deep sense of purpose, whether that is helping others, raising children, cleaning up the environment, supporting other creatives, working with the disabled, making inspiring music or art, or collecting donations for the poor, have a stronger sense of fulfillment, and that doubles when they blend their inherent talents and skills with their purposeful goals.

American comedian Eddie Cantor (1892–1964) made a career doing what he loved best. He also had the wisdom to note you need to not rush through life but slow down and enjoy it.

What gives your life meaning? That simple question is at the heart of identifying our purpose, if we don't know what it is. In "Seven Ways to Find Your Purpose in Life," Jill Suttie wrote for the August 6, 2020, University of California–Berkeley' *Greater Good* that many people come to know their purpose after hardship, giving the examples of a kid who was the victim of racial abuse or someone who overcame a devastating illness. But that is not the only way. She identifies steps you can take to find your purpose, including identifying things you care about. "Purpose is all about applying your skills toward contributing to the greater good in a way that matches you. So, identifying what you care about is an important first step."

Suttie also suggested doing a lot of self-reflection on what matters most, which will be as individual as the person doing the reflecting. What are your values? When you understand that, it will help narrow down your purpose. She also suggested a wonderful exercise called "the magic wand exercise" in which you imagine yourself at a later time in your life as if everything has gone as well as it could have. You can journal what you are doing, who you are with, what your daily life is like, and get into the details and the emotions behind living your best, most meaningful life.

It might not be all about just getting what you want. In "7 Tips for Finding Your Purpose in Life," Amy Morin, L.C.S.W., editor-in-chief of *VerywellMind.com*, wrote: "Researchers at Florida State University and Stanford found that happiness and meaningfulness overlapped somewhat but were different: Happiness was linked to the person being a taker before a giver, whereas meaningfulness went along with being more of a giver than a taker. The givers in relationships reported having a purposeful life more often than the takers did."

Other obvious ways to find your purpose is to consider the injustices you feel strongly about and see where that leads. You can also explore your interests from childhood to the present and see if any of them feels like something you would do for free. Are you a good information spreader? Do you bring people together in your community or job? Are you a great mediator or diplomat?

Again, your purpose doesn't have to be about changing the entire world, unless that's what you feel strongly about. It can be something unique to you; what gives one person meaning might not do so for the next. You were born with talents and gifts to share with the world, and purpose tends to reveal itself when you use those to your own benefit and to the benefit of others.

In *Happy for No Reason*, Marci Shimoff described purpose as the roof upon your Home for Happiness. "When you don't have that sense of purpose, it's like having a leaky roof: it can rain unhappiness over every other aspect of your life." As William F. Buckley Jr. once said, "There are two great days in a person's life–the day we are born and the day we discover why." Shimoff wrote, "Being connected to purpose expands you and helps you feel inspired in each moment, which naturally leads to more success."

We feel purposeless when we lead an uninspired life, as if we are just going along with everyone else, on autopilot, until the day we die. Having a sense of something greater and grander than ourselves helps us find a reason and purpose for being alive. When we understand that we are here to thrive, not just to stay alive, we can look deeper than the physical and material world and reach into our souls to see what we have to give to that greater, grander universal allness. Like a drop of water in the ocean or a blade of grass in a field, we are all important and all here to do our part to leave the world a little better and brighter than we found it.

Shimoff cautions against attaching purpose to an external thing like a person or job because if that person leaves or that job ends, we

William F. Buckley Jr. (1925–2008) was a conservative political commentator, founder of the *National Review*, and longtime host of TV's *Firing Line*.

feel like our purpose does, too. Instead, it's about finding our own North Star, or our own inner GPS that we follow no matter the external circumstances.

It's important to identify your passions and your purpose, but even more important to choose them every day. Make the conscious decision to move in the direction of your passion and purpose and stay on track. Don't listen to naysayers or give into judgment or criticism, and when times get tough (and they will), hold onto your purpose like a life raft because that is what it is. It keeps you from drowning in regret, meaninglessness, and apathy. Hold on tightly to it.

IS PURPOSE DESTINY OR CHOICE?

There are those who seem to have been destined for a great purpose since birth, and those who find their purpose later in life, sometimes by accident. Most people have an inkling of their purpose but for many reasons don't pursue it.

Fear of failure is a huge reason people don't pursue their purpose. People are taught from birth that getting a "good job" is the ultimate. Making a great deal of money, they believe, is far more important than feeling vital and alive. The number of people who are doing jobs that bring in a lot of money but make them dissatisfied and miserable may outweigh those who are doing what they truly love. Given that scenario as a possibility, why wouldn't we fight tooth and nail to try to do what gives our life deep meaning and satisfaction?

Whether it is something on a grand scale or something more humble, your life has purpose. Simply by being here on Earth, you have a purpose, even if it is just being a good person to friends and family.

If you are alive, you have a purpose. Again, that purpose can be as simple as living your best life (which inspires others around you to do the same) or it might be as complex as discovering a new solar system in the far reaches of the universe where first contact will be made. Purpose is yours and yours alone to find.

Is it all about a predetermined "destiny" or do you have some choice in the matter? This age–old debate between destiny and free will is frustrating and confusing for purpose-seekers. "I don't feel called to anything," you might say and assume you have no purpose because you don't feel a sense of "Luke, it is your destiny," as in *Star Wars*. You might also have had a strong inner knowledge and drive toward a particular vocation since the day you came tumbling out of the womb or told everyone that becoming the next great horror author "is my destiny."

Maybe we all have a destiny that we are born with, but few of us allow ourselves the inner reflection to hear it calling our names. Maybe it's all about choice and free will and we can choose whatever the heck we want as our purpose and change it whenever we feel called by our passions to do something else.

It could also be a little of both. We may be born with gifts and talents that incline us toward being a singer or an accountant. We might have had a burning desire to perform as a dancer since toddlerhood, or maybe we've always been building things with our hands. We might know "what we want to be when we grow up" from an early age and never waver.

Then again, we might not have a clue.

If we look at those gifts and talents and ask ourselves if we love doing them, it can point us in the direction of our purpose, knowing we alone have the choice to move toward it or away from it. Destiny may be predetermined, but it might not be fixed; we can create our own future based upon the choices we make and their consequences. The idea that we are all born with a fixed destiny might have some appeal, but it also takes all the fun out of being in the pilot seat of our own plane.

Motivational author and speaker Debra Poneman, known for her hugely popular YES to Success trainings, calls it our "dharma," the reason we were born on Earth at this time. She refers to the Eastern traditions and how dharma is interpreted in one way as the guided right action we are called to take to fulfill

The ancient Hindu scripture known as the Bhagavad Gita wisely advises us to search for our own dharma and not those of other people.

our purpose. She believes we each have our own particular dreams and that we are meant to live them, and just having the dreams means we also have access to the people and circumstances that will help us achieve them. Why else would we have those dreams and not the dreams of the person standing next to us? Poneman also refers to teachings in the ancient Hindu scripture, the Bhagavad Gita, that tell us not to pursue another person's purpose or dharma. We have our own for a reason.

Destiny, yes. Choice, yes. When it comes to finding our purpose, the most important thing is to make sure it's what you truly feel called to do and not something you feel you have to do or must do or that others expect you to do. Life may have dealt you a certain hand of cards, but you alone get to choose how to play them.

Think of purpose like a ladder. You may place your ladder up against a wall and spend years climbing it to reach the top only to find that you hate the view. You have the power to climb down and move your ladder to a different wall with a different view, one that might align more closely with your soul's deepest desires.

AUTHOR INSIGHTS

Marie's Story

I was always one of the "lucky ones" who knew what I was destined to do from early childhood. It combined my passion for everything from science to reading and my sense of purpose as a world-class kid storyteller. I wanted to be a writer. Well, not exactly true. I wanted to be everything. I wanted to be a jockey, an astronaut, a teacher, a scientist, a tap dancer, and a movie star, but the one thing I was doing consistently was writing about all the things I wanted to do. My passion for expression and my purpose as a writer were set in stone, and I have pursued them relentlessly to this day.

I thought many times about trying to do something else. I really did want to be a jockey but grew too fast and too tall. I toyed with going to college to be a physicist like my father, but I hated math. I looked into being a movie star and decided I preferred anonymity and privacy. One thing never failed me, and that was writing. I was born to be a writer. I am lucky in that I rarely deviated from that passion and purpose, even when it looked like my dream might never come true.

Today I look back and wonder how different life would have been had I not gone along with the strong inner drive, which kept me writing during good times and bad. All the rejection I faced was painful, but I picked myself up and moved on by continuing to write and expanding into different formats of self-expression.

People today will find out I've been writing since childhood and ask, "How did you know?" I tell them, "I just knew." Nobody told me. It was an inner certainty and it lit me up and allowed me the freedom I desired to become anything I wanted to be through stories or learning and writing about my favorite subjects. I saw it as a way to be everything I wanted to be without having to choose one thing to be. That was a choice I knew I could never make and be happy with.

Truth is, I have strong intuition, and when I listen to it, it leads me right where I need to be. When I ignore it, my passion and purpose is derailed. It's that simple. I have many past regrets of times when even with my writing career, I chose to ignore that inner voice, that inner compass telling me where True North was. And I paid the price for it.

When I did listen, it always led me to writing.

Pay attention to your personal compass and where it is leading you.

How to Live a Mindful, Meaningful, Magical Life

I will be writing until the day I die and imagine that on my deathbed I'll be working on the ending of the great novel that is my life, minus the editing. I'll let God do that. Am I one of the lucky ones who was touched with destiny since birth, or just someone who paid close attention to my inner compass?

I sense it is a bit of both. I know that I could choose tomorrow to stop writing and become a dolphin trainer. But I won't because I know it won't make me happy or fulfilled, and also because I know that if I want to become a dolphin trainer for a little while, all I need to do is find a way to combine that with my writing career. See how that works?

Denise's Story

I've already bombarded you in previous chapters with my passions and purposes and how I was able to discover a few years back that I'd fulfilled many of my passions and purposes more than once, even if I'm not doing some of them now. Why am I not doing them right now? In some ways it is because I am pursuing new passions, or those old passions have transformed. For example, I used to participate in archaeology, including digs (which, by the way, are not the biggest part of archaeology). Physically I wouldn't be up to that part of archaeology these days. So now I'm enjoying reading about it and sometimes writing about it. One of my passions, archery, is also not a physical possibility for me now because of arthritis in my hands and a wrist. But I am so glad that I pursued it while it was right in front of me! I can say I have no regrets.

Some new purposes, such as utilizing my mediumship and writing screenplays, came to me in the last few years. I've discovered that there are new passions arising all the time, if I only keep my eyes, ears, and thoughts open to the possibilities. Who knows what new passions will find me tomorrow?

MAGICAL TIPS

You Are a Cork

Imagine you are a cork from a wine bottle floating on a creek or river. You go with the flow and don't fight the current. But when something or someone, including you, presses down on the cork, it doesn't go anywhere but underwater. Think of living a life of purpose as what you would do if nobody or nothing was pressing down on your cork.

What would you be in the flow of? Where would the river of life be taking you? Use this visual to allow yourself to dream of a life of free–flowing energy and then jot down small steps you can take to begin living that life.

Listen

Slow life down long enough to really listen to the musings and desires of your heart. You can do this by taking a long bath or a long walk, meditating or daydreaming, going for a swim or lying in the warm sun. Anything that stops the train of life long enough for you to breathe is a great way to hear the still, small voice within that is trying to tell you what your purpose is. What–ever you choose to do, do it with mindfulness and be sure to note down later any ideas, inspirations, or imagery that came to you, because it all holds clues.

One of the best ways to turn off the world and tune in to your inner self is through deep breathing. Sit comfortably and do some deep belly breaths. Focus your attention on the in hale and the exhale and let thoughts come and go without forcing them to stop or paying them too much attention. Your subconscious mind will be sure to store anything important for later, and you can always journal afterwards to capture anything of note. Right now, just breathe, and just be. Try to do this whenever you need a break from the busyness of life, but aim for at least three times a day and make it a daily prac-tice. This is how the inner voice makes itself known and tells you what you need to do next to fulfill your dreams, goals, and purpose.

The inner voice also speaks through symbolism via images, songs, phrases, synchronicities, and surprises that occur through–out your day, so pay attention and listen for the whispers of the divine spirit inside you. It may not be as loud as your conscious mind is, but it usually has a lot more of value to tell you.

Make a Boat–Float List

What did you love doing as a child? Why did you abandon it? Perhaps it is time to rediscover that joyful sense of play and apply it to your life today.

Make a list of things you loved to do as a child. Make a list of things you currently love to do. See any repeat offenders? They hold the key to a possible purpose. Is there a way to make a living doing them? What could you see yourself doing even if you didn't get paid for it?

Identify what floats your boat and why. Your passions might also contain the seeds of your purpose, or they might just be stuff you love to do now and then. You'll know. You can rate each one from 1 to 10 in order of boat–floating intensity. The magic of making lists is that something will usually jump out at you from that list and demand to be seen, heard, or attended to. If that happens, explore even further where that passion might lead to a purposeful goal.

One Year

If you had the gift of one whole year to spend any way you'd like, with all your bills and expenses paid for, what would you do? Where would you be? Who would you be with? We tend to factor the need to make money and pay bills into our purpose, and unless your means of doing so is also your passion in life, it is doubtful that that is how you really want to spend your time and energy.

Imagine 365 days of pure freedom with nothing in the way of finances to worry about. Everything you need is taken care of in terms of food, shelter, and basic necessities. You can spend that year doing anything you want, pursuing any passion you desire. Write down everything that comes to mind and put an asterisk next to the things that really set your heart on fire. They will be indicators of your purpose.

For example, you might list bungee jumping, traveling to the Amazon forest, and whitewater rafting in the Rockies. Is there a pattern or link between these desires that might translate into a deeper passion and a possible purpose? Maybe your passion is adventure travel. Maybe your purpose is to start a blog or video blog of traveling around the world on various adventures. Maybe you can combine the two and start your own adventure travel company.

This is a great exercise for excavating the desires we have that we might be suppressing or putting off for another time because we are so consumed with making a living. There are clues here. Explore them.

The Magic of Creativity and Imagination

Everything you can imagine is real.

Pablo Picasso

To practice any art, no matter how well or how badly, is a way to make your soul grow.

Kurt Vonnegut

Imagination is everything. It is the preview of life's coming attractions.

Albert Einstein

Creativity. Imagination. What is the first thing you think of when you hear these two words? Purely in the definition, creativity is the ability to generate and form from original ideas and use imagination to bring into being something that is physical or mental in property. Creativity comes from the necessity of solving a problem or bringing something to life. Some might argue against using the word "imagination" as a part of it. Assumptions about how creativity works play a large part in this attitude.

Often imagination is looked upon with a lightness that can border on dismissive. After all, when we are children, we are boundlessly creative, but by the time we reach adulthood we may believe the time for creativity and play is over. We may have been scolded at home and in school about daydreaming and told that coloring pictures outside the lines was childish and silly. Maybe we even were told we couldn't make the sky pink and the sun green. Our inherent and innate desires to imagine and to create were dampened and dismissed by the people around us who had lost their ability to imagine and create.

We abandoned creativity because we harbor acknowledged or unacknowledged beliefs that adults "shouldn't" be creative but logical and constrained. Sometimes we do not even understand that in many cases logic doesn't have to be thrown out in order to use creativity and imagination. It's as if we must choose one over the other and we can never go back and forth from logical pursuits to creative endeavors because it might disrupt the balance of the planet itself, even though we have the capacity for both (thus why we have a right brain and a left brain).

Yet there is another subset of internal beliefs that can derail creativity.

We think we aren't creative because we are not an artist, painter, sculptor, singer, actor, or writer, as if those labels alone de-

People make the mistake of thinking that creativity only applies to the arts, such as writing, painting, music, etc. Actually, creativity has its place in all types of areas, even in business, politics, and economics.

Everyday Magic

fine what it means to create. We all have an imagination, and we are all creative if we allow ourselves to be. How that creativity manifests can be in countless ways. Lest we think developing problem-solving abilities is only for kids, adults can grow their capabilities as well, if they tap into some of the childlike elasticity and willingness to pursue and think about things with an open mind.

IN THE BEGINNING

Early on, a child's creativity can give parents, a childcare provider, or a teacher an opportunity to understand what the child is thinking or perhaps feeling. Children do not always understand what they are feeling in clinical terms, but they may be able to act it out in their creativity.

Denise's Sidenote: I vividly recall a time when I took a baby doll and treated it very harshly. It's obvious there was some big anger going on there. What that anger was, I don't recall. I just know I was intent on giving this baby doll the "what for!" An adult looking at that would probably have to wonder what was going on in my young mind.

Children who are given an opportunity to play and create are also developing problem-solving abilities, as well as other important things such as gross and fine motor skills.

Adults can support this creativity by encouraging children to read, join in art projects, explore the outdoors, and ask questions. Allowing a kid to take the lead in their play, rather than taking over as an adult, can be a huge way to generate creativity in the child. Adults often have the temptation to instruct and guide, and while there has to be some of that, we can often overdo it. Time constraints and frustration can encourage the adult to take over and show a child how to do something even if it means the child misses an opportunity to be creative and learn self-reliance, self-esteem, and self-worth.

We've all laughed at the scenario where the three-year-old goes on a "why" rampage of asking why about everything. The fact that the child is asking why a lot is a reason to celebrate. True, some children might do it to get attention and/or annoy an adult, but many times it is a genuine desire to understand the world. Curious kids can prove to be wonderfully intelligent and creative adults.

Another childhood creative outlet is doodling, and who hasn't gotten busted in school for drawing stars and moons and bunnies and cars on their notepaper when they should have been paying attention to the teacher? Doodling, ironically, is a fantastic way to entertain our creative right brains while allowing our intellectual left brains to focus more on the task at hand. Doodling is productive and meditative, much like doing a jigsaw puzzle or crossword, and allows us to process information. It also has a calming effect that relieves symptoms of anxiety by refocusing our fearful and anxious monkey mind onto drawing a house with two chimneys or an intricate pattern of circles and lines.

Adults in our world can choose to stifle the tools of creativity and the imagination or they can choose to use those tools to help the world grow. Even if an adult attempts to block this creativity, it is often within the child to continue to imagine and create within their own heads. There is no way to stop it if a child wishes to continue with that process.

YOU ARE CREATIVE, TOO. YES. YOU ARE.

Just because you're an adult working a 9 to 5 job doesn't mean you have to be boring! Everyone has creativity within them. You just need to figure out a way to let it out. Toss out your inhibitions and let yourself fly!

Some people believe creativity belongs to only some humans. That mysterious person who just has what it takes. Yet everyone is imaginative and creative. The degree of imagination and creativity can vary, but it is boundless to all who wish to utilize and find it and who are not afraid of allowing themselves to engage in daydreams and wild imaginings and creating things that did not exist before.

A child or adult must believe in the first place that there are any number of possibilities in the world.

Without this willingness, there is little creativity. Some will argue that constraint can bring about creativity. This can also be true. Perhaps it means a person works harder to find that creativity. The bottom line is the desire of the individual to recognize and understand possibilities and have the belief that it is good to venture in mind and action toward creating the new.

LEFT BRAIN OR RIGHT BRAIN?

We've all heard of the theory of right brain and left brain, which says the store of creativity is in the right brain and the logic process in the left. This theory has been somewhat debunked in recent years in some research avenues. As with many things, there are differing opinions.

In "Why Creativity and Analysis Aren't Mutually Exclusive," a July 22, 2016, posting on *TechnologyAdvice.com*, author Zach Watson says there is a fallacy in business and technology sectors of dividing people's abilities in this way. He quotes Dr. Jeff Anderson of the University of Utah as saying, "It is absolutely true that same

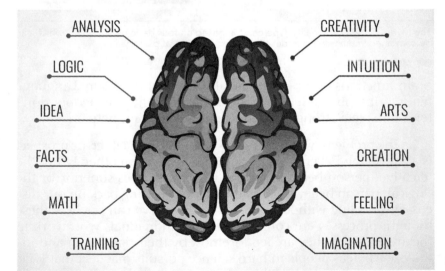

ANALYSIS   CREATIVITY
LOGIC   INTUITION
IDEA   ARTS
FACTS   CREATION
MATH   FEELING
TRAINING   IMAGINATION

Describing people as being either left- or right-brained is misleading. Sure, it seems that the right side of our gray matter leans to the creative and the artistic, while the left side is more analytic and objective, but it doesn't mean we're all one or the other. You might *lean* toward one of these, but you still have both sides.

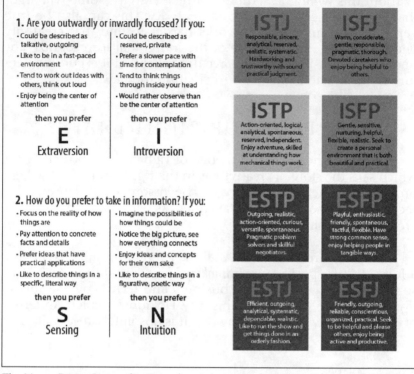

The Myers–Briggs Personality Type chart is based on four basic dichotomies, which can be combined in many ways to describe a broad range of personalities.

brain functions occur in one or other side of the brain. Language tends to be on the left, attention on the right. But people don't tend to have a stronger left–or–right–sided brain network."

The problem with looking at creativity as an either–or prospect is a prevailing belief in the virtue of one over the other. Either the "creative" person believes their way of thinking is superior, or the "logical" person believes theirs is superior. Looking back on our discussions dealing with logic versus intuition, we can see how these thought processes are connected. Many individuals who work in the arts may feel they are led foremost by their right brain and intuition, whereas people in hard science pursuits may feel that logic and the left brain provide the correct way to do their job effectively.

Regardless of all this, if we explore our own brains/minds and how we believe they work, most of us can identify and ac-

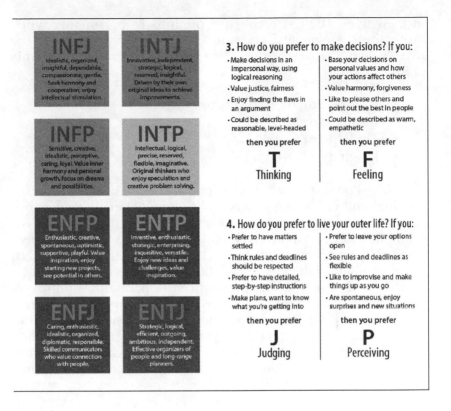

INFJ
Idealistic, organized, insightful, dependable, compassionate, gentle. Seek harmony and cooperation, enjoy intellectual stimulation.

INTJ
Innovative, independent, strategic, logical, reserved, insightful. Driven by their own original ideas to achieve improvements.

INFP
Sensitive, creative, idealistic, perceptive, caring, loyal. Value inner harmony and personal growth, focus on dreams and possibilities.

INTP
Intellectual, logical, precise, reserved, flexible, imaginative. Original thinkers who enjoy speculation and creative problem solving.

ENFP
Enthusiastic, creative, spontaneous, optimistic, supportive, playful. Value inspiration, enjoy starting new projects, see potential in others.

ENTP
Inventive, enthusiastic, strategic, enterprising, inquisitive, versatile. Enjoy new ideas and challenges, value inspiration.

ENFJ
Caring, enthusiastic, idealistic, organized, diplomatic, responsible. Skilled communicators who value connection with people.

ENTJ
Strategic, logical, efficient, outgoing, ambitious, independent. Effective organizers of people and long-range planners.

3. How do you prefer to make decisions? If you:

- Make decisions in an impersonal way, using logical reasoning
- Value justice, fairness
- Enjoy finding the flaws in an argument
- Could be described as reasonable, level-headed

then you prefer

T
Thinking

- Base your decisions on personal values and how your actions affect others
- Value harmony, forgiveness
- Like to please others and point out the best in people
- Could be described as warm, empathetic

then you prefer

F
Feeling

4. How do you prefer to live your outer life? If you:

- Prefer to have matters settled
- Think rules and deadlines should be respected
- Prefer to have detailed, step-by-step instructions
- Make plans, want to know what you're getting into

then you prefer

J
Judging

- Prefer to leave your options open
- See rules and deadlines as flexible
- Like to improvise and make things up as you go
- Are spontaneous, enjoy surprises and new situations

then you prefer

P
Perceiving

knowledge our personal preference to use one or the other approach to "thinking." How about you? Do you lean toward logic and left-brain thinking or intuition and right-brain thinking?

There are few people who do not utilize creativity in some way, even if it is not recognizable to the individual or to outsiders looking at what the person is doing. We most certainly use both sides of our brain even if we tend to prefer to use one side more than the other sometimes. One test that has been used over the years to give individuals an understanding of their minds is the Myers–Briggs test. In this test the right–brain/left–brain controversy is played out in discovery of brain preferences. In other words, how do you like to do and process things?

Many of the tenets and theories surrounding Myers–Briggs are based on the studies of Swiss psychiatrist Carl Jung. This test, in simplistic terms, explains how people tend to prefer to interact in their lives. The test breaks people into 16 personality types. (Note: these personality types are also used by Socionics and the Keirsey Temperament Sorter.) The types are determined by a mix of four qualities: .

- Introversion or Extraversion
- Intuition or Sensing
- Thinking or Feeling
- Judging or Perceiving

Based on responses to questions answered in the test, an individual will fall within a personality type. Along with the personality types there are variations in strength of preference. For example, a person who is INFJ tends to deal with life on the spectrum of Introversion, Intuition, Feeling, and Judging. Within each of these qualities there is a scale of strength. Someone might be an INFJ with a very strong preference to operate from introversion, intuition, and feeling. Perhaps the judging part of their personality is more balanced with the perceiving side of them, but the judging part is strong enough to show a preference. Hence, they are a J rather than P because of this preference. This does not mean the INFJ person is never extroverted, sensing, thinking, or perceiving.

An introversion approach describes someone who would prefer working alone and may find frequent exposure to people and the outside world draining. They are thought–oriented. An extraverted person is more likely to enjoy working around and with people, energized by and engaging in more frequent social events. As a result, they are generally more action oriented. An INFJ may go with their gut and trust intuitive perception more than a thinking approach. A thinking approach lends itself toward logic and "just the facts." An INFJ may approach life with the desire to do something based on judging rather than perceiving. The judging part says, "I judge this to be worthy" and may take a considered, cautious approach to a person, place, or thing based on those judgments. Someone who leans more heavily toward perceiving can be more spontaneous and laid–back in their approach to the same person, place, or thing.

None of these "letters" are inherently better or worse. They are simply preferences for dealing with and interacting with the world. Some of the types are rarer. INFJ is considered to be the rarest.

What does this have to do with creativity? There is a larger tendency for people with a preference for the INF profile to be artistic and creatively motivated individuals. This is not across the board, but it is prevalent.

FORGET THE FEAR: LIFELONG CREATIVITY

Creative people must create, or the host of mental and physical problems that come from denying their creativity can be enormous. Creative truth is surrendering to the understanding that for some creativity is vital to physical and mental health. Creative people often talk themselves into a restrictive box filled with "shoulds." Some creative truths that are vital for lifelong creativity are:

- Any impulse to create should always be honored.

- Stifling creativity because of outside expectations is often damaging to free expression.

- Individuals must discover which creative method motivates them and recognize there is no wrong way to create.

- Acknowledging a childlike desire to play (have recess, if you will) usually results in joyful creation.

- Problems with inspiration begin when you talk yourself out of being who you are as a creator.

- Refilling the creative well often gives the creative individual what they need to boost them over any roadblock.

- Creating what you believe is interesting and meaningful is top priority. Creating what someone else deems worthy will eventually be unsatisfying.

ENGAGING IN THE "AWE-SOME"

In order to be creative, we must imagine because what we seek to create may only exist in our minds. To envision something and then make it real, whether it's a painting or a poem, we have to be able to experience a sense of awe that opens us to the possibilities of what only exists, for the moment, in the depths of our minds.

When we feel awe and wonder, which is the magic of life itself, we are straddling the fence of what we know exists and what we hope to one day manifest or see come into existence. It's the line that divides the reality we are living in with imagined worlds and alternate realities that our minds create and embellish. Without a sense of awe, without being able to wonder, we cannot imagine that which does not yet exist.

Awe cannot be forced, but it can be cultivated, and one of the best ways to do that also increases our ability to be creative. Daydreaming is taking time to remove ourselves from the world at hand and enter a world we wish were at hand, to imagine something that is not yet real, and to envision an experience we have not yet had. Daydreams, unlike the dreams we have at night, are perfectly under our control and we can be anyone, do anything, and go anywhere our minds can take us because we are not bound by the laws of physics or external rules. If we want to daydream we are eagles, we can. If we want to daydream we are race-car drivers, nothing stops us.

To daydream is to escape the real world for a time and indulge in a fantasy land of what we feel the world could or should be.

Daydreaming is unlimited and opens the doorway through which our imaginations can enter realms far beyond the confines of day-to-day living. In our daydreams we may come up with amazing and creative ideas or solutions. We may determine that our goals are no longer the same and set about creating new goals. We may realize that the desires of our hearts are much closer than we first thought. So much is possible when we daydream.

AUTHOR INSIGHTS

Denise's Story

Imagination is a rich resource for our well–being on every level, but most of us don't know it. From the time I was a little kid I've been plugged into my imagination, and it has never stopped for me. It's like breathing air. I don't know how to *not* use my imagination. My imagination wasn't hamstrung by my parents, so early on it was extremely easy for me to enjoy my own imagination. Another advantage is that I grew up in an age where there was no internet and only four TV channels (where I lived in particular). It was a rural setting, and there were no cell phones or personal computers. This isn't to say that I think people should return to decades in the past and lack of resources, only that it made it easier to tap into imagination at that time. Even before I took pencil and pen to paper, my mind was already designing stories in my head.

> *My imagination wasn't hamstrung by my parents, so early on it was extremely easy for me to enjoy my own imagination.*

My guess is that a lot of kids do, but somewhere along the way that desire to use imagination is ignored and perhaps even short–circuited by the messages children receive about the value of imagination. This ability isn't just for us artsy types; it is also a powerful component for children who lean into sciences. That kid who dreams of building rockets to go to Mars? The one who goes beyond string theory or designing a huge skyscraper? She might be the one who actually does it if her imagination is encouraged from the time she is a child.

Marie's Story

As a single mom who worked over a hundred hours a week while also caring for my homebound child full time, I had very little energy left in my days for things like awe and wonder. My son had been in a wheelchair for months after a botched pre–surgical procedure, following years of surgeries and treatments for a disability, and with chronic stomach pain that also kept him un–

able to go to "real" school. Instead, he was home with me every day taking online charter classes while I worked in the next room of the condo we rented.

My son had tons of physical problems since birth, but now and then he could walk fairly well and was able to get out and enjoy life and be a normal kid. He was obsessed with *Star Wars* for a time and wanted to go to Comic–Con, which takes place in San Diego every year. I knew he was feeling pretty good but wondered if he could handle all the walking, as he had a very pronounced limp. He did not want to take his walker and agreed to only go for as long as his legs would hold out.

We rode the trolley to the Convention Center and began the trek to get to the entrance and register inside. I could see my son was struggling, but he was so excited because he had on his *Star Wars* costume and mask and kids were stopping him to say hi. He was in heaven. Once we got inside, it was a full–on assault of costumes and cosplayers, and many of them were in *Star Wars* regalia.

San Diego Comic-Con is the largest pop-culture convention in the world, a place full of fantasy, imagination, and wonder for all ages. But you don't have to go to a comic book convention to experience such wonder. Just stop and look around you.

Everyday Magic

We stayed for four hours, which at the time was pretty amazing considering my son's challenges. He had a blast. Despite the heat in the exhibition hall, he refused to take off his costume or his helmet. Because his limp was bad, recovering from surgery, people generously made space for him to get through the crowd, always complimenting his awesome costume.

I watched as he soaked in sights and sounds of the massive science fiction and comic book convention as if he were standing at the gates of heaven. For a kid who dreamed at the time of one day creating his own video games, he was, indeed, in heaven. I kept asking him if he felt okay, if he wanted to sit down and rest, but he was a trouper and kept on going.

All around us, people milled, like a sea of costumed humanity. But at one point, my son stopped to watch a preview for an upcoming *Star Wars* animated show and was just transfixed. For that moment, he appeared to be in total awe, in a state of rapturous wonder that caught my breath, and luckily, was captured on film as I had the good sense to take a photograph.

Where had my own sense of awe and wonder gone? Why could I not ever just STOP and become enraptured by something in my environment, especially since we lived in the paradise that is Southern California?

> *Where had my own sense of awe and wonder gone? Why could I not ever just STOP and become enraptured by something in my environment...?*

I watched, becoming transfixed myself, but I was not watching the show preview. I was watching him—his eyes, his face—as he lost all sense of the ear-splitting noise and chaotic movement around him and enjoyed the present moment as I had seen few adults be able to do. He looked so ethereal that soon others stopped to watch him, smiling and nodding, as if they understood. People stood beside him, watching the preview, and he became a magnet for anyone who wanted to transcend reality for a moment and become daydream believers.

How to Live a Mindful, Meaningful, Magical Life

His imagination in those moments no doubt was taking him on his own adventures in space with the characters on the screen. I could almost sense him imagining he was manning a Millennium Falcon–style ship with an assortment of crazy aliens and a big Chewbacca sitting in the copilot seat, roaring and barking. He lost all sense of the space and time he was in and entered a place that I, as an adult, often struggled to access.

The realm of pure imagination.

The magic of make–believe.

We rode the trolley back to the car with huge smiles on our faces. I could tell he was exhausted and his legs hurt, but it didn't matter. He chattered on and on about all the amazing things he saw in the few hours we were there.

Today, each time I look at that photo, I feel a sense of that same awe and wonder myself when I look at his face and the way it glows, and I thank my son for slowing us down long enough that day to experience it together.

MAGICAL TIPS

Use Your Imagination/Connection with Nature

Combine some New Age or easy listening music with journaling to connect to nature.

When we see children at play, we see something that adults internalize as "childish." They think they can't connect or shouldn't connect with this childhood element in adulthood. Or as adults we might think of play as participating in sports. While participating in sports is a great way to generate good physical and mental health, what can someone do if they aren't into or capable of physical play? You can take up a hobby that excites you, and this is an excellent idea, but there is also an additional way you can generate feelings of well-being through imagination. This process can be easy or a little complicated, depending on how far you wish to venture into your imagination.

The easiest method requires pen or pencil, paper, and music. Yes, be sure it is an old-fashioned pen or pencil and paper. No cheating with a computer or other electronic device where you can write notes. If you have a phone or other electronic device that has music on it, you can certainly use that for the music. Even if you aren't a big listener of classical or New Age/easy listening music, go on a hunt for music that is interesting or peaceful to you. Make certain there are no lyrics (unless you pick something like a Gregorian chant). Settle in a room or space where you won't be disturbed. You can use headphones to listen to the music if you wish. Listen to this music for a few minutes. Note any images or thoughts this music brings to mind.

Write down these images. Go freeform without regard to what the images might mean. Think of it as a way to free your imagination. Most anyone can do this. The point of the exercise? To prove to yourself that you have an imagination.

Oracle Cards

Whether or not you believe that oracle cards can enlighten you about everyday personal matters, they can help you tap into intuition and your creative center. If a project is giving you fits, snag an oracle deck. Whatever questions or concerns you are wrestling with in relation to a creative project, write them down.

Shuffle the cards and select three cards from various spots in the deck. Turn over each card and note the symbolism in them. Does anything jump out to you? If it does,

Oracle cards are different from tarot cards in that the cards are much less structured than in tarot; they may have a wider range of meaning, and you are not limited by the usual 78 cards found in tarot.

write it down. Do this with each of the three cards. Afterward, consult the book that comes with the deck and look up the listed meaning for each card. If there is other wisdom contained within the book for the meaning behind each card, also write this down. Often you will find a new kernel of inspiration each time you use the cards.

Discover Your Negative Belief Points: Countering the Negative and Creating a Benevolent Self

You don't have to be a painter, sculptor, or writer to allow negative belief points to keep you from completing any type of project. Remember what it feels like when your creative juices are flowing. You're rolling along, and the sensation is so fantastic it's better than a slice of cake. When creativity is working well, you feel like you're on top of the world. Yet, when you're not creating consistently, or when you're not rolling along, negative feelings can start, initiating a downward spiral that makes it that much harder to create.

While not everyone's life is the same ... you can take concrete steps to identify the thoughts and beliefs in your life that are impacting and sabotaging your creative journey.

Few people take time to notice how their current thoughts influence their creative ability. While it is impossible to stay positive every minute of the day, the amount of negativity you introduce into your thoughts will directly impact your mood.

Maybe you start to get anxious. Angry. Depressed. The variety of reactions can range far and wide. Most of the time it isn't the outside world making your creative journey difficult. Often what you're thinking about and how you're reacting to it, or how you feel about creating, can mean the difference between creating one day or not, or having success or frustrations.

Creative people can spend as much time thinking of ways not to create as they can spend creating. While not everyone's life is the same and the issue is complex, you can take concrete steps to identify the thoughts and beliefs in your life that are impacting and sabotaging your creative journey. Creative people tend to be hard on themselves *all* the time. We dredge up perceived faults we have against our creative abilities one after the other and beat ourselves bloody.

What if you could call on a benevolent and confident self (call it your future self if you like) to get you through any negative self-talk? What if you could journal your way from negative thinking that tanks your creativity toward an encouraging and confident self that uplifts your creativity?

If you've journaled before, take a quick peek at it. Did you fill it with a plethora of negative highlights, such as what didn't go right or your judgments about and grievances with yourself and others? Journaling like this might relieve the pressure, and in some cases it can free up your creativity. In Julia Cameron's *The Artist's Way*, she encourages writers to start their morning with stream-of-consciousness writing. The idea is to get down all of your gunk, good or otherwise and without censoring or holding back. Many writers have gained perspective and benefit from this technique. The process of letting it all out can open our eyes.

For some writers, journaling what isn't working for them is enough. Often the barriers we place on our writing abilities come from childhood experiences or other situations through life where something went wrong. Getting it out helps, as we assume that the same type of negative thing will occur again—and sometimes it does, but we can be better prepared.

However, beyond that is our own internal thought process where, if we focus on the negatives, we often then only see the negatives in everything, and we repeat negative patterns and belief systems in an endless cycle. It's a self-fulfilling prophecy. We say we can't. So we don't.

To reverse this, we should step into our power and create a benevolent self that can flip the negative thinking. One way to do this is journaling.

If you don't already have a journal, now is the time to grab one specific for this assignment. Find one that appeals to you in color/fabric/material and paper. Use a favorite pen or buy a new one to use just for this journal. This can pump up your enthusiasm to stick with it.

Below are journal prompts designed to open your mind to new creative possibilities. Take as much time and as many pages as needed to thoroughly explore each of these possibilities and questions.

- What negative things do you tell yourself most frequently about your creative abilities?
- Are there similarities between the negative things?
- Where and when did you get these ideas about your ability to create? Don't be shy. Lay it all out here. You may not have taken much time to think about these things before, so don't be surprised if it takes a while to pinpoint them.
- What are the patterns you see? Are these things someone else told you about your abilities or things you assumed entirely on your own?

Now that you have some idea of the negative beliefs about your writing that bother you, let's work on the one that bothers you the

most. Of the negative things you've listed, is there one that sticks out to you as the most painful? Highlight that. Then you will ask, is it actually true? How do you know it isn't true? Would you say this to a close friend?

Now that you've highlighted the one negative, let's analyze the truth of it. Let's work through the process using this example: I can't write at all.

Do you tell yourself negative things about your creative abilities? Writing down just what they are might help you to overcome this obstacle to success.

With the highlighted negative thing you've told yourself, answer the following question:

- Is it actually true? No, it isn't true that I can't write.

- How do you know it isn't true? Because I have written and published books.

- Would you say these things to a close friend? No, I wouldn't. In fact, I think it is horrible to say to my friend that she can't write, because it isn't true. I'd be angry at anyone for saying this to my friend.

When it is apparent that your negative belief is most likely not true and why, it can help you attack each negative belief you have with regard to your creativity.

Go back through each negative you wrote and ask/answer the questions for each one. Is it actually true? How do you know it isn't true? Would you say these things to a friend?

Now there is one more step to take, which is to take the negative things that bothered you and shift this thinking. What would a benevolent, loving self say to you? Basically, turn that negative into a positive.

Example: I can't write at all.

Benevolent self: I am a talented writer with many stories to tell. I'm particularly good at telling XYZ type of stories.

Example: I can't write historical fiction because it is hard to write, and I was never any good at research.

Benevolent self: I love reading historical nonfiction. It fascinates me. Knowing that, I'd find reading research on the time period I want to write extremely interesting. I can research the time period and facts I find intriguing with ease.

If you have difficulty getting to an uplifting statement, go for a middle ground that is neutral such as, "I enjoy writing stories. XYZ stories intrigue me the most." This neutral ground points out to you that you enjoy writing and what you want to write, which is more encouraging and not a negative.

Dream a Little Dream

Take some time to daydream for 15 minutes a day. Let your mind wander to where it seeks to go, and do not stop or censor the journey of your imagination during the process. Dream big, dream wild, dream crazy. Then write down your daydream and any nuggets of wisdom or creative inspiration that came to you during or afterwards. If you have children, encourage them to daydream and write down their thoughts. Let them know how important imagination and creativity are to live a full, happy life, and never scold them for sharing their own dreams with you. It's a privilege when someone shares their dreams and imaginings with you.

Don't be afraid to daydream because others will judge you or say you are wasting time. You don't have to tell anyone what you are doing.

Don't be afraid to daydream because others will judge you or say you are wasting time. You don't have to tell anyone what you are doing. If once a day is challenging, start with twice a week. Note any ideas or inspirations that come to you even in the following days and weeks as your mind merges your dreams with your logical goals and comes up with all sorts of cool ideas you had never thought of before. How could that be a waste of time?

Night dreams hold a lot of wisdom, too, and can spark the imagination and creativity. Write them down upon waking and review them later to look for patterns or repeating imagery that jumps out at you.

Dreams are as important as reality, because if you think about it, everything starts out first as a thought or a dream or a creative urging in the mind before becoming manifest in the physical world. Without daydreams and imaginings, we would never have any new inventions or gadgets or movies or television shows. There would be no new books written or stories told, no new buildings erected, no cures for diseases or treatments for medical conditions. Stop for a moment and think about all that would be missing from your world if someone out there had not been creative or imaginative enough to come up with a method, service, or product that offered a new way of doing things or a solution to things that did not work.

Life would be awfully bland and boring if we did not ever dream up new dreams of what could be or act on them by creating something no one ever thought possible before. Over 100 years ago, people could only imagine that one day they could talk into little boxes to people across the globe, or send text messages, or work on computers and laptops, or stream movies 24/7 whenever they wanted to watch something.

We are driven to create, and our imaginations are where we generate the ideas behind those creations.

The Magic of Miracles

Infuse your life with action. Don't wait for it to happen. Make it happen. Make your own future. Make your own hope. Make your own love. And whatever your beliefs, honor your creator, not by passively waiting for grace to come down from upon high, but by doing what you can to make grace happen … yourself, right now, right down here on Earth.

Bradley Whitford

I do not at all understand the mystery of grace—only that it meets us where we are but does not leave us where it found us.

Anne Lamott

Miracles, in the sense of phenomena we cannot explain, surround us on every hand: life itself is the miracle of miracles.

George Bernard Shaw

THE MAGIC OF AN OPEN DOOR

Grace is one of those hard–to–define states that you know when you experience it, yet when asked to describe it you fall short. Grace often gets grouped with miracles because they both involve a mysterious, profound divine or otherworldly interven–

tion. Some people believe that grace is the force that opens the door through which a miracle enters.

Grace is often associated with religion. In Christianity we talk of God's grace bestowed on lowly spirits to lift them up in hope and in strength. The Old and New Testaments of the Bible are filled with references to grace. "For the grace of God has appeared, bringing salvation to all men" (Titus 2:11) is one example. Catholics pray "Hail Mary, full of grace" to the mother of Jesus, who loved unconditionally and sacrificed everything for the greater good of the world.

The concept of grace exists in most major religious or spiritual traditions, such as *kripa* in Hinduism or the Buddhist concept of "merit," which refers to the power of good karma that builds over time through meditation, effort, and spiritual practices. In Judaism, it is *chesed*, which means loving–kindness and mercy.

In Wicca there is the concept of power of the individual to bring things about in their own lives and/or for those who wish assistance. Even in that, there is the concept of God (not the Christian God) and Goddess as two sides of a higher power/force. If someone is drawn to a particular deity or deities and works with them most often, they may find magical workings proving more fruitful and may see any grace as a generous flow of positive energy and results by appealing to the deity. Or they may see the positive flow of results equally attributed to the source of their power within. There is a combined effort in the willingness of the deity and the power you own as an individual. Christopher Penczak says in his book *The Inner Temple of Witchcraft: Magick, Meditation and Psychic Development*: "When I say witchcraft is a spirituality, I mean it is a spiritual path. You walk it for nourishment of the soul, to commune with the life force of the universe, and to thereby better know your own life." And if you are brought closer to understanding yourself, you are bringing a force for good to you and those around you.

The concept of God's Grace is key in Christianity but also in many other religions and beliefs across the globe.

Many New Age practitioners, whether they adhere to a particular organized religion or not, may recognize an equivalent in the concept of alignment of body and spirit and a recognition that things work for them in a marvelous (if not 100% predictable) way when this alignment is flowing. There may also be the idea/concept/belief of natural divine power residing in Gaia (the Earth) and Mother Nature as a whole. If one knows that Mother Nature cannot specifically and totally be controlled and will do what she will, we are more likely to accept that lack of control and creatively see how we might accept and work with such a divine and powerful force.

Many Native American/First Nation cultures believe a higher power to be the Great Spirit. Some consider the Great Spirit to be both male and female yet one divine force. With 574 recognized tribes, there is a true diversity of beliefs. Within that framework is the concept of the connection of all things in nature, including humans, who are not separate from nature.

Knowing there are so many varieties of approaches toward grace, is there anything specific we can say about it? We could look at grace as a universal force that brings fruitfulness into our own lives despite our mistakes, sins, and misfortunes. In some recovery programs, grace is seen as the presence of a higher power needed to help achieve and maintain sobriety. Addicts and alcoholics surrender to this power because they have not been able to get sober of their own accord despite their many attempts. They set ego aside and give themselves over because nothing else has worked. They open the door to grace.

We sing "Amazing Grace" to give thanks for this enigmatic force through which some part of us is saved from the world and from ourselves. We call someone gracious when they extend a supportive hand to us or show us kindness. We say,

First Nation cultures believe in the Great Spirit, which is both male and female in a manner similar to Wiccan beliefs.

228 The Magic of Miracles

"There but for the grace of God go I" when we hear of a friend who is suffering hardship or see a homeless person begging for food.

Someone who is graceful is described as light on their feet, walking with angelic, ethereal movement, or as having a gentle and nurturing manner. Grace isn't clunky like wisdom. Wisdom can come as a stumble or a gut-punch as easily as it can a quiet "aha" moment. Grace doesn't stumble or punch. It flows and caresses the spirit.

Perhaps grace is being touched by the hand of the divine, however you choose to describe or define the divine. In her book *Happy for No Reason*, Marci Shimoff wrote about a great spiritual mentor of hers named Bill Bauman, a former priest who once told her that grace "is just a fancy word for the infinite, unconditional, all-responsive love of God flowing in our lives." Like the unconditional love a mother has for her child, flaws and all, the mother wants nothing more than to give and give and give. If you don't believe in God or Goddess, replace that word with life force, higher power, inner spirit, or whatever suits you best. It all means the same thing.

Bauman told Shimoff that the best way to allow grace into our lives is this: "By practicing surrender. Look for opportunities to be open to blessings, without defining too clearly what they should be, and then trust and let go." Having an "I'm in charge" mindset could impede grace by putting up obstacles and blocks to that free flow. Our Higher Power, he continued, will respond only when we are open to the flow of grace when it comes.

This concept echoes the idea of generating creativity and how, if we erect too many rules in how that fine art painting is going to work or outline too much of the story we're writing, we might miss the creative spark that can come through releasing hard-core expectation and allowing an answer to come to us out of our internal creativity and wisdom.

If we are pedantic on the subject, we might think that allowing things to happen goes against the concept of alignment or intentions. In truth, having intentions about what is going to happen in your day increases your chances of those outcomes being possible. Having intentions doesn't mean constructing every aspect of how your day might look. Most likely you'll find "grace" happens because you made the intentions and then noted that if that grace didn't look a certain way, it might come another way and still fulfill your intention.

For magic to occur in our lives, we'd be wise to allow it to come without putting up fences and walls of "this is how it must look" and "I only want this specific thing." It sounds simple yet is one of the hardest things for us control–hungry humans to do. We hate to let go and let God/Goddess/Higher Power take the wheel. Marianne Williamson wrote in her seminal book *Everyday*

Marianne Williamson is a former spiritual leader for the Unity Church, is a bestselling author of self-help books, and a former spiritual advisor to Oprah Winfrey.

Grace: Having Hope, Finding Forgiveness, and Making Miracles that "The door to God swings open at the slightest knock." How many of us are too arrogant, controlling, or afraid to knock in the first place, or we knock and then demand it open in our timing? When it doesn't, we lose all faith and trust and take back the reins of control, which rarely ends well.

Williamson continued, "The portal that takes us from the hysteria of the fear–based world to the peace and love of God is any moment of pure and sacred silence. It only takes one moment, perhaps one good deep breath, in which we inhale the love of God and exhale the madness of world." We can receive grace from our creator, in this silence where we are open and willing to let the light of love shine through and fill the dark places in us. That is the miracle of grace. It is an abstract thing, but we can bring it into our world through our own experience of it and become, as Williamson said, "agents of the sacred" bringing wisdom of the abstract into the realm of reality. It can happen in an instant and usually when we have given up or given in.

So, grace is our connection to and experience of the divine or the force of creation as we see it, and the allowance of it to flow in our lives and extend outward through our own spiritual

good works in the world. It is the energy of creation itself, bringing with it the magic and miracles of life especially at a time when
we might feel as though no magic or miracles exist, but only
when we open the door and let it come through. And if the door
closes, there will no doubt be a window that flies open at the
same time. If we are only focused on the door, demanding our
happiness or joy come through that door and that door alone,
we might never see the open window through which grace can
fly in and offer us even greater gifts.

> *That act of surrendering ... is what allows them*
> *to finally stop the workings of their*
> *dysfunctional ego and allow spirit to flow in*
> *them and through them.*

Like synchronicities and serendipities, we see the results of
grace but not the causes and understand that because we, too, are
divine, we have the power not only to receive grace but to give it
to others who need it. People tend to experience grace more often
when all hope seems lost because that is when they are more
likely to surrender and give up control of what they cannot control. That act of surrendering–that rock–bottom experience–is what
allows them to finally stop the workings of their dysfunctional ego
and allow spirit to flow in them and through them.

Ego isn't a friend to creativity or grace. Ego keeps our focus
off of the spirit and keeps us feeling separate from the divine or
creative force. Ego is driven by materialism and what we can see
and has little room for trust, and no room for surrender. Williamson wrote, "Listening to the ego–for whom separateness is not a
problem but a goal–we allow mental conflicts to separate our
hearts. This divides us not only from one another, but from the
experience of God." She refers to this as our exile from the Garden
of Eden. We become terrified, and in our willingness to see things
differently and give up the egoic control, we are able to welcome
grace into our lives. "Whatever we focus on is bound to expand.
Where we see the negative, we call forth more negative. And
where we see the positive, we call forth more positive."

You don't have to be suffering extreme pain or grieving a
loss to have grace enter your life, though suffering has a way of

Wicca is a spiritual belief focused on unifying the spirit with nature. It is possibly the fastest-growing religion in the United States today.

opening us up to things we might be closed off to, such as giving up control of the Universe. Grace can come to us any time we are fully and completely ready, willing, and able to get out of our own way and receive it. It could just ask us to shift our perspective or embrace a new one altogether. If we ask, it knocks, and we let it in.

The meaning of life. The wasted years of life. The poor choices of life. God answers the mess of life with one word: "grace."

Max Lucado

That perhaps is at the core of Wicca—it is a joyous union with nature. The earth is a manifestation of divine energy. Wicca's temples are flower-splashed meadows, forests, beaches, and deserts. When a Wiccan is outdoors, she or he is actually surrounded by sanctity, much as is a Christian when entering a church or cathedral.

Scott Cunningham, Wicca:
A Guide for the Solitary Practitioner

How to Live a Mindful, Meaningful, Magical Life

IT'S A MIRACLE!

Marianne Williamson wrote in *Everyday Grace* that there is only ever one problem: "That we are separated from the thinking of God ... Miracles can come from anything, anywhere, anytime. There is no situation that ties God's hands. He is bigger than lay-offs, or recessions, or stock market losses. Every ending is a new beginning. Through the grace of God, we can always start again."

As with grace, you don't have to be religious to believe in miracles. They are all around us when we have the eyes to see them with. A miracle is described in the American Heritage Dictionary as:

> An event that appears inexplicable by the laws of nature and so is held to be supernatural in origin or an act of God.
>
> One that excites admiring awe, a wonderful or amazing event, act, person, or thing.
>
> Synonym: wonder.
>
> A miracle play.

It is an act of divine intervention, an effect where we do not see the cause. It is magic because we feel like it came from something or someplace beyond ordinary, mundane reality. People from all walks of life believe in miracles and many have experienced them firsthand. From the family whose house burned down only to win the lottery and buy an even bigger house, to the woman with stage 4 breast cancer who wakes up one day in total remission, to the child who was told he could never walk who becomes a marathon runner, miracles happen all the time.

Because we cannot fathom or describe how they happen, we label them as something supernatural, above and beyond what is natural. They don't make sense or they come out of the blue, and we call them miraculous, even if we cannot see all the invisible machinations that led to their manifestation.

In the December 6, 2017, *HuffPost* article "How to Create More Miracles in Your Life," blogger and lifestyle writer Rachael Yahne described miracles as "a welcome and surprising result not explicable by science. By its very definition, miracles require that we welcome them into existence." Remember the definition of grace? Grace welcomes miracles in. Yahne adds that positive and happy miracles occur with our help and it all comes down to our energy and the mindset we create our reality with. That positive mindset "constantly works miracles to bring you what you want. In turn, this universe is so giving and loving, it gives just the reality you asked for with your beliefs. Life loves you that much."

It also helps to feel open to and worthy of miracles, so it's imperative we do the work of excavating old beliefs and blocks that keep us from feeling deserving of such wonderful, magical surprises. We are living today's reality based on the beliefs we had in the past, and it might be time to let some, if not all, of those beliefs hit the highway in favor of more empowering ones. The past is dead, and we can choose to not allow it to shape our future.

REGRETS BE GONE!

One of the biggest blocks to living a miracle-filled life is wallowing in past regrets. We waste so much time and energy trying to redo or fix the past and we will never succeed. It's done and gone, yet we allow ourselves to be anchored to it. It's dead weight that robs us of the present moment and the possibility of a more magical future.

Writer Victoria Holt once said, "Never regret. If it's good, it's wonderful. If it's bad, it's experience." All of the "if onlys" that plague us and steal our peace need to be reframed as powerful lessons and experiences that brought us wisdom and more grace, but only when we finally make the commitment to release them for good. We might still need to process some of the trapped emotions like sadness, grief, and re-

The regret we feel for things we've done in the past and cannot change can really set up a blockade to forward progress in our lives. Don't let regret bog you down. Learn from past mistakes and take them as growing experiences.

morse, but when we do, we see that they hold lessons for us on how to live better now that we know better.

The best way to live is with no regrets, to follow our bliss and go for our dreams. To live our wildest and best life so that when we are on our deathbeds, we feel like we are full and there's room for no more. We lived to the fullest and we loved to the fullest. But few of us can go through an entire lifetime never making a mistake or doing something stupid. If we want to invite miracles in, we must accept those mistakes and stupid moves and let them go because no matter how hard we try, we cannot bend time and go back for a do-over.

Miracles need fertile soil to grow and bloom. A mind and heart filled with regret over the past is not fertile and will not bear fruit. Do some inner work if you need to, or talk with a therapist or close friend, and bring those regrets to the surface where they are exposed to the light of day. Then, accept them as they are, thank them for the lessons they imparted, and say good-bye. Remember, when the past comes calling, don't answer. It has nothing to say to you.

THE MAGIC OF WISDOM

Processing regrets creates more wisdom. Lucky for you, the key to recognizing grace and miracles in life is wisdom. Otherwise, we might miss the magic because we are focused elsewhere. Wisdom comes from experiencing life. It is knowledge, but not brain smarts or even street smarts. It's the kind of smarts we get when we have survived and thrived, learned lessons, and attained a deeper understanding of ourselves and what it means to be alive. It is also, for many, linked to a stronger relationship with God or Source or spirit, and it gives our lives meaning and depth. We go through life with good times and bad times, but wisdom is the education we get from the bad times so we can learn from them and hopefully avoid them in the future.

Hopefully, an older person will possess wisdom because they've lived longer and experienced more, but it also comes to the young any time they experience something profound that teaches them a life lesson. Some believe that we acquire wisdom when we overcome some challenge or traumatic experience, but that is not always the case. Wisdom can come from happy times, too. A wise person may just be someone who is more alert and aware and who possesses more self-knowledge than others of the same age. We can be quite intelligent, yet not possess a lick of wisdom if we don't learn to incorporate past experiences and the lessons we learned from them into who we are and how we view the world in the present.

Wisdom often follows experience, which is why we typically consider older people to be wiser than the young, although that's not always the case.

The greatest wise men and women have always been those who have their eyes wide open, and that includes using their "inner vision" that allows them to see the bigger picture the rest of us may ignore.

RISING SUN WISDOM

Every new day is a miracle waiting to happen. We don't usually see that because we are too focused on all the stressors we brought over from yesterday and the worries we have about tomorrow. Rising sun wisdom asks that we look at each new dawn, when the sun is coming up again after a long, dark night, as a brand-new slate for magic and miracles.

Most people wait for a birthday or New Year's Day to start over with new goals, but there is no time like the present. Anything we want to do in life can be started at any moment. The first light of morning when the sun begins its ascent into the sky reminds us that we can experience a renewal and clear out the old energy of yesterday. As the sun's light increases and the rays warm our skin, we can move forward into the possibility that each day holds, making different choices than we did the day before, focusing our attention on the power we have in this new day to experience magic and wonder.

How to Live a Mindful, Meaningful, Magical Life

Honor the rising sun by getting up a few mornings a week and going outside to watch it move up over the eastern horizon. Let the light dissipate all darkness and fill your spirit with healing, love, joy, potentiality. If going outside is impossible because of the weather or where you live, find some screenshots for your phone to gaze upon or put a gorgeous sunset image on your desktop as a screensaver. Any reminder will do, including some bright orange and yellow fresh flowers to greet you upon waken.

If going outside is impossible because of the weather or where you live, find some screenshots for your phone to gaze upon or put a gorgeous sunset image on your desktop as a screensaver.

The sun rises, then sets, then rises again. So, too, do our lives, and with each new sunrise we can start all over and dream a new magical dream. Our coldest, most frigid winters are always followed by the magic of gentle spring and summer breezes and sunny afternoons. No matter how dark life seems, if we hold our focus on the light, we allow ourselves to be made new.

LIVE FOR TODAY, BUT PLAN FOR TOMORROW

It might sound contradictory to live in the moment or live for today and also make plans for the future. Which one is it? Live now? Plan for later? It's an age-old dilemma that often leaves us confused.

There is a fine balance between experiencing the joy of the present moment and also making goals and plans for the future. You might think of it this way: living is all about today; planning is all about tomorrow. The good decisions and goals we set today benefit our dreams coming true tomorrow, and there is no reason to be deprived of the joy of the moment stressing over all the things you want to achieve next year.

It seems like a choice between instant gratification and long-term happiness, and it is. You can gratify your instant desires without sacrificing your life goals as long as you always ask yourself if the choices you make today will affect the life you get to live tomorrow, then choose accordingly. It's like eating and exercising. You may decide today to eat a piece of cheesecake and plan tomorrow to work out a little extra, so this way you get to enjoy both. You are out of balance if you have a long–term goal of losing weight and yet you are eating an entire cheesecake every day. A good decision today is a good decision for the future.

In the fable "The Ant and the Grasshopper" the ant works hard all summer to save food for the winter, while the grasshopper enjoys the summer and starves in the winter. The real trick is to juggle the pleasures of the present with the wisdom of planning ahead.

EVERYTHING HAPPENS FOR YOU

Such a powerful shift occurs when you learn to look at the things that happen in your life as happening for you, not to you. This takes away the feeling of being a victim and places the power back in your court to take responsibility for how you will react and whether or not you can turn a difficulty into a miracle. Feeling as though life is happening to you makes you powerless to be in the driver's seat of your own destiny.

Miracles occur when we realize we are responsible for where we are in life right now and what we have around us. It is all the manifestation of past beliefs, actions, and responses and the awesome thing is, we get to make new choices and invite miracles in when we understand on a deep, gut level that we have so much say in how our lives unfold. Marci Shimoff and Dr. Sue Morter teach in their course Your Year of Miracles about allowing yourself to make choices from the place of what is possible for you, which gets you into your Miracle Zone, not from the place of lack and limitation. They point out that you can take responsibility for your life by being aware of how you give your power away via blaming, shaming, and complaining.

Becoming more aware of when you blame others, take on shame yourself, and complain about everything that isn't working opens the door to the Miracle Zone they teach about, where every day can be ripe with amazing possibility and potentiality. It's about changing how you show up in your life and aligning yourself with the flow of magic and blessings that are always available when we aren't actively blocking or disallowing them. Taking responsibility for your own power removes any need to point the finger of blame at others, especially when we are often projecting our own faults onto them. Sometimes those who blame the most are the most to blame for how their lives have turned out.

Taking responsibility is one of Five Foundations for Living in the Miracle Zone, the others being trusting in the Universe, living from the soul, choosing where to put your energy and attention, and leading with an open heart.

Louise Hay once said, "Be willing to take the first step, no matter how small it is. Concentrate on the fact that you are willing to learn. Absolute miracles will happen." Jack Canfield, the mastermind behind the *Chicken Soup for the Soul* franchise, called it living from this equation: $E + R = O$. Events plus response equals outcome. Events happen, we choose how to respond to them, and that manifests an outcome. We can choose miracles if we want to.

Jack Canfield (pictured) co-created the *Chicken Soup for the Soul* book series along with Mark Victor Hansen. Canfield is also the founder of the Foundation for Self-Esteem and of the Canfield Training Group.

It often comes down to where we focus our attention. We have a say in making miracles happen. Our energy aligns with the energy of the Universe through our thoughts, attention, and actions, and we can manifest miracles and change our lives. When we are out of alignment, miracles are blocked or suppressed until we clear our intentions and step back into our own power. A little faith goes a long way, too, to make miracles an everyday reality by extending our belief to include that which we cannot yet see.

Don't let the limits of your human mind keep you from the unlimited blessings of an abundant and creative Universe. Be open to surprises, however they look.

People reject miracles because they see so much suffering around them. How can you believe in a miracle when children are suffering and dying? Or when animals are abused? When families lose their homes in a natural disaster? We don't know the answer, except to say that miracles and grace both require trust in what we cannot know or see or touch. They require us to suspend our belief in reality being only what we can see, hear, smell, taste, and touch, and embrace the unknown mysteries of life. They ask us to see beyond physical reality to the unseen world where, as in quantum physics, all potentiality exists at once until observed into a fixed state. They demand that we accept life on its terms without regret over what was, while at the same time placing our intention on the life of our dreams, knowing that where we put our attention grows and expands.

We cannot explain why tragedy occurs, but we can trust that there is something behind it all, that life is not punishing anyone or singling anyone out for pain and suffering. There is a grander scheme underlying all things.

YOU ARE THE MIRACLE!

Do you know how your existence is itself a miracle? Your heart can pump over 2,000 gallons of blood around your body every day without you forcing it. Your eyes can discern more than 7 million color variations. Your skin can detect sensations and send information to the brain in a nanosecond. Your brain stores as much information as over 20,000 dictionaries. Your lungs know how to breathe in and out without your assistance. Just the fact that your father's sperm met your mother's egg amidst many obstacles and challenges is a miracle when you realize that there were anywhere from 40 to 150 million more sperm that didn't make the cut. But the one sperm that did made you as the unique individual you are.

You are a divine expression of the Universe wrapped in an individual package that is unlike any other on Earth.

In *Happy for No Reason*, Marci Shimoff urges us to "incline our mind toward joy" to experience more happiness. We have the

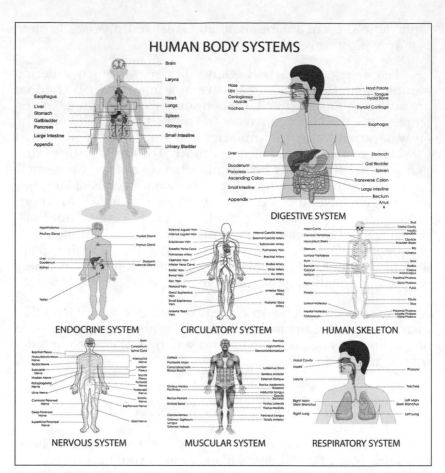

The human body is a mind-bogglingly complicated biological machine. It's truly a miracle, let alone the millions of years of evolution that resulted in our current species.

power to incline our mind in any direction we want. When we incline negative, we won't feel much joy. Our tendency, Shimoff suggests, is to make our brains "Teflon for positivity," which allows happiness to slide away. Instead, we can even the score by focusing on the good and become happier as a result.

Albert Einstein said, "There are only two ways to live your life: One is as though nothing is a miracle. The other is as though everything is a miracle."

Which will you choose?

Everyday Magic

AUTHOR INSIGHTS

Marie's Story

I am no stranger to the recovery world, having been through 12-step programs several times. The concept of grace plays a huge role in the success of an addict or alcoholic because without it, the person can never be free from the control of an ego that thinks they can get well on their own. I've seen grace work wonders, and I've also seen people die because they either didn't believe it could work for them or didn't know how to accept it.

For me, grace has always been those quiet moments when I can hear the whisper of something bigger than me directing me toward what would make my authentic spirit sing. Grace has been the quiet workings of that inner GPS that says "Go here, not there" or offers me support when I feel completely alone and without an anchor in the world.

I remember sponsoring an addict who was so far gone, she could not see any good ahead of her in life. We did the step work and she kept going back out and drinking, and I felt like a failure to her as a sponsor. But we kept doing the work. Eventually, she had a bottoming-out experience that almost killed her, and something inside her snapped—or opened might be a better word for it. She suddenly became willing to have her Higher Power step in and help her. She had not been willing before because of her ego telling her she could white-knuckle her way sober.

It was strange, yet so thrilling, to see how one moment could change someone so deeply. I knew it could happen, but trying to help someone else have that same experience is difficult. My words fell on deaf ears until she was willing to hear them, just as the grace of the God of her belief fell upon infertile ground until she was able to allow herself to be fertilized by it.

So many times in my life I go back to that as a reminder that grace happens in the blink of an eye, but only because the groundwork was done first to make the "host" ready, willing, and able to receive it. That only happens through a surrendering and giving over of the problems and blocks, admitting that we cannot

Have you ever passed by a homeless person and thought to yourself, "There but for the grace of God go I"? Sometimes, the difference between a comfortable life and a much sadder state of affairs can be just a roll of the dice.

fix them of our own accord, and asking the higher power of our understanding for some divine intervention.

It doesn't work for everyone, and it may not always stick the landing, as many addicts use again, but it is a start and a road map toward eventually kicking the addiction for good and walking in alignment with a higher power that fills the void the drugs or drinking or food or gambling or sex never could.

There but for the grace of God go I.

Denise's Story

We are much more in control of our own ship than we might realize. At the same time, there are these little instances that if I look back, I can see where something bad that happened was really coming from a good place. I might not have even liked it when it happened, and I certainly didn't understand it. Yet it was a bit of grace that would help me later.

When I was about 10 years old, I was talking with a friend during recess. I don't recall the subject, but it must have been around things not working for me. I might have been whining, and maybe my friend was sick and tired of hearing me bellyache. To this day, I remember the shock when she said something like, "It's not everyone else. It's you."

Boom! That hurt like all holy you know what. Stinging. Burning. Mortification. A big ol' gut punch.

I'll never forget it. A confirmation of everything I already believed about myself. My stripped-bare insides filled with self-loathing were laid out for me to see. A self-hate exposed.

Granted, it didn't make the lightbulb illuminate for me at the time. In fact, it may have set me back a little more. Was it mean for her to say? At the time, I thought so. I didn't rage at her. Maybe I wanted to, but I was into making people like me, so I didn't. It wasn't until I was much, much older that I realized that 10-year-old girl was right in a lot of ways. I mean, she was only 10 years old, but dang if she didn't have some wisdom beyond her years. She was asking me to think about how I was contributing to my own issues. A lightbulb offering.

If no one ever brings to their attention that they are not powerless, they might never see it and do anything about it.

Up until then I'd spent a lot of time in "survival mode." Through a combination of family dynamics and outside dynamics, I'd gotten it into my head that life was always against me. Now I'm not saying this is unique. Many kids get that impression for a variety of reasons, and it becomes the default mode in which they operate into adulthood and maybe old age. If no one ever brings to their attention that they are not powerless, they might never see it and do anything about it. This isn't to say people can't have that flash of BOOM where they figure it out themselves without anyone telling them. They can.

My default mode, though, was, "How do I survive?" You could say I was taking care of myself but not designing my life by authentic means. I became a master manipulator at surviving absolutely every contingency imaginable. Most of it was designed around placating and appeasing everyone else and becoming so good at reading people I knew exactly what to say and do to avoid a bad outcome. This worked at the time, but it didn't serve the authentic me. Now, every day, I work on authenticity.

How does this figure into grace and miracles? Years later I realized my young friend saying I was contributing to my own disaster was actually an opening for me to understand I could do something about my situation. At the time I didn't understand it, and she certainly didn't give me ideas on how to fix my disaster–prone thinking. Yet it was the very beginning. That opening to "grace," if you will.

For me grace is tied more to a belief that we can act from a position of personal power. From a position that says *I am who I am and I am worthy*. What we do and say and how we act have an effect on our outside world and will help create the environment for how we are treated by others. It does not absolve us or others from bad behavior, but it puts the onus on us to start out on good footing. The grace comes in connecting to that power that is within us, the part of us that is divine and a part of the whole. Accepting the grace that is already authentically us.

MAGICAL TIPS

You Are Divine

It is easy to blame everything but us for what is happening in our lives. While there are things beyond our control, there is a way to take back some power. I hate to use the words *easy* and *simple*. Yet there are some easy, simple ways to start identifying where we are not being authentic and true to that which is divine within us. If you aren't being true to you, chances are a happy life is going to prove a lot harder. By "true to you" we mean honoring, accepting, and showing who you really are. You might be saying that's all well and good but where do I start? It doesn't have to be enormous gestures. Start by asking yourself:

1.   Am I fawning, placating, and appeasing everyone
     and everything and putting myself last? If so, time

to find out why and understand that while self-sacrifice is lovely in many
ways, if you are sacrificing
everything for everyone else,
you are not honoring the
divine and grace within
you. Your being miserable
isn't divine. It's crushing the
divine.

2. What are some things I've
    wanted to do but have con-
    sistently shoved away be-
    cause other people either

Each of us—you, me, everyone—is
a divine being with more power
within us than we realize.

don't approve or insist "aren't worthy"? You get to
decide what is worthy of your time and enjoyment.

3. Am I avoiding doing things like reading books or
    watching television/movies because other people I
    know say those things are not worthy? Again, what
    I want to read and watch is your own personal
    business.

These questions might seem simplistic, and they are. Yet they
are the start of opening yourself up to the grace that is you.

Surrender, Dorothy!

Whether your name is Dorothy or Dale, surrendering to life
is a great way to invite grace and miracles. This means getting
quiet in meditation or silent contemplation and letting go of all
that clutters the mind, including regrets of the past and worries
of the future. Surrender your spirit into the present moment. Stay
in that space where you feel in close communion with the divine
or your inner self and let thoughts move across the screen of your
mind without paying them any attention. In this sweet spot,
where you experience calm and centeredness and feel no resistance to what is, envision opening a doorway through which miracles can enter. Don't try to dictate the whens, hows, and wheres.
Just open the door and let it be.

How to Live a Mindful, Meaningful, Magical Life

The Magic of Prayer and Ritual

Prayer and ritual are methods of quieting and grounding the mind in the realm of spirit. Through the use of repetition, symbolism, and the power of words, you can rise above the physical demands of your life and enter the fertile ground where miracles are born. Praying is not about begging; it's about stating and declaring your intention and giving thanks for it already existing even if you cannot yet see it. Ritual can involve anything that feels powerful and symbolic to you, such as burning candles while chanting a mantra, creating a sacred outdoor space where you can meditate daily, or spending 15 minutes every night writing out your gratitude list. Ritual is structured and repetitive to train the mind and spirit, but you can do whatever turns you on and aligns you with spirit.

Some people find that listening to music is a ritual, allowing them to let go of the daily concerns and melt into the notes and melodies. Others might enjoy an herbal bath with scented candles that puts them in a light meditative trance. Rituals can be done

Rituals can be traditional and elaborate, or they might be something more simple and personal. The point is to create something using symbolism, repetition, and perhaps a verbal element that helps ground you to a world open to miracles.

Everyday Magic

alone or with a like–minded group of people and should be reverent and sacred. The key is to create a space where the unlimited possibility divine grace and miracles can come into a fertile mind and spirit unencumbered by the normal and mundane grind of life. Rituals and prayer also bring us into a higher state of consciousness where we can access divine guidance, inspiration, and knowledge–blessings that we rarely experience or pay attention to when we are stressed about getting dinner on the table or commuting through heavy traffic.

Elevating our conscious awareness into the miracle zone on a consistent basis is a must for setting the stage for those miracles to appear in our busy, crazy lives. It's a spiritual practice that, like a good recipe, mixes together all the necessary ingredients to create magic.

Marianne Williamson wrote in *Everyday Grace* that "[s]acred ritual illuminates the meaning with which we imbue an experience, raising it to the realm of divine understanding." Through any kind of practice that brings us more in tune with the sacred and divine, we find genuine connection. "They are portals to divine radiance, and the light we receive through them remains inside us."

Be a Miracle

Like energy attracts like energy. If you want miracles, be a miracle to someone else. If you want blessings, be a blessing to someone else. Don't do it just for the return on investment but for the joy of being a force for good in the lives of others. The Universe knows the difference between when we do something to get something and when we do something because we love to do it and want to spread happiness to others.

Get creative. There are a million ways to be a miracle to another person or living thing. Try doing one thing a week and see how it uplifts your own spirit. Before long, you will be doing it every day until being a walking miracle to others is just a part of who you are.

How to Live a Mindful, Meaningful, Magical Life

Amazing Graces

If you are struggling with the concept of grace, get out a journal and make a list of all the times in your life when you thought it was game over, and then something happened that lifted you up and out of the darkness. Reach back as far as you can into your past. When did you feel as though there was no way out, and then a door or window opened and a new solution to an old problem suddenly appeared in the form of an idea, a person, a thought, or something physical and tangible? It could even be a book that leapt off a shelf when you were in the bookstore, or a song that came on the radio with just the message you needed to hear. This is one time when looking backward can be helpful, because we have all been touched by grace. We just forget about it as time goes on, or we rationalize it away as coincidence.

List every synchronistic, serendipitous, surprising, and supernatural way that you were assisted by unseen forces out of the shadows and into the light. If you can, identify a specific person who helped you and write their name on the list, because grace, like miracles, often takes on human form.

The Magic of Death

Death is not the greatest loss in life. The greatest loss in life is what dies inside us while we live.

Norman Cousins

After your death you will be what you were before your birth.

Arthur Schopenhauer

There is no such thing as death. In nature nothing dies. From each sad remnant of decay, some forms of life arise so shall his life be taken away before he knoweth that he hath it.

Charles Mackay

We know, we know. How could we possibly write about the magic of … death? And leave it for the end of the book to boot. Death is scary. Death freaks us out and we don't want to think about it. Death is an unavoidable curse we are all under. Why write about death?

Magic exists in every corner of life, and that includes death. It's a natural part of the cycle of life, and until we realize its importance we fail to truly embrace the gifts in front of us. Death is what makes life so darned precious and immediate and reminds us to live in the moment and to do so fully and with our whole hearts and souls.

Many cultures around the world look at death with a lot less fear than we Westerners do. We tend to think of death as something to be terrified of when it is a part of nature that everything alive experiences. Because it is the "greatest of the great unknowns," we assume it will be horrible and do everything in our power to avoid it. Our pagan and primitive ancestors saw it as part of the cycle of birth, life, death, and rebirth. They observed the natural world around them and saw that what looked as though it were no longer flourishing or bearing fruit in the cold of winter would begin to sprout new life and fruit in the spring and become more abundant in summer. What looked desolate would be made lush with life again.

What if death is just a door we go through to continue the experience of existing, but not in the same body or form we are in now? What if we do, indeed, come back again and again in a form of reincarnation, and sometimes with the same people we knew in this life? Would we fear death as much if we knew that what lay on the other side of that door was even better, more joyful, filled with peace and happiness? No, we'd no longer fear it, but we might stop living THIS life as fully as we could in anticipation of it.

The whole mystery of death serves us. It's to our benefit not to know the great mystery, so that we can fully experience the life we are living right now and not put off everything until the next go-round. It is a secret for a reason, and that reason is to push us to awaken to the amazing, miraculous, magical life we have been blessed with.

Death, especially in Western cultures, is feared and misunderstood. This is exacerbated by the fact that no one knows for sure what comes afterwards, if anything.

Death is a critical reminder that life is not forever in the current form we are experiencing it, and that it should be lived with passion, purpose, joy, and love, to the fullest each day because we don't know when our last day alive will be. Death reminds and teaches us how important it is to engage and not wait to love others, love ourselves, connect with Source, follow our bliss, enjoy well-being and creativity and nature and all the other things we've written about in previous chapters.

We don't want to dwell on death or stress out over the fact that it's coming for us at some point along our journey. Doing so would be a waste of time and life. But being aware of it sure does add a depth and sweetness to being alive that nothing else can.

> *We die to different ages and milestones. We die to different loves and careers. We die to who we were to become who we are now.*

ONE LIFE, MANY DEATHS

Truth is, we die many times throughout our lives. We die to different ages and milestones. We die to different loves and careers. We die to who we were to become who we are now. As we move from infancy to toddlerhood, part of us dies to who we were as we age and grow. When we graduate school and get a job, get married maybe, and have kids of our own, we die to the old ways we once lived and embrace a new life with new meaning and purpose.

When loved ones die, our lives change. We feel the grief of loss, but we know a part of them lives on within us, even if they are not physically present. Some of us even have contact with those who pass on, or experience life after death in a near-death experience. Others simply live with the faith that life does not end but changes, just as energy does not cease to exist but changes form, as basic physics teaches us. Why, then, would we not change form as well? We are made up of energy, too.

Maybe we will live and die a thousand times, or a million, before we merge with all there is and become a part of the universal life force. Maybe we only live this once. We don't know, and those who have died and come back only have their subjective experiences of what occurred in the moments after death, not what happens two weeks or a month later. We either don't believe them or we take it on faith with a side of hope.

OUR GREATEST FEAR, OUR GREATEST HOPE

Death is our greatest fear, but it's also our greatest hope. It's inextricably tied to the fear of the unknown and the hope of the possible. Depends on your perspective. The younger we are, the more distant death seems, so we are more willing to take risks and go for our dreams. As we age, death becomes a next-door neighbor we are always aware could knock on our door at any time, so we tend to get more conservative with taking risks and the goals we think we have time enough left to achieve. We stop dreaming big and dream in "I may have time for this" instead. At the end of our lives, we either go to our death feeling as though we lived well, with few if any regrets, or we cling to life in desperation, suddenly and acutely aware of all the things we didn't do or say or make time for. It's our choice which of those we experience.

The young tend to ignore the inevitability of death, planning for the future; the old feel its presence more palpably and consider carefully the time they have left. Those who fear death might take the strategy of pretending it just doesn't exist for them.

In the December 3, 2017, *Psychology Today* article "The Psychology of Death and Dying," Ronald E. Riggio, Ph.D., wrote about his own research into how people feel about death. He pointed out how some people fear death to such an extent that they ignore it and don't think about it. Other people are motivated by it. "According to some psychological theories, imminent death motivates us to leave a legacy behind." That legacy might be something we do or make that we might leave for our children and grandchildren.

Those who ignore death, Riggio stated, never come to grips with it, and he believes contemplating death is a healthy exercise for learning to come to terms with the inevitable. Even though people claim to not think about death consciously, it's easy to see by their actions and behaviors that they are deeply aware of it on a subconscious level. Fear drives so much of our behaviors, especially the apprehension that we will be killed or someone we love will be. At the heart of all human existence, on a biological level, is the need to survive.

Death does have many lessons to teach us, as Prabha Rao found out. In "6 Empowering Lessons Death Taught Me About Life" for *Tiny Buddha*, Rao talked about all of the family member deaths that created fear that more things could and would go wrong. There was a sense, Rao stated, of being singled out by the universe for punishment. "By then, I had decided that the Universe was conspiring against me. I did not think anyone cared, and I put on an act, pretending to be happy. The truth was that I was buried under the rubble of my fearful thoughts, and constantly worried that something would go wrong."

Rao had an awakening. "I realized that I was not singled out for anything bad." This awakening allowed Rao to see the many blessings in life and to focus instead on the good, as there is always something going right in our lives. We are survivors, and it isn't our fault when things happen beyond our control, such as the death of a loved one. "As long as you are living, something wonderful could happen at any moment," Rao said. This is how we stay open to miracles and allow death to be a positive impetus for growth and expansion, not something scary that has us cowering in fear, afraid to go outside and live.

The brilliant American author Mark Twain understood that death was necessary and that those who live a fulfilling life do not fear the inevitable.

We are all going to die. All living things do. Nature teaches us that life goes on and that in some form, we do, too. We have the power to choose how we view death and whether or not we will give into the fear of a looming unknown we cannot stop or understand it and accept it and let it be a motivating force for making our lives just the way we want them.

Mark Twain summed it up perfectly. "The fear of death follows from the fear of life. A man who lives fully is prepared to die at any time." Science agrees, as in the February 26, 2022, *Lancet* study titled "Report of the *Lancet* Commission on the Value of Death: Bringing Death Back into Life." The study authors examined how death and dying has changed over the generations, finding: "Philosophers and theologians from around the globe have recognized the value that death holds for human life. Death and life are bound together: without death there would be no life. Death allows new ideas and new ways. Death also reminds us of our fragility and sameness: we all die."

LIVE LONG AND PROSPER

To quote a famous Vulcan, death urges us to wake up and live, and to make the most of the moments we have been given. To prosper and thrive, not just be alive. Life is a magical gift, and so many of us just coast on through on autopilot, day in and day out, like worker bees doing what we did yesterday and will probably do tomorrow.

Either you have one life and that's all you get, baby, so why not make it the best you can?—or you have more than one life, but guess what: you are only conscious of one of them at a time, so why not make it the best you can? It's a no-brainer when you think about it. Wasting your life, no matter what comes after, only leaves you with regret, fear, and emptiness when the Grim Reaper comes calling.

In looking at reincarnation a little closer, there are many, many different belief systems on how it all works. Pierre Teilhard de Chardin said, "We are not human beings having a spiritual experience. We are spiritual beings having a human experience." With that in mind, one thread does run through several philosophies. We come back again and again to experience all the things. All the possibilities and opportunities. We may choose, on the other side, to come back as the opposite of what we were before to experience everything and every possibility. Only by doing so can we understand all facets of life. Only then can we transform and learn the lessons and reach a new rung in our evolution as a spiritual being. If we knew that was what we were doing, we would put gusto into our human experience and embrace many more experiences to make certain we were learning things we wouldn't have to do again the next time around.

Pierre Teilhard de Chardin (1881–1955) was a Jesuit priest, scientist, and philosopher from France who famously said, "We are not human beings having a spiritual experience. We are spiritual beings having a human experience."

AUTHOR INSIGHTS

Marie's Story

I take my dog out to pee beside the house several times a day. There is a huge, vine-covered wall between my house and the one next door, which happens to belong to my sister. During the cold winter months, there is no green, no life, and I often contemplate how the vine looks dead. There is no sign of any waiting buds from which the green leaves will soon spring. It's a tangle of gray branches that look like long fingers covering the wall.

When spring arrives, tiny buds of green appear. They stand out like sore thumbs against the gray backdrop. By the end of spring, the entire wall is covered from end to end with giant, lush green leaves and tiny purple "berries." I marvel. Where on Earth did those leaves and berries come from? I recall how during the winter I couldn't even find a little bud here or there. It was just a mass of seemingly dead branches.

Yet the leaves came forth as they do every year, and it reminded me again of the cyclical nature of life and death. What struck me the most was how I could not see any signs of life on the wall, but when it got sunnier and warmer, it bloomed like crazy from the very places I could not see. Had I not known of this natural cycle, I might have torn down the entire wall of ivy in the winter thinking it dead and thrown it in the compost pile.

I love perennial flowers for the same reason. I plant buds in flowerpots, and they bloom months later, then the stalks and flowers wither away come winter. During winter, the pot looks like it's just filled with dirt. I once had a less-than-experienced gardener throw away a whole pot of dirt, not realizing there were bulbs down in that dirt that would come out to play when spring arrived. I have one plant that comes out every year with awesome flowers, and I've had the pot outside my front door for over eight years now. Normally, perennials might last a couple of years, but not this one.

Look at a tree in summer, filled with leaves. Birds nest and critters hide out in the branches, under camouflage of green. Then when the cold months arrive, the leaves fall and the birds and critters find shelter and the tree looks void of life.

Gray. Dead.

Until the days become warmer and the blooms of green begin to show.

Life and death and life again. Nature reminds me that nothing ever dies. Nothing alive ceases to exist; it just might cease to exist in the current form it's in. But perhaps, like the ivy and the perennials, it comes back exactly the same in another season, in another Universe or timeline or reality.

Denise's Story

I have a weird relationship with death. Well, perhaps it isn't strange, because we all deal with the ultimate great unknown in a different way. My philosophy for most of my life has been that everyone says they know what comes after death, but we do not actually know until we get there.

It could be that I'm actually obsessed with death. From the time I was a little kid I was intrigued and excited about ghosts and all things macabre in my television, movie, and reading choices. No one influenced me to be like that. It was always there, as far back as I can possibly remember. My fascination with mortality endures to this day.

When I realized my mediumship abilities back in 2018, it was like a huge lightbulb turned on. I'd realized, in the popular words of the young boy in the movie *The Sixth Sense* ... I see dead people.

> *My philosophy for most of my life has been that everyone says they know what comes after death, but we do not actually know until we get there.*

Wait.

Don't mediums know that they see dead people from the time they are little kids? Many do. Some don't. I fell into the didn't-get-what-was-happening category. To make a long story short, I've always had a huge imagination. So, the stuff I saw and heard in my head I attributed to my imagination. I understood that I had psychic abilities, but I didn't think I had the ability to talk to the dead. It wasn't until I took a class on intuition from a medium that she helped me recognize the ability. When I began to do readings for people, I was able to confirm many things for people I could not possibly have known any other way other than by talking with deceased relatives, friends, ancestors, and acquaintances.

Part of me felt tremendously dumb because I thought mediumship looked a certain way. After all, in popular literature and televisions/movies, the only way to portray mediumship and make it interesting to the general public is to dramatize it. I have no beef with that, but now I have an understanding that mediumship looks different to every medium.

Death from suicide or murder is a touchy subject for many, yet I have also realized that spirits who have experienced these types of passing are drawn to me. When I asked another medium/coach why this was so, she told me that these spirits knew that I would understand them and could speak with them, and that my vibration matched and attracted them. My experiences with talking to those who have committed suicide or been murdered have also brought tremendous understanding to me and others. In these readings I've learned that those who have passed on in these circumstances are fine on the other side. They wish to reach out to loved ones and friends the same as anyone else who has passed on. With this knowledge, I have felt an additional ease with the concept of my own mortality.

MAGICAL TIPS

Write Your Own Obituary

How do you want people to remember you? How do you want to have lived? This is a great exercise that allows you to imagine what will be said about you when you have moved on to the other side. It also helps clarify the most important dreams and goals you have in this life that you would love to leave behind as your legacy. Don't hold back. Be bold and dream big and get into the whole spirit of imagining how you wish your life was and what you would like to be remembered for, and then find ways to begin to live that way today. Why wait until you die? Take that amazing vision of your death and see how you can begin to fulfill it with small goals you can work toward in life.

Deathly Questions

If you are struggling to see how death can be a magical blessing, try answering these two questions.

If you knew that when you died there was nothing else—final, finite, fade to black—how differently would you live your life today? Would you be so afraid of that finality that you'd be rendered helpless, wondering what the point of life is? Would you throw in the towel on your dreams because it wasn't worth the limited time you have? Or would you make this one life you've been given a magical, kick-ass rollercoaster ride and experience as much as you possibly could? Think about all the ways you might act, think, and behave if you truly knew that life ended for good and you were never coming back in any form.

If you knew that beyond death, there was something equally or more wonderful, and that you would exist, albeit not in the same body with the same circumstances, how differently would you live your life? Would you get lazy about pursuing dreams and goals, thinking

Whether there *is* something after death or there is only oblivion, how would knowing the true answer affect how you live today?

you have all the time in the next life and the one after that? Would you want to make your mark so it carried over in the next life? Would you accept yourself as you are and embrace each ride as it came, or would you be so overwhelmed with fear of what might come next that it would immobilize you? Think about how differently you would live today if you knew you were eternal.

Conclusion: Everyday Magic Is Right Where You Are

"I don't believe in magic."

"Magic is for kids. It's not scientific."

"Magic is all about stage tricks."

"There's no such thing as real magic anyway."

Sound familiar? The word "magic" brings up all kinds of connotations that turn us away from what everyday magic really means. We are not talking about stage tricks, although you can pull a rabbit out of a hat if you know the sleight of hand behind it. We are not talking about doing a wrinkle of the nose and transporting yourself to a beach in Aruba or folding your arms and turning a goat into a box of chocolates. Or having some kind of spell or wand that you can use to drive back a horde of Orcs or demons.

The magic we are talking about here is the energy of joy and bliss that occurs when we tune in to the wonders of the world around us that we ordinarily ignore or don't see because we are too busy working or on our phones or stressing out over some past or future event. We've talked about our personal journeys to find magic and the many methods you can employ to find it. Yet

Everyday magic isn't about casting spells like a character in the *Harry Potter* movies or a Halloween witch. No, it is the magic that comes with the bliss and wonder we gain when we are in tune with the Universe.

when it comes down to it, the formula for success can be broken into four major components.

Magic only requires:

• Awareness

• Attention

• Mindfulness

• Intention

That's about it. Here's the thing. Everyday magic is easier to access than a good chocolate chip cookie recipe, yet it's one of the hardest things we can do because of three of the above requirements: awareness, attention, and mindfulness. Maybe we can sum it all up by saying that everyday magic is always there, that we are surrounded by it all the time, that it comes from within and also from our external environment, yet it is the hardest thing to pinpoint … until we do.

Ever hear someone say, "I never saw it until I saw it and then I could never unsee it again?" That's how everyday magic works. It's a shift or change in perspective from what we normally see, our default worldview, to what is all around us. It asks us to look at things we see all the time with fresh, new eyes, like the eyes of a child seeing things for the first time. Remember that feeling when everything felt amazing and filled with unending wonder and awe? Then as we got older it turned boring and rote and we became jaded.

The things that filled us with amazement did not change. We did. We stopped looking.

Magic hides in perspective. Say you have a huge wall of ivy outside your bedroom window. In the winter, you can see right through your neighbor's kitchen window and he into your bedroom. In the spring, as the leaves sprout and grow, turning lush and green, you cannot see into your neighbor's window, nor he into yours. You have privacy now. You also might have allergies or lose sleep listening to critters crawl through the ivy. There are positives and negatives to everything in life.

Magic comes from looking at the positives. Yet this isn't one of those things where you ignore all the negatives. It's about shifting perspective from seeing a wall full of critter-laden ivy to an awesome green privacy screen so that our neighbors cannot see us walking around our bedroom.

Living in a busy urban environment may be all about noise and crowds and busy streets. Shift the perspective a little and you have an environment rich with culture, restaurants, shops, and museums to explore. One pair of eyes might see too many people they want to avoid. Another pair might see many people they cannot wait to meet and learn from. Yet a third might recognize that balance is the ultimate key to magic, and life will have ups and downs, but the more we concentrate on creating the positive, the longer we can stay in the positive.

Everyday life is filled with stuff we have to do that bores us to tears. Laundry, paying bills, trying to decide what to make for dinner, working at jobs that pay the bills but don't feed our

The "real world" can often seem dreary, workaday, but changing our perspective and searching for the wonder in life even slightly can help reveal the magic that is all around us. Embrace it!

How to Live a Mindful, Meaningful, Magical Life

souls.... Yet if we could simply shift our perspective ever so slightly, we might see magic dancing just beneath the surface of the illusion of boredom we have bought into.

Doing the laundry means we have great clothes to wear, and it makes them smell so good. Paying bills means we make money to take care of our basic needs and we can be thankful for the services we receive. Working at a job we hate may hold hidden gems of opportunities to learn what to do to discover our true passion and purpose. We might also come to like the challenge and fun of coming up with great new recipes to make for dinner instead of the usual.

Life can have a way of turning us jaded and doubtful as we get older. But we can learn to look at life again through the eyes of a child by getting out of the rat race and the past- and future-fo-cused anxiety and become mindful of the moment at hand. The air that we breathe that moves through our lungs and our blood, giving oxygen to our brains. The sights and sounds and smells around us in that moment. The life outside our window that goes on without concern for our petty differences and daily frustrations.

If we get up and go outside and stand in the sun, all the boredom and jadedness melts away as we feel the life-giving warmth. We hear the chirp of birds–oh how lovely they are, although that ONE in that tree is quite annoying. We watch butterflies flit from flower to flower, their beautiful wings gently carrying them on the light breeze. We smell delectable flowers and plants that we never stop long enough to enjoy, and our senses are assaulted with beauty and wonder and joy.

Nature is frikkin' awesome! And filled with magic.

Yet magic exists not just in nature. It exists wherever we are if we have the inner vision to discern it. We might go play with our dog or our child. Or cook something we've never tried before or clean out the garage and get a pile of stuff ready for a charity pickup. Anything that brings us to the moment is where the gift is. The present of the presence, to get clichéd. That shift in perspective allows us to see things we once considered chores or obligations as the true experiences of joy and being alive that they are, including cleaning out the garage to help others use and enjoy all the things we no longer need.

Awareness of our surroundings and ourselves, attention to the things happening in the now, and mindfulness to stay focused on that now–that magical present because that and that alone is where we live life–are how we stay in the magic. Not in the past, which happened and is now gone. Not in the future, which hasn't hap- pened yet and which we cannot predict. No matter what is going on in our lives, good, bad, and ugly, we find some gift of the present moment, some silver lining or wisdom or positive aspect we can focus our awareness and attention on. We come to realize that our lives are lived moment to moment. We live in the now.

With these concepts, the idea of intentions has to again be mentioned. Without our intent to bring about good outcomes in our own world and that of others, no progress can be made. The Universe responds to wishy–washy with more wishy–washy. We need to get clear on what we want, and not on more of what we don't want, to see magic afoot and miracles abound.

If we don't know what we intend each morning, our lives can go out of control. We can find that the whims of the world around us can lead the show, rather than us doing all we can to form and create the lives we desire. The resulting chaos of this can make it harder to find magic in our lives, and we are back to abandoning ourselves, our dreams, and our lives to external forces.

Sometimes all it takes is a small shift in perspective to create big changes. Magical living doesn't ask us to leap off of huge cliffs, unless we are ready. It's about taking that first step, then the next, and the next, and staying aligned and open to guidance from within.

Stepping into each day with intentions, awareness, mindful- ness, and attention can bring better outcomes and more magic into our lives and those of our fellow human beings.

That's where the magic is, and once we see it we can never unsee it.

Eckhart Tolle said, "Life is the dance and you are the dancer." You get to choose how you wish to dance. It just doesn't get any more magical than that.

FURTHER READING

Babauta, Leo. "9 Tips On How to Find Passion in Life." *LifeHack*, November 2, 2022.

Beck, Martha. *Finding Your Own North Star: Claiming the Life You Were Meant to Live.* New York: Harmony Books, 2002.

Brooks, Arthur C. *From Strength to Strength: Finding Success, Happiness, and Deep Purpose in the Second Half of Life.* New York: Portfolio Books, 2022.

Brown, Brene. *Daring Greatly: How the Courage to Be Vulnerable Transforms the Way We Live, Love, Parent, and Lead.* New York: Avery Books, 2015.

Buddhist Society. *1001 Pears of Buddhist Wisdom: Insights on Truth, Peace and Enlightenment.* Toronto, Ontario: Duncan Baird Publishers, 2006.

Cameron, Julia. *The Artist's Way: A Spiritual Path to Higher Creativity.* New York: TarcherPedigree, 2016.

———. *Seeking Wisdom: A Spiritual Path to Creative Connection.* New York: St. Martin/Essentials, 2022.

Cherry, Kendra. "6 Types of Relationships and Their Effect on Your Life." *VeryWellMind*, September 21, 2022.

Colier, Nancy. "What Is Forgiveness and How Do You Do It?" *Psychology Today*, March 15, 2018.

Costa, Ken. *Know Your Why: Finding and Fulfilling Your Calling in Life.* New York: Thomas Nelson Books, 2016.

Cunningham, Scott. *Wicca: A Guide for Solitary Practitioners.* Woodbury, MN: Llewellyn Publications, 1989.

Dalai Lama and Howard C. Cutler. *The Art of Happiness: A Handbook for Living.* New York: Riverhead Books, 1998.

Davidson, Richard J. "The Four Keys to Well-Being." *The Greater Good Magazine*, March 21, 2016.

DeBecker, Gavin. *The Gift of Fear: Survival Signals That Protect Us from Violence*. New York: Back Bay Books, 2021.

Field, Barbara. "7 Surprising Ways to Make Your Relationship Better." *VeryWellMind*, November 16, 2022.

Flaxington, Beverly D. "The Importance of Self-Love." *Psychology Today*, January 17, 2019.

Forleo, Marie. "The Secret to Finding Your Passion (Hint: It's Not What You Think)." *Oprah.com*, November 14, 2012.

Frankl, Viktor E. *Man's Search for Meaning*. Revised edition. Boston: Beacon Press, 2006.

Goddard, Neville. *Law of Assumption*. Andura Publishing, 2020.

Greenberg, Melanie. "8 Powerful Steps to Self-Love." *Psychology Today*, June 29, 2017.

Harvard Medical School, "The Power of Forgiveness." *Harvard Health Publishing*, February 12, 2021.

Hoffman, Bobby. "3 Reasons Why People Refuse to Help Others." *Psychology Today*, October 3, 2013.

Holmes, Ernest. *The Science of Mind: A Philosophy, A Faith, A Way of Life*. New York: Tarcher/Penguin, 1926.

Honda, Ken. *Happy Money: The Japanese Art of Making Peace with Your Money*. New York: Gallery Books, 2019.

"How Being Thankful Makes You Happier." *Arizona Heart Foundation*, November 2, 2022.

Isaacson, Walter. *Steve Jobs*. New York: Simon & Schuster, 2021.

Jonas, Wayne. "The Power of Relationships as We Age." *Psychology Today*, March 9, 2021.

Jones, Marie D. *Destiny vs. Choice: The Scientific and Spiritual Evidence Behind Fate and Free Will*. Franklin Lakes, NJ: New Page Books, 2011.

——. *Natural Health: Your Complete Guide to Natural Remedies and Mindful Well-Being*. Detroit, MI: Visible Ink Press, 2022.

Junttila, Henry. *Find Your Passion: 25 Questions You Must Ask Yourself*. CreateSpace Independent Publishing, 2013.

LaMott, Sandee. "The Benefits of Owning a Pet and the Surprising Science Behind It." *CNN.com*, February 20, 2020.

Martin, Sharon. "How to Stop Being Codependent." *LiveWellWithSharonMartin.com*, January 14, 2021.

Maslow, Abraham. "A Theory of Human Motivation." *Psychological Review*, 1943.

Millaci, Tiffany Sauber. "What Is Gratitude and Why It Is Important." *Positive Psychology*, February 28, 2017.

Morin, Amy. "7 Tips for Finding Your Purpose in Life." *VeryWellMind*, December 26, 2022.

———. "How to Improve Your Psychological Well-Being," *VeryWellMind*, February 10, 2022.

Nierenberg, Cari. "Scientists Measure Intuition." *Live Science*, May 20, 2016.

Ornish, Dean, and Anne Ornish. *UnDo It! How Simple Lifestyle Changes Can Reverse Most Chronic Diseases*. New York: Ballentine Books, 2019.

Penczak, Christopher. *The Inner Temple of Witchcraft: Magick, Meditation, and Psychic Development*. Woodbury, MN: Llewellyn Publications, 2002.

Pratt, Misty. "The Science of Gratitude." *Mindful.org*, February 17, 2022.

Rao, Prabha. "6 Empowering Lessons Death Taught Me about Life." *Tiny Buddha*. Accessed October 4, 2023.

Riggio, Ronald E. "The Psychology of Death and Dying." *Psychology Today*, December 3, 2017.

Robinson, Ken, and Lou Aronica. *Finding Your Element: How to Discover Your Talents and Passions and Transform Your Life*. New York: Penguin Books, 2013.

Sallnow, Libby, and others. "Report of the *Lancet* Commission on the Value of Death: Bringing Death Back into Life." *The Lancet*, February 26, 2022.

Santi, Jenny. "The Secret to Happiness Is Helping Others." *Time Magazine*, August 4, 2017.

Seetubtim, Mo. "7 Rules to Live By for Those Who Live with Passion." *HuffPost*, June 6, 2015.

Shimoff, Marci, and Carol Kline. *Happy for No Reason: 7 Steps to Being Happy from the Inside Out*. New York: Free Press, 2008.

Suttie, Jill. "Seven Ways to Find Your Purpose in Life." *GreaterGood UC Berkeley*, August 6, 2020.

Tsipursky, Gleb. "Is Serving Others the Key to Meaning and Purpose?" *Psychology Today*, July 14, 2016.

Warren, Rick. *The Purpose-Driven Life*. New York: Zondervan Publishing, 2002.

Watson, Zack. "Why Creativity and Analysis Aren't Mutually Exclusive." *Technology Advice*, July 22, 2016.

White, Matthew P., and others. "Spending at Least 120?Minutes a Week in Nature Is Associated with Good Health and Well-Being." *Scientific Reports*, June 13, 2019.

"Why Giving is Good for Your Health." *Cleveland Clinic*, December 7, 2002.

Williamson, Marianne. *Everyday Grace: Having Hope, Finding Forgiveness, and Making Miracles*. New York: Riverhead Books, 2004.

Wilson, Matthew, "15 Reasons Why Having a Pet Is Good for You and Your Family." *Insider*, July 2, 2020.

Yahne, Rachael, "How to Create More Miracles in Your Life." *HuffPost*, December 6, 2017.

INDEX

Note: (ill.) indicates photos and illustrations

A

Abraham, 128–29
abundance, 134–35, 146–48
Ackerman, Diane, 184
Agnew, Denise A.
  creativity and imagination, 213
  death, 256–58
  giving and service, 177
  grace, 242–44
  gratitude, 160–62
  nature, 118–20
  passion and purpose, 198
  relationships, 41–43
  self-love, 14–17
  source, connecting to, 69–72
  Universal Laws, 140–42
  well-being, 92–94
alignment, 57, 74
alignment inventory journal exercise, 74
Amiel, Henri Frédéric, 56
Anderson, Jeff, 207–8

Aristotle, 99
Assumption, Law of, 130, 131, 137–39
Atkinson, William Walker, 128
attention, 83
Attraction, Law of, 128–30, 131, 137–39
authenticity, 44–45
awe, 212

B

Babauta, Leo, 190
Bacon, Francis, 169
Bailey, Donovan, 183
barefoot, 108–9
Bauman, Bill, 228
Baumeister, Roy, 169
benevolent self, 218–21
Bernstein, Gabrielle, 79
Bhagavad Gita, 56
Blavatsky, Helena, 128
boat-float list, 200
boundaries, 8–9
breathing, 94–95
breathing and grounding meditation exercise, 77–78
Brown, Brené, 34, 34 (ill.)
Buckley, William F., 193, 193 (ill.)
Buddha, 1

Buddhism, 226
Buscaglia, Leo, 23
Byrne, Robert, 183

C

Cameron, Julia, 219
Canfield, Jack, 238, 238 (ill.)
Cantor, Eddie, 191, 192 (ill.)
Cheeke, Robert, 79
Cherry, Kendra, 27, 28
childhood inventory quiz, 19–20
choice, 194–96
Christianity, 226
Churchill, Winston, 169
clouds, 113–14
clutter, 90
codependency, 27–28
Cohen, Alan, 12
Colier, Nancy, 10, 11
comfort of home, 89–91
Comic-Con, 214 (ill.), 214–16
community, 35–36
Complex Post-Traumatic Stress Disorder (CPTSD), 4, 132, 133
Confucianism, 168

Confucius, 167
cork, 198–99
count the grass exercise, 148
Cousins, Norman, 249
creativity and imagination, 203–5
  Agnew, Denise A., 213
  awe, 212
  children, 205–6
  daydreaming, 222–23
  Jones, Marie D., 213–16
  left-brain vs. right-brain, 207 (ill.), 207–11, 208–10 (ill.)
  lifelong, 211
  nature, 216–17
  negative belief points and benevolent self, 218–21
  oracle cards, 217 (ill.), 217–18
  tips, 216–18
  universal, 206–7
Creed, Linda, 1
Cruise, Tom, 40
Cunningham, Scott, 231
Cutler, Howard C., 32
cynic, 55

D

Dalai Lama, 32, 33 (ill.), 33–34, 125
D'Angelo, Anthony J., 23
David, Brother, 157

Davidson, Richard J., 82–83, 169
Day, Doris, 154
daydreaming, 212, 222–23
death, 249–51
  Agnew, Denise A., 256–58
  fear and hope, 252–54
  Jones, Marie D., 255–56
  life, 254–55
  multiple losses, 251–52
  questions about, 258–59
  tips, 258–59
destiny, 194–96
diaphragmatic breathing, 94–95
Donne, John, 23–24
Dunbar, Mary, 1
Dyer, Wayne, 49, 125
dyscalculia, 15, 16, 42

E

earthing, 108–9
Eckhart, Meister, 166
ego, 230
Einstein, Albert, 49, 52, 54, 54 (ill.), 68, 203, 240
electronics, unplugging, 95–96
Emerson, Ralph Waldo, 99, 100 (ill.), 167
Emmons, Robert, 150
extraversion, 208 (ill.), 210–11

F

"5-3-1" daily practice, 96–97
failure, 185–87
fawning, 132
fear of missing out (FOMO), 59–61
feeling, 209 (ill.), 210–11
Flaxington, Beverly D., 11
focus, 164
fog, 111
foraging, 102–4
forest bathing, 109–10
forgiveness, 9–11, 37–40, 84
Forleo, Marie, 190 (ill.), 190–91
Fortier, Verla, 121
Frankl, Viktor, 139–40, 140 (ill.)
free will, 139–40
frenetic energy assessment exercise, 75–77

G

Gaia, 227
gardening, 102–4
generosity, 83
Gibran, Khalil, 99
giving and service, 167–69
  Agnew, Denise A., 177
  health benefits, 168–69
  helping without hindering, 174–77

Jones, Marie D.,
177–79
kindness jar, 181
reasons to par-
ticipate in,
170–72
small types of,
172–74
tips, 179–81
God, 61–63, 126
Goddard, Neville
Lancelot, 130, 130
(ill.)
grace, 225–31
Agnew, Denise
A., 242–44
Jones, Marie D.,
241–42
journaling, 248
tips, 244–45
gratitude, 149–51
Agnew, Denise
A., 159–60
attitude of, 156–
59
exercises, 164–66
Jones, Marie D.,
162–64
locating, 154–56
opposite of, 159–
60
saying "thank
you," 166
science of, 151–
54
tips, 164–66
well-being, 84
Great Spirit, 227, 227
(ill.)
Gretzky, Wayne, 185
grounding, 109

H

Hansen, Mark Victor,
186, 186 (ill.)
Hay, Louise L., 3, 3 (ill.),
238
Hegel, Georg Wilhelm
Friedrich, 183
Herzog, Harold, 31–32
Hesse, Hermann, 35
Hicks, Esther, 49, 128–
29, 129 (ill.)
hierarchy of needs, 25
(ill.), 25–29
high tides, 112–13
Hill, Gene, 30
Hinduism, 226
Hoffman, Bobby, 170
Holmes, Ernest, 176
Holt, Victoria, 233
Honda, Ken, 136 (ill.),
136–37
Houston, Whitney, 1
hugs, 37
human body, 239–40,
240 (ill.)

I

imagination. See crea-
tivity and imagina-
tion
Ingle, Kent, 63–64
instant gratification,
236–37
intentions, 146–48
intimacy, 32–34
introversion, 208 (ill.),
210–11
intuition, 52–56, 72,
73–74, 208 (ill.), 210–
11

intuition inventory,
74–75
ions, 107–8
Isaacson, Walter, 53

J

Jerry Maguire, 40
Jobs, Steve, 53, 53 (ill.),
185
Jonas, Wayne, 26
Jones, Marie D.
creativity and
imagination,
213–16
death, 255–56
giving and serv-
ice, 177–79
grace, 241–42
gratitude, 162–64
nature, 116–18
passion and pur-
pose, 196–98
relationships,
40–41
self-love, 12–14
source, connect-
ing to, 73–74
Universal Laws,
143–44
well-being, 91–92
journaling exercise,
20–21
Judaism, 226
judging, 209 (ill.), 210–
11
Jung, Carl, 209

K

Kabat-Zinn, Jon, 88
Kant, Immanuel, 126,
126 (ill.), 127
karma, 131–33

kindness, 84
kindness jar, 181
Koontz, Dean, 49

L

lack, 133–34
Lamott, Anne, 225
LaMotte, Sandee, 31
Lao Tzu, 149
laughter, 85–86
Law of Assumption, 131, 137–39
Law of Attraction, 128–30, 131, 137–39
Law of Reciprocity, 131–33
laws. *See* Universal Laws
left-brain, 207 (ill.), 207–11, 208–10 (ill.)
letting it be, 86–87
Li, Qing, 110
life, 254–55
listening, 199
"live for today, but plan for tomorrow," 236–37, 237 (ill.)
long-term happiness, 236–37
low tides, 111–13
Lucado, Max, 231

M

Mackay, Charles, 249
magic, everyday, 261–65
Mann, Denise, 108
Martin, Sharon, 28
Maslow, Abraham, 25
Maslow's Hierarchy of Needs, 25 (ill.), 25–29
meditation, 57, 58, 66–67, 77–78

mediumship, 257
Merton, Thomas, 23
Millacci, Tiffany Sauber, 150
mindfulness, 56–59, 84, 87–89, 97–98
Mindfulness-Based Attention Training (MBAT), 59
miracles, 232–33
    human body, 239–40, 240 (ill.)
    regrets, 233–34
    responsibility, 237–39
mirror exercise, 18–19
money, 135–37
Morin, Amy, 83, 192
Morter, Sue, 237–38
Mostafa, Ahmed, 125
Mother Nature, 227
murder, 258
Murphy, Joseph, 51
Myers–Briggs Personality Type chart, 208–9 (ill.), 209–11

N

Native American/First Nation cultures, 227, 227 (ill.)
nature, 99–102
    Agnew, Denise A., 116–18
    clouds, 113–14
    creativity and imagination, 216–17
    earthing and forest bathing, 108–10

foraging and gardening, 102–4
    indoors, 105–6
    Jones, Marie D., 115–16
    medical benefits of, 115–16
    outside mindset, 121–22
    presence in, 114–15
    sunlight and water, 106–8
    tips, 120–21
    walking, 122–23
    wisdom of, 110–13
negative belief points, 218–21
negative low tide, 112–13
New Age, 227
"No Man Is an Island" (Donne), 23–24

O

obituary, 258
optimism, 93
oracle cards, 217 (ill.), 217–18
Ornish, Dean and Anne, 45
outlook, 82
oxygen mask, 92

P

Parks, Rosa, 149
passion, 183–85
    Agnew, Denise A., 198
    failure, 185–87

finding, 188–91
freedom, 200–201
Jones, Marie D.,
196–98
Paul, St., 63
Pearson, Joel, 53
Penczak, Christopher,
226
perceiving, 209 (ill.),
210–11
pets, 30–32
Picasso, Pablo, 203
Piff, Paul, 102
Pilates, Joseph, 79
pollinators, 104
Poneman, Debra, 195–
96
positive thinking, 84
prayer, 61–64, 246–47
prosperity, 135–37
purpose, 184
Agnew, Denise
A., 198
destiny or
choice, 194–96
failure, 185–87
finding, 191–94
freedom, 200–201
Jones, Marie D.,
196–98
tips, 198–200
well-being, 83–
84

R

Ram Dass, 1, 30, 30 (ill.)
Rao, Prabha, 253
Reciprocity, Law of,
131–33
regrets, 233–34
reincarnation, 255

relationships
Agnew, Denise
A., 41–43
authenticity, 44–
45
community and
tribe, 35–36
forgiveness, 37–
40
healthy, 29–30
hugs, 37
importance of,
23–25
intimacy and
vulnerability,
32–34
Jones, Marie D.,
40–41
Maslow's Hierar-
chy of Needs,
25 (ill.), 25–29
pets, 30–32
roles and pat-
terns, 46–47
saying no, 45–46
tips, 44–45
religion, 226–31
resilience, 82
responsibility, 237–39
Richards, Stephen, 127
Riggio, Ronald E., 253
right-brain, 207 (ill.),
207–11, 208–10 (ill.)
rising sun wisdom,
235–36
ritual, 246–47
Rumi, 12

S

Sadhguru, 130
Sagan, Carl, 73, 73 (ill.)
saying no, 45–46

Schlitz, Marilyn, 63
Schopenhauer, Arthur,
249
Sedaris, Amy, 31
Seetubtim, Mo, 189–90
self-care, 6–7
self-love, 1–4
Agnew, Denise
A., 14–17
boundaries, 8–9
childhood in-
ventory quiz,
19–20
forgiveness, 9–11
importance of,
11–12
Jones, Marie D.,
12–14
journaling exer-
cise, 20–21
mirror exercise,
18–19
self-care, 6–7
somaticizing, 7–8
tips, 17–18
what it is not, 4–
6
sensing, 208 (ill.), 210–
11
sensitivity, 15–16
service. See giving and
service
Shaw, George Bernard,
225
Shimoff, Marci, 19, 157,
193–94, 228, 237–38,
239–40
skeptic, 55
Socionics and Keirsey
Temperament
Sorter, 210
somaticizing, 7–8

source, connecting to, 49–52
  Agnew, Denise A., 69–72
  alignment, 57, 74
  alignment inventory journal exercise, 74
  breathing and grounding meditation exercise, 77–78
  fear of missing out (FOMO), 59–61
  frenetic energy assessment exercise, 75–77
  intuition, 52–56, 72, 73–74
  intuition inventory, 74–75
  Jones, Marie D., 73–74
  meditation, 57, 58, 66–67, 77–78
  mindfulness, 56–59
  perspective, 68–69
  prayer, 61–64
  tips, 74–77
  trust, 67–68
  tuning in, 64–67
sticks and stones exercise, 144–46
strengths, 84
suicide, 258
sun, 235–36
sunlight, 106–7
surrendering to life, 245

Suttie, Jill, 192

T

Teilhard de Chardin, Pierre, 255, 255 (ill.)
"thank you," 166
thinking, 209 (ill.), 210–11
tides, 111–13
Tolle, Eckhart, 51, 73, 149, 265
trauma, 4
tribe, 35–36
"triggered," 144–46
trust, 67–68
Tsipursky, Gleb, 168
Twain, Mark, 254, 254 (ill.)

U

Universal Laws, 125–27
  abundance, lack, and staying centered in the present, 133–35
  Agnew, Denise A., 139–40
  count the grass exercise, 148
  Frankl, Viktor, 139–40, 140 (ill.)
  intentions and abundance exercises, 146–48
  Jones, Marie D., 143–44
  karma and Law of Reciprocity, 131–33
  Law of Assumption, 130, 137–39
  Law of Attraction, 128–30, 137–39
  money and prosperity, 135–37
  sticks and stones exercise, 144–46
  tips, 144–48

V

VanderWeele, Tyler, 38
vitamin D, 107
volunteering, 177
Vonnegut, Kurt, 203
vulnerability, 32–34

W

Walker, Alice, 64, 99, 187
walking, 122–23
The Walking Dead, 33
water, 107–8
Watson, Zach, 207
well-being, 79–82
  Agnew, Denise A., 92–94
  comfort of home, 89–91
  cultivating, 82–84
  Jones, Marie D., 91–92
  laughter, 85–86
  letting it be, 86–87
  mindfulness, 87–89, 97–98
  tips, 94–97

Whitford, Bradley, 225
Wicca, 168, 226, 231,
    231 (ill.)
Wilde, Stuart, 126
Williamson, Marianne,
    229, 229 (ill.), 230,
    232, 247

Wilson, Matthew, 32
wisdom, 234–36
witchcraft, 226
words that trigger,
    144–46
writing, 42–43, 177–79

Y

Yahne, Rachael, 232–33